A Room Forever

Thomas E. Douglass

A Room Forever

The Life, Work, and Letters
of Breece D'J Pancake

The University of Tennessee Press / Knoxville

Frontispiece. "Breece" by Rick Gerber—block print from woodcut, April 1993.
This woodcut won first prize in printmaking at the annual Marblehead Festival
of Arts, Marblehead, Mass., 1993. Courtesy of Rick Gerber. Illustration on page 156
courtesy of Kent Williams.

Library of Congress Cataloging-in-Publication Data
Douglass, Thomas E.
    A room forever : the life, work, and letters of Breece D'J Pancake/
Thomas E. Douglass. — 1st ed.
      p. cm.
    Includes bibliographical references and index.
    ISBN 1-57233-001-5 (cloth: alk. paper)
    1. Pancake, Breece D'J, d. 1979—Biography. 2. Authors, American—
20th century—Biography. 3. Pancake, Breece D'J, d. 1979—Correspondence.
4. Authors, American—20th century—Correspondence. I. Pancake, Breece D'J,
d. 1979 Correspondence.
Selections. II. Title.
PS3566.A559Z64 1998
813'.54—dc21
    [B]   97-21171

In memory of
Robert "Doc" Bain
and Jim Wayne Miller

Contents

Preface   xi

Chronology   xiii

Part I Breece D'J Pancake's Life and Writings

1 A Partial Portrait   3

2 Nowhere on Earth   16

3 Cadillac Cowboy   33

4 Aristocrat in Blue Jeans   58

5 A Room Forever   89

6 "The Only Value": Pancake's Moral Vision   106

7 The Prisoning Hills of Home   120

Notes to Part I   137

Part II Selected Letters and Fragments

8 1970–1975   157

9 1976–1977   188

10 1978–1979   214

Bibliography   251

Index   257

Illustrations

"Breece" by Rick Gerber—Block Print from Woodcut *frontispiece*

Following Page 32
The Pancake Home on Route 60 in Milton
Covered Bridge on the Mud River
Tom Roach, Robert Pancake, "Sug" Newman, Bill Weeks,
    and George McComas
Pete Perry and Gally Pancake
Helen Jean Frazier Pancake, 1944
Clarence Robert "C. R." Pancake, 1944
C. R. and Breece in Seneca State Forest, W.Va., 1953
C. R. and Breece, 1957

Following Page 57
Fossil of a Trilobite
Milton High School Graduation, 1970
Breece Pancake, Self-Portrait, 1970
1920 Underwood Number 5 Typewriter
Breece and C. R., Christmas 1971
Capt. Breece Pancake, Fork Union Military Academy, 1974–75
Breece's Father's Day Gift, June 1967

Following Page 88
Breece Pancake, 1977 Portrait
Breece Pancake, 1979 Portrait by Carlos Santos

Breece and Emily Miller in Washington, D.C., 1978
"Faraway" Hunting Cabin in Middlebrook, Va.
Sarah Nutt's House in Staunton, Va.
Breece with "Papa," Winter 1979
Pancake's Grave at Milton Cemetery

Preface

This story of Pancake's life is based mainly on the hundreds of letters and the few assorted notebooks and manuscripts belonging to the Pancake family estate and to John Casey and the Pancake manuscript collection at Alderman Library, University of Virginia. Also essential in drawing a more complete portrait of the author are the hours of videotape recording made by Russ Barbour and Marty Buchsbaum of WPBY television in Huntington, West Virginia. Those videotaped conversations with teachers, friends, and people who knew him or his work were invaluable in corroborating the image of the author as it was projected in his own personal letters to his family.

Pancake was a prolific letter writer, though many of his letters are more informational than lyrical, more business-minded than literary. He wrote most of them on an antique "hunt 'n' peck" Underwood no. 5 typewriter given to him by his Aunt Julia "Pancake" Ward, and with characteristic good humor he unconsciously proceeded to chronicle the joys and anxieties of a young writer coming of age during the 1970s. His letters home to his parents provide the most complete chronology and picture of the young artist. They are an impeachable resource no doubt, but the letters also make up a story written by the author himself and not a story pieced together by opinions or impressions of people who may have known him only a short while.

Pancake's relationship to his parents appears to be straightforward, but his father's alcoholism and early death and his own suicide may suggest a more complicated emotional relationship, something that may never be fully known. The story fragment included in this volume entitled "The Conqueror" suggests how complicated this relationship may have been. Two other story fragments included here, "Shouting Victory" and an untitled piece, help illustrate some of Pancake's consistent themes of failure and impotence of escape.

Pancake loved his family and feared disappointing them. His ambition and drive for success, his insistence on making it on his own, and his obsessive dread of economic and personal disaster are recurrent themes in his letters. In some respects, the profile that emerges resembles that of Sylvia Plath, someone who was also a "dutiful achiever," and who felt she could never fit in, and who became depressed by less than perfect-results in her writing. Some of his letters exhibit a hopelessness like that of Plath, who, after her first suicide attempt, believed that "There was no more sanctuary in the world," that everyone in her family would die, and that she would be left alone.

In addition, the details in the selected letters that appear in the second half of this book provide a rare and explicit view into graduate school life, an experience becoming quite common for writers born after the 1950s. Of further interest are the Appalachian touchstones mentioned, the books and people and places of and about the region that became resource material for Pancake's fiction. The few letters included here not written by Pancake help chronicle the events of his life from Milton to Charlottesville and confirm those personal qualities evident in his letters.

I am indebted to Helen Pancake for allowing me access to her son's correspondence, which was in considerable disarray. The task of compiling and accurately dating letters was complicated by incomplete dates, missing pages, and general disorganization. In transcribing the letters I have provided accurate dates as they appeared on the letters and have placed question marks next to those dates which had to be provided through calculation by content or by reference to other correspondence. I have included typing errors and misspellings as they appeared in the originals and have deleted portions of letters that are redundant or too mundane for purposes of a literary biography. The deleted portions are indicated by a series of four ellipses.

I would like to thank Fred Hobson, Linda Wagner-Martin, Alex Albright, Rick Wilson, Russ Barbour, Rick Blenko, Elizabeth Toney Reese, Charles Perdue, Richard Jones, Jim McPherson, Eleanor Ross Taylor, Ruel Foster, John Casey, Janet Lembke, Sarah Nutt, Joe Nutt, John Shaffer, Carlos Santos, Dan Patterson, Jack Higgs, Townsend Ludington, Chuck Kinder, Denise Giardina, Lisa Koger, Meredith Sue Willis, Jayne Anne Phillips, Richard Currey, Pinckney Benedict, Lee Maynard, Newton Smith, Meredith Morris-Babb, Jerry Wayne Williamson, and Susen, Rachel, and Abigail Douglass for their help and support during the making of this manuscript.

Chronology

June 29, 1952	Born Breece Dexter Pancake in Charleston, W.Va.
June 1970	Graduates from Milton High School.
1970–71	Attends West Virginia Wesleyan College, Buckhannon.
Sept. 1972	Attends Marshall University, Huntington, W.Va.
Jan.–Apr. 1972	Marriage plans disrupted, goes west and works odd jobs in and around Phoenix, Ariz., travels to Mexico.
June 1972	Re-enrolls at Marshall University.
1973	Makes second trip west, hitchhikes, works on story manuscripts "Stuart" and "Rat Boy."
June 1974	Graduates from Marshall University.
Sept. 1974	Accepts post to teach middle grades 5–8 at Fork Union Military Academy, Fork Union, Va. Meets and befriends Matthew Heard.
Nov. 1974	Applies to law school and the graduate school of English, West Virginia University.
Jan. 1975	Buys 1964 Cadillac convertible and calls it the "Great Blue Whale." Begins driving to Charlottesville to attend John Casey's writing classes at the University of Virginia.
June 1975	Completes "Fox Hunters."
Aug. 1975	*Cabell Record* of Milton publishes five of Pancake's local character profiles.
Sept. 1975	Accepts teaching post at Staunton Military Academy, Staunton, Va. Completes "The Scrapper."
Sept. 8, 1975	C. R. Pancake dies of complications resulting from MS.

Sept. 29, 1975	Matthew Heard dies in a car crash.
Oct. 1975	Begins writing "The Mark." Meets distant Pancake relatives in Staunton. Meets Mary Lee Settle and Peter Taylor in Charlottesville.
Nov. 1975	Moves to 324 East Beverly St., Staunton, the home of Sarah Nutt.
Feb. 1976	The University of Virginia awards him Emily Balch fellowship for the fall semester. Begins writing "The Way It Has to Be" under the title "Cowboys and Girls." *Rivanna* publishes "The Mark."
Mar. 1976	Begins writing "Hollow."
May 1976	Staunton Military Academy closes.
Aug. 1976	Moves to One Blue Ridge Lane, Charlottesville.
Sept. 1976	Begins work with Peter Taylor, writing "Trilobites" and "The Honored Dead" under the title "Will o' the Wisp."
Oct. 1976	Meets and befriends Richard Jones. Reads Tom Kromer's "Waiting for Nothing."
Nov. 1976	Plans project on collecting Tom Kromer's work. Begins attending Catholic mass at St. Thomas Hall.
Jan. 1977	Begins working with Jim McPherson and Richard Jones.
Mar. 1977	Submits "Trilobites" to the *Atlantic*.
Apr. 1977	Begins writing "Time and Again." Redrafts his Will. Begins working at the "19th hole" at the Penn Park Golf Course.
May 1977	The *Atlantic* accepts "Trilobites" for publication in December. Edward Weeks solicits story collection from Pancake.
June 1977	Becomes a novitiate in the Catholic Church, changes his name to "Breece D'J Pancake," keeps "John" for his confirmation name. Begins writing "In the Dry."
Sept. 1977	Meets Emily Miller.
Nov. 1977	Daniel Menaker of the *New Yorker* solicits Pancake's work.
Feb. 1978	The *Atlantic* accepts "In the Dry" for publication in August.
Mar. 1978	*Nightwork* accepts "Time and Again" for publication in September.
June 1978	Proposes marriage to Emily Miller.
July 1978	Travels to Telluride, Colo., as chaperone to inner-city children for a summer trip. Marriage proposal is rejected.
Nov. 1978	Wendy Jacobson of Doubleday solicits a novel from Pancake.
Jan. 1979	Plans story on yellow slave trade in the Pacific Northwest for the *Atlantic*.
Apr. 8, 1979	Commits suicide at One Blue Ridge Lane.
Apr. 20, 1979	Millay Colony for the Arts offers Pancake a fellowship.

Jan. 1981	The *Atlantic* publishes "The Honored Dead."
Dec. 1981	*Antaeus* publishes "A Room Forever."
Oct. 1982	The *Atlantic* publishes "Hollow."
Feb. 25, 1983	Little Brown publishes *The Stories of Breece D'J Pancake.*
Apr. 14, 1983	"The Way It Has to Be" appears in *Rolling Stone.*
June 15, 1983	The *Atlantic* nominates the *Stories* for the Pulitzer Prize.
Dec. 1983	Berea College nominates the *Stories* for the Weatherford Award as the best in Appalachian literature.
1984	Rinehart and Winston publishes the *Stories* in a paperback edition, and it stays in print up to the present.
1986	Marshall University sponsors a Breece Pancake Symposium, Nov. 4–6, Huntington, W.Va.
1993	Secker and Warburg of Great Britain publishes the *Stories* under the title *Trilobites and Other Stories,* which features a cover photo by Walker Evans.
1994	The University of Tennessee Press publishes *Appalachia Inside Out: A Sequel to* Voices from the Hills, edited by Robert J. Higgs, Ambrose Manning, and Jim Wayne Miller, which includes "First Day of Winter."
	Bertrand Brasil issues Portuguese edition under the title *Contos Cortantes* ("Stories of the Heart") bearing a cover painting by Edward Hopper, "7 a.m."

Part I

Breece D'J Pancake's
Life and Writings

1

A Partial Portrait

[W]e are the sum of all the moments of our lives—all that is ours is in them:
we cannot escape or conceal it. If the writer has used the clay of life to make
his book, he has only used what all men must, what none can keep from using.

—Thomas Wolfe, *Look Homeward, Angel!*

Milton Cemetery rests above the town on a little knoll. Graves line this
rolling plot of land in undulating rows, and aging cedars stand like
sentinels near the surrounding chain link fence. In this cemetery on a clear
and sunny April 12, the body of Breece Pancake was laid to rest among the
flat bronze markers and upright granite slabs of stone. His grave, immediately adjacent to those of his father, Clarence, and his grandfather Robert is
simply marked with his adopted pen name, "Breece D'J Pancake," and the
cardinal dates of his life, "June 29 1952–April 8 1979." Underneath this, a
small bronze cross is raised in relief against the black rough finish of the
grave marker. From this spot one can see Company Hill to the southeast and
the railroad tracks running through the town of Milton, West Virginia,
where he was born; and far off to the north, one can see highway 64 point-
ing west toward Huntington and Marshall University and east toward the
University of Virginia and Charlottesville, where he died.

Father Pat O'Connor of St. Thomas Aquinas Church in Charlottesville
had traveled to Milton to give a eulogy service earlier that spring day at
Heck Funeral Home to a small group of friends and family, but a few days
before, at services in Charlottesville, O'Connor saw hundreds of people
come to pay their last respects, many people who knew Pancake well and
some who only knew of him. At the memorial service in Charlottesville,

John Casey, fighting a stutter, read excerpts from Pancake's stories, and friends Carl Beckman and Mike Jennings read scripture. In both services O'Connor praised Breece Pancake for his fine qualities and pointed to the importance of his writing—"the search for the best language, the best way of communicating ideas,"[1] but O'Connor also warned that dwelling on his loss would "make Breece's death larger than his life."[2] At the graveside in Milton, "Father Pat" said a brief prayer as the body descended into the grave, then Pancake's sister Donnetta interceded and insisted that she be able to bury her brother. She and Mike Jennings, John Casey, and Carl Beckman took shovels in hand and threw the freshly dug earth onto the lowered casket. His mother, Helen Pancake, watched and vowed that somehow she would see a book of her son's stories published.

On that Palm Sunday, the evening of his death, Mrs. Pancake says she saw her son's ghost at the foot of her bed where she was resting, just before the phone call came. In Charlottesville, upon hearing the news, Emily Miller, whom Breece had wanted to marry, urged John Casey to just "go see" if it were true.[3] And Casey, with a sense of urgency and fear, hurried to the apartment at One Blue Ridge Lane and found his former student and friend cradling an over-and-under 30-30/20-gauge shotgun, his body slumped over in a lawn chair underneath an apple tree. Behind the chair stood a whitewashed wall flecked red from a self-inflicted shotgun wound to the head.

Pancake left behind bewildered friends and family who were unable to understand his suicide. Rick Blenko, his boyhood friend from Milton, said, "I can't believe he would kill himself. He was fooling around or playing around with a bullet in a gun."[4] Emily Miller claimed, "His death was a freak accident. He loved life too much for his death to have been anything but an accident."[5] And his grief-stricken mother, looking for the answer in his papers and notebooks, found a letter addressed to her, half-written and not sent, that told of a dream he had only a few weeks before about a mythical place, "a happy hunting ground," where you could shoot a rabbit and the rabbit would come back to life again. "I don't think he intended to take his life," she insisted. "Maybe he thought if he shot himself he would jump up and run away again. Who knows what he thought!?"[6] Pancake's letter to his mother follows:

> Last night I dreamed of the "happy hunting ground." I passed through a place of bones that looked human, but weren't—the skulls were wrong. Then I came to a place where the days were the best of every season, the sweetest air and water in spring, then the dry heat where deer make dust in the road, the fog of fall with good leaves. And you could shoot without a gun, never kill, but the rabbits would do a little dance, all as if it were a game, and they were playing it too. Then Winter came with heavy powder-snow, and big deer, horses, goats and buffaloes—all white—snorted, tossed their heads, and

I lay down with my Army blanket, made my bed in the snow, then dreamed within the dream. I dreamed I was at Fleety's,[7] and she told me the bones were poor people killed by bandits, and she took me back to the place, and under a huge rock where no light should have shown, a cave almost. was a dogwood tree. It glowed the kind of red those trees get at sundown, the buds were purple in that weird light, and a madman came out with an axe and chopped at the skulls, trying to make them human-looking. Then I went back to the other side of both dreams. . . .[8]

Pancake also left behind those who half expected an ending like this. Casey remembers, "There were some people who felt that he was *fay*. I use the word in its older sense, meaning somehow touched already by death or in touch with death."[9] Family friend Sam Harshbarger reached the same conclusion, reflecting on the day Pancake's father had died four years before in 1975. "I know he took his father's death very, very hard," said Harshbarger. "I think that's what killed Breece. I think it caused him to mourn greatly."[10] Recalling his moodiness and alienation, school friend Julia Morgan merely said, "I wasn't surprised. I was very saddened, but I wasn't surprised." She explained, "I don't think he ever really learned how to have skin on so that he didn't feel everything so intensely. I think as good as he was at holding other people away from him, that he felt himself much more vulnerable than other people perceived him to be. I think it just hurt too much to keep seeing things the way he saw things."[11]

It was in the way in which he saw things that explains how his collection of twelve stories, *The Stories of Breece D'J Pancake* published posthumously by Little, Brown in 1983, came to be regarded as a watershed of contemporary Appalachian fiction, but it was in the way he felt things so intensely that underlines the necessity of understanding the relationship between an author's life and his work, to see how the realities of biography may have influenced his art. Pancake's suicide spawned a new version of the romantic legend about the author as the tragic artist; an artist whose creativity is found in giving way to uncontrolled internal forces that might yield annihilation as easily as transcendence and rebirth; whose creativity manifests itself where the light and the dark, life and death, meet. Pancake also became known as the writer's *writer*, the stylist to be emulated, the courageous writer from whom emotional strength can be borrowed to stare at the things that most frighten us, and the moral penitent who attempted to exorcise his own demons through his art.

Compared to the early work of Hemingway, Joyce, Steinbeck, Anderson, this small book from a young writer not yet twenty-seven years old attracted an extraordinary amount of attention from reviewers and the reading public. Nominated for a Pulitzer and a Weatherford Award, *The Stories of Breece D'J*

Pancake announced a revival in regional interest, and its publication focused national attention on an unusually large number of emerging writers from Appalachia—Bobbie Ann Mason, Denise Giardina, Richard Currey, Lisa Koger, Jayne Anne Phillips, Pinckney Benedict, Marsha Norman, Cormac McCarthy, Chris Holbrook, Lee Maynard, Meredith Sue Willis, among others.

During the years following his father's death, Breece Pancake struggled to become the writer he had dreamed of becoming, and he did so with the purity and fire of his own Appalachian vision. While presenting the West Virginia Literary Award to Pancake posthumously in 1984, State Librarian Frederic Glazer prophesied Pancake's influence. "Should there be an Appalachian Renaissance in letters," Glazer said, "Breece D'J Pancake could well be the rejuvenated pioneer spirit who turned the trail into a thruway and took us to a new literary frontier."[12] His work was praised for its controlled, "muscular" style that reminded people of Hemingway, its strong undercurrent of emotion, and its evocation of the blighted lives of the mountain poor. Pancake's themes of loneliness, failure, loss, frustrated escape, and the need for redemption demanded comparisons with an earlier generation of southern writers as well—Faulkner, Wolfe, and O'Connor; yet, as Helen Pancake remembers, it was always her son's aim to combine the old with the new. The newness of Pancake's fiction lay in his ability to capture, in part, the mind of the Appalachian of the 1960s and 1970s—the frustration of dysfunctional families in a place where, historically, family has been all that matters, the geographic and economic isolation, the conflicts of desire imposed by the suburbanization of the mountains, the desire of wanting more than the past or region could offer yet wanting to hold onto things of traditional value, and the resulting generational turmoil—all inevitably leading to the wholesale flight of young people to find opportunity in other cities and towns throughout the nation. Some of these ideas had already been sounded by Wolfe and Faulkner, and in some ways Pancake is a throwback to that earlier generation, which created deeply conflicted characters like Eugene Gant and Quentin Compson.

It is no coincidence that the Milton Public Library dedicated a copy of Thomas Wolfe's *You Can't Go Home Again* to the memory of Breece Pancake. The self-conscious impulses and needs of Wolfe's mountain boyhood were the same as those for Pancake—and both yearned to transcend "The Buried Life" closed-in by mountains, surrounded by the limits of possibility, suffocated by the knowledge of the past and the history of failure. Despite the closeness and familiarity of family and town—in fact, because of it—their individuality, stifled by the unchanging sameness and expectation around them, struggled to emerge in full knowledge of what it would cost, only to live a life of isolation and regret. "Naked and alone we came into exile," Wolfe wrote in his epigraph to *Look Homeward, Angel.* "In her dark womb we did not know our mother's face; from the prison of her flesh have we come into the unspeakable and incommunicable prison of this earth. Which of us has known his brother? Which of us has looked into his father's heart? Which of us has not remained forever prison-pent? Which of us is not forever a stranger and alone?" Pancake shared this same kind of longing and sorrow, this common shadow with Wolfe.

Lewis Simpson's observations about the character of southern fiction of Wolfe's generation also helps in understanding the work of Pancake. "Southern fiction," Simpson wrote, "derived from visions in which faith in the American's ability to make his own world has had an entangled confrontation with an experience of memory and history that tells him he cannot do it."[13] All of Pancake's protagonists, whether they are conscious of it or not, are faced with this same "entangled confrontation," and they are frustrated with their resulting failure. This is the seed of Pancake's tragic sense in his fiction and in his life. What is left for the writer facing this circumstance, of course, is the escape or flight of imagination. When the flight is over, the same tragic sense often returns, sometimes with a deepening and more isolating resonance than it had before. Pancake's solitary nature, though well suited to his vocation as writer, caused him to go deeper into a cave of solitude and darkness.

Furthermore, what Simpson has observed about that earlier generation as reflected in the work of Robert Penn Warren is directly related to Pancake's dark vision. Simpson wrote that Warren "envisions the southern experience, the southern white experience, as not one of enveloping community but one of ineffable loneliness."[14] Ottie of "In the Dry," Colly of "Trilobites," the second mate in "A Room Forever," Reva of "The Mark"—in fact, all of Pancake's characters—are terribly lonely, isolated not only by economic and social circumstances but also by their own belief in tragedy. Even though Pancake, in life, had many friends and a loving family, he was spiritually a loner, able at any moment to put a wall up around himself, but unable to escape his claustrophobic loneliness. As his friend and teacher James McPherson observed, "[C]onstitutionally, Breece Pancake was a lonely and melancholy man."[15] Pancake's characters, naturally, mirror the interior self of the author, though not in particular details. It is the legendary aspect of Pancake's life and work that most troubles critics and readers trying to assess his achievement and to understand what his work means.

"Pancake's work is not armchair ready," Pinckney Benedict has said. "It's going to be hard and tough like a good teacher. It's not fluffy. It's not nice or kind. It's not entertainment. It's terrific art. Good art is almost always very hard—is almost always tough to deal with. Beautiful because of its hard form, the toughness of its surface."[16] What one first notices in a Pancake story is the careful attention to concrete detail, but underneath lies the drama of the story where he works the extremes of internal experience. Pancake's romantic imagination allowed something beautiful to be rendered from the terrible, something good from something sad, painful, difficult. For example, his descriptions of the Appalachian landscape yield a bleak effect, yet the beauty of the mountain twilight and sunrise, the in-between light of the romantic artist, shines in his prose.

British novelist Richard Jones, who befriended Pancake at the University of Virginia, commented about him: "Creative people are sometimes quite incomprehensible. They set up currents releasing forces within themselves that are not easily tamed. Unhappily, most of life as we live it consists of what you might call tamed forces. How otherwise could society continue?"[17] Pancake left the mountains to go to the University of Virginia to study with John Casey, Peter Taylor, James McPherson, and Jones, and to become a "finished" writer. When he arrived, they immediately recognized his talent; they also recognized the chaos in him. "He was a student for an eyeblink," Casey recalls. "He showed up, and right off the bat he was devouring so much on his own. It wasn't a question of teaching him. It was a question of deflecting some of his energy and skill."[18] Along with this enormous creative energy, there was an unpredictable wildness to him to which the people of Charlottesville were not accustomed. He was known to be "difficult." Libby Wilson, one of Pancake's friends in Charlottesville, observed something unsettled in him: "He was chaotic. You never knew what kind of mood he was going to be in, or if he were going to end up storming out. I didn't resent it because I always thought he was struggling hard within himself."[19] And novelist Jane Barnes recalls, "When he first came on the scene in Charlottesville he was innocent and outlandish and loud-voiced. It was easy to feel affection even in his gaucheness. But the longer he was there, the more complicated he became in manners. In the two years before he committed suicide, he became increasingly antagonistic in his social behavior. He would inflame people against him—which would make him more defensive. But only in retrospect did I realize how much he had changed from being the refreshing country boy. The longer he stayed, the more complicated his social performance became."[20]

Casey himself admits that Pancake "was difficult, very passionate, short tempered. He would apologize eventually, but he was somewhat mysterious. There was something that was unreachable. He became the severe nun who would rap my knuckle with a ruler. I never quite knew what he was up to."[21] Perhaps Pancake's difficult behavior was something that resulted from being far from home in the strange, more cultured land of Jefferson's university. Grace Toney Edwards, then a student and colleague at the University of Virginia, remembers: "[H]e said he felt out of place at UV; he thought he ought to go back to West Virginia. I can't sit downstairs in the lounge with those people (the graduate student lounge). I don't know what they're talking about."[22]

However, the people who knew him in Milton also noticed that, along with his dry, witty sense of humor and good nature, he, at times, was aloof, intense, shy, sensitive, possessing a mercurial temper, and an ability (as Julia Morgan remembers) to put "you right on the spot with something real accurate, but doing it in a way that it could hurt and doing it in front of a lot of people." Morgan, one of Pancake's high school friends, also remembers that "he could be really funny, real bright, quick, but he could be real quiet. He tended to be loud when he talked. He laughed loud. He had a larger than life feel to him and he studied you when you talked, but his face didn't give a lot back to you. . . . He could close it down so you didn't know what he was thinking."[23] Whatever troubled Pancake may have been exacerbated by being an outsider in Charlottesville, but his sense of things, his personality, had been molded long before in Milton.

Boyhood friend Robert Jackson describes Pancake as "very serious, very cerebral," as someone who "didn't laugh easily" and that "once we got into puberty he became a loner."[24] His mother describes him as "neat, clean, obedient, and never talked back." She says that "he didn't have any bosom buddies," that when he and his friends got together, it was Breece who was the teacher: "He was the instructor, he was the storyteller."[25] Other friends relate that he could be "dry, cynical, fascinated with things that other people didn't understand, fascinated with Germans." Once he made a charm for a girl made of an Iron Cross and bullets "that had killed a man" he told her.[26]

At Marshall University in Huntington, W.Va., where he received his undergraduate degree, Pancake was remembered as "moody," often running the gamut of emotions from exuberant to depressed and withdrawn. When asked what characters in his stories most resembled the author, John Teel, one of Pancake's former professors at Marshall, pointed to the flamboyantly funny hillbilly in "The Salvation of Me" and the alienated adolescent in "Fox Hunters."[27] Pancake, of course, was not any of his characters. Other than setting and inherited social and economic history, he did not share the same physical circumstances; Pancake was never a coal miner, for example, or a farmer or a mechanic, and certainly he was more articulate than any of his characters could reasonably be. Yet, it seems that in life Pancake may have been as alienated as his characters, desiring in a desperate way to belong, to be loved, and to be accepted.

Julia Morgan remembers that "he really didn't like being here, being in Milton. It was very difficult being in Milton being the kind of person he was.

It was a pretty conservative town. He wasn't part of the 'in crowd.' You didn't see him at many of the games or the school dances, and he didn't hang out at the swimming pool in summertime." She remembers that he wanted to be accepted but went to extreme lengths to show that he didn't care about it one way or the other.[28] It was this feeling of always being the outsider that made it difficult for him to fit in at Charlottesville or Milton, but perhaps for different reasons in those different places. "It wasn't easy for him," Jackson surmises. "I think he chose not to try to be all things to all people. This is me. This is Breece Pancake and if you don't like it, I am not going to accommodate myself to find a common ground between us . . . and he didn't feel like he could come home because he was different . . . growing up here, he did walk with a different step."[29]

Mary Lee Settle has suggested that Pancake apparently was suffering from what Tolstoy called the great "wound" that happens in an artist's life, something that provides the compulsion and obsession to explain and to heal the self through the practice of art.[30] Whether the wound resulted from a specific event or trauma, or some psychic way of seeing is a question for this biography, yet it appears Pancake never got over whatever it was that drove him. Rather, he succumbed to it. Looking for an answer to the death of his boyhood friend, Robert Jackson soberly points out that "when someone takes their life, you have to go back and look at each event in their life to explain it. It isn't one thing."[31]

Some of Pancake's early poems written in 1973 when he was only twenty-one reflect some of the personal chaos that would resurface throughout his life. "The poems which I read and then read again. It's all there, the pain, the shame, the fear and even the plan starts to take shape," wrote his sister Charlotte.[32] From the very first line of the untitled poem, "Ghosts always followed him and," his intense preoccupations with the past and the inability to come to terms with the past become apparent.

> Ghosts always followed him and
> Spoiled the cream of life for
> Him with their highcheeks and
> Passionless faces. And he thought:
> "We asked for bread and they
> Took the grain. We asked for
> Peace and were given red alerts
> We cried in the rain and
> Were given . . . Oh, to hell
> With poetry." And when he
> Was balanced on the breast
> Of his plan took a card

From the shelf. The glitter
Stuck to his hands. He sighed
And mailed it, but never
Read the rhyme. Tomorrow
He would have a party peopled
With war-dead ghosts—and
He would join them.

In this poem, the ghosts negate Christmas card wishes for peace and happiness.

In another untitled poem, written in 1973 at about the same time, the poet is again haunted by ghosts, but the window ghost, a reflection of himself, fears the creative impulse, "zeal uncontrolled," and to what it might lead, the fatal diminishment of value and beauty.

"It is fear," the window ghost complained,
"Not for lack of zeal, but for zeal uncontrolled."
"Our dialogues are few," I blushed.
"Impotent squirts," he answered.

"And when one finds a pearl too large
to carry, must it be chipped into buttons?"

Haunted by the past and fearing the impulses within him encouraged a sense of isolation, but there is also a resignation in these early poems. Irreconcilable grievings, muted yearnings for redemption, grim portents of violence fill the lines. The mourning that follows "the Blood soaked earth" in "Starlings" (written in January 1973) and the crucifixion of the vixen on the "Mail Pouch barn" in "Song of the Road" (May 1973), and the dreaded lines of violence in "Let It Flow" (June 1973) tell of Pancake's struggle to live in spite of fear, in spite of loss and disillusion. Pancake's poetry corroborates John Casey's description of him as someone who "struggled hotly to be a gentle person."[33]

Starlings

The starling was happy
With her mate
In the spring-bud maple.
She was happy—if illusions
Are known to starlings—
When my tallons [sic] squeezed
The trigger and told all
For a mile of her falling.
I took her up from the
Blood-soaked earth,
And for a day, wore
Her feathers. But

In the black wing
Beat of night I hear
Her mate's mourning and
Draw my hands closer
To my fire.

Song of the Road

I am of that collied race
Of soiled nomads seeking shelter.
They taught me to read the ancient sign—
To mark if the moon is sifted through
Lacy shadows of trees, to defend
Myself against storm, sand, and man.
I have seen that race glued to the berm;
Their weathered faces touched with pain
She sang her song and they followed
To tour her honor guard of telephone poles,
To catch a glimpse of the vixen's breast,
To be crucified on a Mail Pouch barn.
I don't blame her for revenge,
She has fallen to their feet many times.

Let It Flow

Let it flow—cut deeper
Let all my hot, free-life flow
To be soaked up by thirsting earth
    Let it flow.

Rage on in pious blankness
Let red paint your suit
Let life feed your trees
    But not your mind.

Chop me to bits and let it flow
Like a monotonous meat grinder
Hungry for every bull,
    Your jaws rattle.

In tone and imagery these early poems introduce what would be fully realized in his fiction.

To his older sister, Donnetta, these poems "are, indeed, beautiful, sad and gripping. It is amazing to me that he was 21 when he wrote most of them and even younger on the others. I suppose it proves out that as Shorty [Hollandsworth, a family friend] has said, 'Helen, Breece was never a baby.' I remember telling my friends when he was young that he did not start out talking by saying a few words, but he spoke complete sentences and they just laughed at me as if I was bragging, but it was true."[34] His nickname, "Old Pancake," given to him by fellow university students, even though he was in his early twenties, demonstrates how he was perceived, as someone in touch with the knowledge of older generations, someone of an older and more distant sensibility than that of his peers. It was almost as if he knew too much for one so young.

Out of personal chaos came creation, came form, and Pancake became a master of the short story form very quickly. Admired for his taut, compressed style, Pancake was able to achieve a maximum emotional effect with a minimum number of words. "Such a great style," Ruel Foster has noted. "Style to me means the process by which the deepest part of you finds its true verbal form. It is a very dense style in the sense that every word is kinetic and potent. The imagery is strong, the idiom and metaphor exact and hard and evocative. Much like the young genius, Stephen Crane, who wrote *The Red Badge of Courage* and died young at 29."[35]

It seems that Pancake's suicide and the circumstances surrounding the posthumous publication of his work focused attention on the emotional energy contained within his work and has surrounded him with a "James Dean" aura. Many people fervently claim him as the touchstone that will return them to the place they have known or had to leave. Among the many artists who have admired him—Jayne Anne Phillips, Sam Shepard, Carolyn Forché, Greg Orr, Anne Applegate, John Casey, Gurney Norman, Chuck Kinder, James McPherson, Andre Dubus, Peter Taylor, Raymond Carver, Denise Giardina—there have been those like Pinckney Benedict, Cynthia Kadohata, Chris Holbrook, G. C. Hendricks, and others who have leaned on his work in the course of their own literary efforts. Hendricks, author of the Vietnam novel, *The Second War*, has said of Pancake: "He was there, he knew, he was in it all the way."[36] What Hendricks suggests and what has been a common sentiment among writers and critics is that Pancake was a "genuine" artist, conveying the truth of emotion and bringing to his stories what Casey describes as the "physical to the felt."[37]

This was his "genius" as Jack Higgs noted in explaining why he selected Pancake's "First Day of Winter" for inclusion in the anthology *Appalachia: Inside Out*. Higgs said, "[T]he story absolutely breaks my heart. It catches the essential core of sadness and pain that lie at the heart of child-parent relationships. This, I think, is his genius, making us feel grief and pain, not so much in catching the 'reality' of Appalachia, which is not to deny him success in that realm. He's like Hemingway who wants to capture experience and make the reader feel what the author felt. . . . There are writers who can make us see a situation, but the best ones tear our hearts out."[38]

Pancake shares with Davis Grubb a heart-rending sympathy for the West Virginian common man, the poor of Appalachia, the confused and disinherited. "If you write about West Virginia and about its people," said Grubb, "you particularly need this instinct for love. I think. For West Virginia is Appalachia—it is a state of poor people. . . . And for me at least only poor people, and, in my case only the poor people of West Virginia—are worthy of my efforts as a writer of tales."[39] That was the subject for Pancake, the poor of West Virginia, and he approached them with a pathos that enabled him to imagine their experience and give voice to their deepest concerns. Jones observed, "[T]here must be very few people who have got under the skins so well of the ordinary people of this state, the inarticulate, and the enduring, and the long suffering, . . . and I think they have to remember when they read these stories that they were a work of a man who was still in his mid-twenties and what he might have done later on is anybody's guess. It's useless to speculate, but you can't help but do so."[40]

At the time of his death, Pancake was on the brink of a promising literary career. *The Atlantic Monthly* bought two of his stories and wanted more. He was working toward a collection of stories for Edward Weeks at the *Atlantic*, planning and beginning to write a novel for Doubleday, and waiting to receive the acceptance he believed would never come, but did come (in some sense) in the few weeks after his suicide. Had Pancake lived, he would have had his choice between a fellowship from the Millay Colony for the Arts or a Provincetown Fine Arts fellowship where West Virginian Jayne Anne Phillips would also be in residence. He was beginning to be recognized, and his talent was in demand. His success overshadowed the efforts of fellow graduate students at the University of Virginia, yet it wasn't enough.

Pancake had been working on a novel, tentatively titled "Generations," which would chronicle the lives of two young men from West Virginia, Ottie and Colly, during the Vietnam War era. According to his notes, it was to have been a story about having to rely on the moral strength of previous generations:

> I want Colly in Mexico there to meet the anger of the "masses," I want Ottie to wander the country, free from the whole great space, an inch of his own. I want Colly in Vietnam's last days, a leg torn off by our own fire, to see again masses in Mexico, to say "the hell with it" and go to see his Pop. I want Ottie tired, alone, to give up the garage in Chicago, to return and find Sheila gone—meet with the strong good woman (a kind of you [Emily Miller]) and begin his small settling—and I believe that would be a book—and a good one to read for any man of any class. The woman will be written up when I return—she must have four stories to her like the two men—and they must never be too innocent or loving or "decadent."[41]

Like his stories, the novel sketch hints at the emotional realities and dreams of his life, and the sketch names the one missing piece he searched for his whole life but could never find—that someplace "free from the whole great space, an inch of his own."

When re-reading her son's book some years after its publication, Pancake's mother could still see her son struggle for its creation: "I can see him pounding that typewriter," she said. "Breaking those pencils, shuffling those cowboy boots on the floor. Really upset, trying to form it together. I know what's in here. His life."[42]

2

Nowhere on Earth

"Because he was born in West Virginia, in the mountains—"

"Not in West Virginia," Shreve said, "Because if he was twenty-five years old in Mississippi in 1833 he was born in 1808 because—"

"All right, all right," Quentin said, "—he was born where what few other people lived in log cabins boiling with children like the one he was born in— men and grown boys who hunted or lay before the fire on the floor while the women and older girls stepped back and forth across them to reach the fire to cook, where the only colored people were Indians and you only looked down on them over your rifle sights, where he had never even heard of, never imagined a place, a land neatly divided up and actually owned by men who did nothing but ride over it on fine horses or sit in fine clothes on the galleries of big houses while other people worked for them; he did not even imagine then that there was any such way to live or want to live, or that there existed all the objects to be wanted which there were, or that the ones who owned the objects not only could look down on the ones that didn't, but could be supported in the down-looking not only by the others who owned objects too, but by the very ones that were looked down on that didn't own objects and knew they never would. Because where he lived the land belonged to anybody and everybody and so the man who would go to the trouble and work to fence off a piece of it and say 'This is mine' was crazy. . . ."

—William Faulkner *Absalom, Absalom!*

Breece Pancake was not born in a log cabin but in a South Charleston Hospital on June 29, 1952, to Clarence Robert "C. R." (1917–1975) and Helen Frazier Pancake (b. June 16, 1922). His mother picked out the name "Breece" from the sports page of the *Charleston Gazette* while sitting in a hospital bed, a day after he was born. The Americanized surname "Pancake" comes from the German *Pfannkuchen* or its Anglicized diminution "Pankake." His middle name, "Dexter," his father's choice, was at times changed to "David," a name Breece preferred. He also adopted the middle name "John" or "Jon" when he became a novitiate of the Catholic Church. The initials "D'J" for "Dexter or David John" come from a printer's error in the galley proof of his first major success, "Trilobites," and when first he saw the error, he laughed and said, "Let it stand."

He grew up in a modest two-story brick-and-wood-frame house along Route 60, which serves as main street for the town of Milton, West Virginia.[1] Built in 1948, the house sits on a two-acre plot of land which once served as a pony pasture when C. R.'s father, Robert, owned it, and which was formerly a part of the Summers family estate. In the early 1950s, a small red barn was built behind the main house to shelter the two ponies that belonged to Breece's sisters. During the late 1950s, Gally Pancake, Breece's uncle and a retired carpenter, remodeled the barn into a cottage. Later, a fireplace was added, and in the 1960s this became Breece's cottage, a place where he could be away from the rest of the family and where he first began writing. He was very protective of this private space. His parents were frequently invited to have dinner in the cottage and Breece would cook, but his mother remembers that before they could enter they first had to take off their shoes. The cottage also served as an extra place to stay during family visits and eventually was rented out to boarders for extra income.

The building of the house and its transformations marked a common beginning for aspiring middle-class families in the Kanawha Valley during the postwar years. Milton today is a town of twenty-five hundred people and includes a glass factory, two banks, a public library, a few restaurants, two funeral parlors, a nursing home, an arts and crafts shop, a few churches, some small beer joints (Rock Camp among them), and a mini-mall. Union Carbide Chemical Company in nearby South Charleston and International Nickel in Huntington serve as the major employers in the area. The town sits between Huntington and Charleston, squarely in the middle of what was once the Teays River,[2] a prehistoric river that had its genesis in the Appalachian Mountains one hundred million years ago. The valley created by this prehistoric river bed extends to Charleston on the Kanawha River and is called "Chemical Valley" because of the many chemical industrial sites located there. Interstate 64 runs alongside the older Route 60 and through the valley, connecting Huntington, Milton, and Charleston. Visible from the highway just west of Milton stands a cluster of crosses—a taller golden cross flanked by two smaller blue crosses known as the "Crosses of Mercy"—erected by West Virginia–born evangelist Bernard Coffindaffer, who has placed thousands of crosses along the highways of

America to remind people of the second coming of Christ. Off the Milton exit, a highway sign reads "Welcome to Milton, Where Living Is A Pleasure."

Established as a railroad town, Milton's original layout ran in a strip parallel to the Chesapeake and Ohio railroad tracks, which were first laid in 1871. The town was incorporated in 1876 and has an odd, one-sided appearance, since the largest buildings of the town were all lined up in a row facing the track from the north; this gives the newcomer the impression that the town is only half-made. The fortunes of the railroads ruled Milton, as they had done in so many other American small towns in the late nineteenth and early twentieth centuries.

The C & O Railway Station was the hub of the town's commercial activity. There, farmers loaded milk, freshly milled flour, newly carded wool, and tobacco (once a major crop in the valley) on railroad cars for markets to the east and west. There, the citizens of the town came to see the faces of the travelers passing through and to receive the news via mail or telegraph. At one time, the telegraph office located in the station was open twenty-four hours a day, and to be the C & O station manager was to equal if not exceed the stature and prominence of the mayor. Milton, in some respects, shares more similarities with towns of the Middle West—of, say, Sherwood Anderson's Ohio—than with the small towns of Appalachia.

In his autobiographical *Tar: A Midwest Childhood*, Anderson describes the effect that his hometown of Camden, the imaginative alias of Clyde, Ohio, and Marion, Virginia, had on the young writer, Tar.[3] "Now Camden had become, for him, a place among hills. It was a little white town in a valley with high hills on each side. You reached it by stagecoach, going up from a railroad town, twenty miles away. Being a realist, in his writing and thinking, Tar did not make the houses of his town very comfortable or the people particularly good or in any way exceptional. They were what they were, plain people, leading rather hard lives, digging a living out of small fields in the valleys and in the hillsides. Because the land was rather poor and the fields steep, modern agricultural implements could not be introduced and anyway the people had no money to buy." Anderson added: "To tell the truth, Tar was trying, through the creation of a town of his own fancy, to get at something it was almost impossible to get in the reality of life."[4] Pancake's "Rock Camp" stories, of course, attempted the same thing through his re-creation of Milton.

Milton, too, was never greatly affected by the boom-and-bust cycles of the coal industry, but was more dependent on logging, farming, and the local flour and wool mills. Later, in answer to the call of the Great War, Union Carbide and International Nickel came to the valley because of easy rail access and the lure of an abundant, inexpensive supply of natural gas. Then

Blenko Glass began its operation in 1922. These three companies, in effect, displaced the former more agrarian way of life and defined the material hopes of the town, especially after World War II. During Breece's boyhood, the importance of C & O activity had become secondary to the demands of Union Carbide, International Nickel, and other industries. Trucking and the newly paved Route 60 had successfully supplanted the need for a railroad, and, as a result, the station depot had deteriorated and was finally abandoned in the 1970s. The decaying building became, as one local journalist noted, "the object of that curious and aimless small-town sport—bottle breaking,"[5] and it served as the setting for Colly and Ginny's pathetic love-making in Pancake's story "Trilobites."

In all respects, Milton has the flavor of a company town. Next to the VFW's Decoration Day parade, hunting season, and the annual arts and crafts festival, the biggest events include the company summer camps, company picnics, company outings, and company target/turkey shoots in which Breece and his family often participated. Along with this congenial (but sometimes stormy) company hegemony has existed a decidedly pro-labor attitude among the population. Perhaps affected by labor attitudes and history just to the south of Milton in the coalfields of Mingo, Logan, and Wyoming Counties, this pro-labor sentiment embraces the belief in a fair wage for honest labor, a belief in a safe and equal opportunity to earn a living, and a suspicion that the company owners and the people who run the companies, given the option, would work a man like a mule, and after the man was all used up, give preference to a mule. C. R. often warned his son, "Never enter the gates of a plant. Once you do, they've got you."[6]

Ironically, William John Blenko of London, England, founder of Blenko Glass and Milton's first bona fide capitalist and aristocrat,[7] in a land where both are scarce, was a close friend of the ardent pro-labor organizer and former Socialist Party candidate for president of the United States, Eugene V. Debs. Blenko visited and corresponded with Debs while the labor leader was incarcerated at the state penitentiary at Moundsville, West Virginia, for instigating labor unrest.[8] Blenko's grandson, who today owns and operates the company, became Pancake's best friend during high school.

Nevertheless, the Pancake family, as did many other families in Milton, shared in the postwar material promise that the companies offered, which was a modest but good living and the opportunity to send their children to college. Beginning in 1942, C. R. Pancake worked for Union Carbide for thirty-two years, and he and his wife managed to support all three of their children through college and pay all their debts. C. R. often wrote to his son during his first year at college and once confided, "I am . . . most thankful you can be exposed to a better living."[9]

The first Pancakes in the New World were immigrants of German-English descent and first arrived in the Trans-Allegheny region in 1758. They followed the classic migration patterns into Appalachia, probably under the auspices of the Ohio Company of Virginia. The Virginia Colony, eager to settle the western mountain territories, encouraged land speculators to settle people in the western parts of the colony to help firm up its territorial claim, yet prohibited speculators from recruiting new settlers from eastern Virginia. As a result, most of the people who settled in the mountains of western Virginia were immigrants newly arrived in Pennsylvania and New Jersey. Abraham Pancake and his brother Isaac settled along the Ohio River a few miles northwest of present-day Huntington, probably following a trail that led them from landfall in Philadelphia through Pennsylvania and south along the Ohio River Valley. Another brother, Phillip Pancake, settled near Romney, West Virginia, following a probable trail from landfall in Philadelphia through Pennsylvania south through Maryland and along the South Branch of the Potomac.

It was a dangerous time in the Trans-Allegheny region of western Virginia. Conflicts between the English and the French and the Iroquois Confederation made frontier life precarious, not to mention the natural dangers that faced the new pioneers from predators and the wilderness. The colonial governments provided little protection for frontier settlers. Abraham, who settled at Storms Creek near present-day Ironton, Ohio, and from whom Breece and his father's family have descended, built his cabin nearly 125 miles from the nearest fort, which was Fort Frederick, located at Ingles Ferry along the New River, south of the Bluestone River. There was, however, a smaller stockade built by Andrew Lewis in 1755 near Huntington which offered settlers some protection. Still, murder at the hands of the French or Shawnee was a real possibility on the frontier at that time. Later, pursuing the prospects of the booming timber industry, the descendants of Abraham Pancake moved east through the Teays Valley and, sometime during the 1880s, settled along Two Mile Creek just outside of Milton.

Helen Frazier's family of Scotch-Irish descent settled in what is known as Frazier's Bottom in Putnam County along the Kanawha River, halfway between St. Albans and Point Pleasant. The Fraziers settled there in 1798 when the land was still a part of Virginia. Helen's father, Fred Lee Frazier (1899–1981), worked a hillside farm, then moved to Huntington to work for International Nickel in the hot mill as a shearer in the manufacture of monel alloy, a material used in airplanes and ships. There is a monel alloy mine east of Milton near Gauley Bridge, West Virginia.

The first Europeans who came to settle in and around Milton displaced the few Shawnee Indians who remained after the Iroquois conquests of the seventeenth century. The new immigrants were chiefly English, German, and Scotch-Irish with names like Gerlach,[10] Jordan, Rece (Reese), Venable, Morris, Everett, Beckett, Harshbarger, Summers, Kilgore, Neal, Blackwood, Parrish, Newman, and Lewis. All of them were Protestant—either Methodist, Presbyterian, or Baptist. The first meeting house in Milton was the Union Baptist Church, established in 1788 and rebuilt in 1849. During the Civil War, the church served as a garrison for a small Union force whose mission was to protect the covered bridge over the Mud River and the James River–Kanawha Turnpike. This history provided background for Pancake's story, "The Honored Dead."[11]

As early as 1826, people began to settle near Milton because of the stagecoach line established along the James River–Kanawha Turnpike. First commissioned by the Virginia Colony to connect Richmond with Virginia's westernmost regions, this road, also known as the Teays River Turnpike,[12] became one of the busiest east-west thoroughfares in America. Among its travelers were Marquis de Lafayette, Andrew Jackson, Henry Clay, Abraham Lincoln, and John Breckenridge. The Turnpike followed the "Old State Road," which was first completed to the falls of the Kanawha River in 1790 and then to the Ohio River in 1800. The Shawnee first cut the original path for this east-west route and named it the "Buffalo Trail" because of the many buffalo that grazed in the valley. The stagecoach line included a covered bridge near Milton built in 1834 (torn down in the 1950s) and a ferry crossing on the Mud River. By 1852 the importance of the Turnpike had declined because of other competing thoroughfares. The Turnpike, its original roadbed paved over many times, is known today as Route 60 and serves as the main street of Milton, along which the Pancake house still stands.

The settlement of the town adds to the rich history of the Teays Valley, and Pancake was very much aware of both its prehistoric and modern history. These historical details and the nuances of them later found their way into his fiction. He had plans to write a history of the town and had researched an extensive family genealogy, which traced his ancestors and their arrival in the mountains.

From early boyhood Pancake was always intent on finding the secrets to the valley's history. He studied the regional folklore, history, and geology looking for secrets. When the cut was made for the interstate in the mid-1960s, Pancake would often come home from school, change clothes, and walk over the gouged earth, looking for fossils and arrowheads, evidence of the prehistoric life of the Teays. Among the kinds of fossils for which Pancake searched were trilobites, the earliest life forms known on the planet. Trilobites were pre-Cambrian creatures over 600 million years old. They survived two near mass extinctions, but finally perished from the earth 250 million years ago, which actually predates the genesis of the Teays River and explains why Pancake had difficulty finding one.

In Pancake's story "Trilobites," a small but detailed interchange between the older Jim and the young narrator, Colly, recalls this boyhood search.

> I pull this globby rock from my pocket and slap it on the counter in front of Jim. He turns it with his drawn hand, examines it. "Gastropod," he says. "Probably Permian. You buy again."
> I can't win with him. He knows them all.
> "I still can't find a trilobite," I say.[13]

Colly's failure to find a trilobite tells how difficult the search must have been for young Breece. In his story "Hollow" the habit of collecting fossils again appears when the short-sighted Buddy questions the young boy Andy.

> "What ya doin' there, Andy?"
> "Rocks," the boy said. "They's pitchers on 'em." He handed Buddy a piece of shale.
> "Fossils. Ol' dead stuff."
> "I'm collectin' 'em."
> "What ya wanna save ol' dead stuff for?" he said, handing the shale back. The boy looked down and shrugged.[14]

Of course, for Breece, the purpose of finding "ol' dead stuff" was to gain the "stuff" of secret knowledge that connected him, at least in a subconscious way, to the land and informed his identity.

Young Pancake also walked among the ancient Indian burial mounds nearby and made up stories of what they could mean and told them to his friends.[15] He not only enjoyed telling supernatural stories of ghosts and curses, but also tried finding logical answers for the mysterious. Pancake's protagonist in his story "The Honored Dead" observes, "The only surefire thing I know about Mound Builders is that they must have believed in a God and hereafter or they never would have made such big graves."[16] The largest mound that has been discovered in West Virginia measures 69 feet high and 295 feet in diameter, archaeological evidence of the Adena Culture, which existed in the Kanawha Valley from 1000 B.C. to 500 A.D.

Pancake also knew of the legend of the Mothman and of Chief Cornstalk's curse, stories which haunt the Teays Valley and southern West Virginia. The Mothman, a giant grayish beast with wings and red eyes, is said to have been sighted throughout southern West Virginia. The sightings began in the mid-1960s and continued throughout the seventies. A connection seems to exist between the Mothman and numerous UFO sightings in West Virginia.[17] When he was fourteen years old, Breece wrote to the *Herald-*

Dispatch in Huntington in an effort to work out a logical answer to reported sightings of the monster. The small news item was entitled "The Breece Pancake Report."

> I have done some research on your article of November 17, 1966, and have come up with this conclusion. I think the "moth man" is a California condor and here are some reasons. Moth man's height six to seven feet, condor four to five feet. Moth man wingspan 10 feet, condor nine feet. Moth man eyes color red, condor black and yellow but when light is shined into them they have red effect.
>
> The thing that whizzed over the car could have been a meteor. I don't know whether or not a condor can fly 100 miles per hour. As for it veering away, if it is a condor it would be afraid of the lights in the city.

[Signed]
A Fellow Reporter (Junior Journal)
Breece Pancake.

P.S.: Please allow for a few feet in my comparison because the sighters were excited.
[Editor's comment:] He has figured out about as logical answer to the Mason County monster problem as anyone. He'll go far.[18]

The curse of Cornstalk, chief of the Shawnee, has its beginnings in one of the bloodiest Indian–white battles in American history. On October 10, 1774, in the battle of Point Pleasant at the confluence of the Kanawha and Ohio Rivers, Colonel Lewis and his Virginians defeated Chief Cornstalk, who, at the time, opposed white settlement. Three years later at the site of the battle, angry white settlers mistakenly murdered Chief Cornstalk and his son to avenge the deaths of several white settlers for which Cornstalk's people were not responsible. In the moments before he died, Cornstalk supposedly cursed forever the land and the people who would live on it. Today, the people of the region superstitiously link the curse to several disasters that have occurred in the Point Pleasant area in recent decades, namely a bridge failure—a minor but significant detail in Pancake's story "The Mark"—a construction scaffolding collapse, and more than one deadly flood. The idea of the curse also appears obliquely in his story "The Honored Dead."

Pancake believed that if he knew the key to the land and its people, the circumstances that brought them there and kept them there, and the region's geology, history, and folklore, then he could more fully understand and embrace his birthright. It seemed an essential thing for him to do. The passion of his search found its way into his fiction and marked the boundaries of his life and work much like a locust-post in the West Virginia soil.

By some chance, here they are, all on this earth; and who shall ever tell the
sorrow of being on this earth, lying, on quilts, on the grass in summer evening,
among the sounds of night. May God bless my people, my uncle, my aunt,
my mother, my good father, oh, remember them kindly in their time of trouble;
and in the hour of their taking away.

—James Agee, *A Death in the Family*

Clarence Robert "C. R." Pancake was born in Milton on April 17, 1917,
at the beginning of the devastating influenza epidemic of 1917 and 1918.
Known as "Bud" or "Whicker" to his friends and family, he spent a
hardscrabble youth growing up in the 1920s and 1930s during the coal mine
wars of the southwestern coal fields and the Great Depression. Fortunately,
C. R.'s father, Robert Pancake (1883–1959), had worked hard to establish the
Pancake Meat Market in the thirties, which enabled the family to be better
off than most and offered C. R. his first chance at employment. C. R. became
a working partner in his father's meat market in the mid-1930s.

In September 1939, on a dare from another couple, "Bud" and Helen Frazier
eloped to Greenup, Kentucky, where they were married after first meeting
in Kennedy's Dairy Bar in Hurricane, West Virginia. She was only seventeen
and a half years old. Their first child, Donnetta, was born a year and a half
later, and in the year following they had their second daughter, Charlotte.

In his mid-twenties and with the country on the brink of war, C. R.
looked for more stability and protection for his young family. He finally sold
his partnership in the meat market in 1942 and took a job with Union Carbide in the labor pool with the hopes of getting a deferment from the draft.
C. R.'s low draft number guaranteed an early call-up. As an employee of
Union Carbide, a company crucial to the war effort, C. R. was allowed a
nine-month deferment, which delayed his induction and, in retrospect,
probably spared him from the Normandy landing. C. R. entered the draft
on April 1,1944, and was attached to Battery B, 2d Field Artillery, in the
Observation Battalion; his military occupation was listed as cook; his com-
bat assignment, sharpshooter with a carbine.

Helen Frazier Pancake remembers C. R.'s induction into military service with some acrimony because it made life difficult for the family. She
bitterly recalls, "Bud was drafted on a low order number regardless of two
baby daughters, while young single men loafed on the Old Bank steps."
With C. R. in the army, she had to provide for herself and her daughters on
one hundred dollars a month from the government and whatever else Bud
could send home. She sold the family car, planted a Victory Garden, and
canned everything she could. She traded her sugar stamps for shoe stamps

because the babies' feet grew so fast. She remembers that life was very stressful because of constant money worries and because of the dread of receiving a telegram from the government.[19]

C. R. saw action in the Rhineland, in Central Europe, and in the Ardennes. By the war's end he received a Good Conduct Medal, The European/African/Middle Eastern Ribbon, and the World War II Victory Ribbon. His war experience appears, transformed, in his son's fiction, in stories like "Trilobites," "The Honored Dead," and "Time and Again." Colly's vision of his father as "a khaki cloud in the canebrakes" in "Trilobites" comes from C. R.'s habit of wearing his uniform for work clothes after the war. C. R. was officially separated from the army on February 28, 1946, and, upon his return to Milton, he resumed his job with Union Carbide in the Bakelite Shipping Department, loading boxcars and eventually working his way up into the office as a shipping clerk; but all was not well after the war. C. R. developed an addiction to alcohol.

In 1953, a year and a half after Breece was born, C. R., now a confirmed alcoholic, sought help at the Alcoholics Anonymous Chapter of Huntington. Outside the AA meeting house, Helen Pancake often sat in the car with Breece on her lap, waiting for C. R. and the half-hour drive back home to Milton.

Despite C. R.'s alcoholism, an unusually close relationship developed between father and son. C. R. had always been an outdoorsman, a gun collector, and a hunter, and from an early age he shared his interests with his son. Together, they would go camping, hiking, and fishing throughout West Virginia. They hunted for turkey, squirrel, and deer at Seneca State Forest, and together they raised a pair of prized beagle pups to show and to help in the hunt.[20] This letter, written by C. R. to Breece in 1970, provides some insight into the closeness of their relationship and how they shared life together:

> Got this out of your desk. You know what. After I left you I went back to the tent and went to sleep untell [sic] about 10 pm. got up, packed the tent and took off. I missed you so much I just could not stay. You know we always camped together. Camping is nothing alone. After I got to Clay, W.Va., I got on the wrong road and ended up in Gauley Bridge. What a night.
>
> Listen Pal I forgot to tell you to call for the money you need for books. Also we need your new address and ext. number And the name and size of the new coat you asked me to get at Robert Halls.
>
> Would you do me a favor? I am going to send you a bottle of vitamins. Would you please take one a day. They won't make you fat but they will keep you strong and build up resistance against colds. Appreciate it, if you would?
>
> It was so nice having you this summer and thank you for all the good thangs [sic] you did for us while you were here. Looking forward to your next trip home. You see I consider you my very best friend as well as my son, (whiskers and all).
>
> Be sure and call the info. I asked for and write soon.[21]

His father taught him the secrets of the woods, the use of guns, and the romance of traveling to other places. C. R. often told Breece of his freewheeling days in Michigan with his friend "Red Top" Hensley before his marriage and before the war, when he worked at anything he could find: picking cherries, mixing cement, serving up beer in a roadhouse. He also told him stories of his soldiering days in Germany, France, and Italy. Although father and son would have their solitary "walks and talks" ranging through the surrounding woods and through the town, together they also shared the company of the older men of the town, stopping off at a local restaurant for cocoa and coffee where the regulars hung their cups and swapped tales. It was in these moments that Breece first heard the storytelling of Fred Ball and Junior Blake, family friends and characters of the town, and it was not long before Breece began telling stories of his own to the men sitting on the stools.

Tall, gaunt, uneducated, C. R. had always worked hard to make ends meet, and he had a hard edge to him. Family friend Sam Harshbarger remembered C. R. as "quiet," as someone who looked for whatever advantage he could find. Harshbarger recalled:

> When I was young, his father had [just] started to work at Carbide and also ran some pinball machines around town that I used to play a lot. His father one time hired a friend of mine and I and another fellow to clean out a privy for him and our pay was to be an old pinball machine that we were to get sight unseen and that he had stored in the loft in the barn there behind Breece's house. We worked at the job and did it, did it well, and when we got the pinball machine out, Whicker, Breece's father, hadn't told us its condition, and it had no glass, only three balls. It was one of these old types that had a spring coil on a post and if the ball hit the coil and made contact with the post, you got a point. We plugged that thing into the back of Breece's house, and blew every fuse in that end of town. It turned out that mice had gotten into the back of that thing and eaten all the wiring off. We finally made a quarter a piece out of a day's work by selling the balls.[22]

Along with his extreme sense of frugality, C. R. had sympathy for the dispossessed and the down-and-out, and this rubbed off on his son, as did his characteristically Appalachian sense of humor, with its dour deadpan and self-deprecating quality of never taking oneself too seriously nor being surprised when the worst always happens. Breece's impression of Mexico, which he visited in 1972, and his experiences in the world of work reflect his father's sympathy for the underdog. While working in Virginia, he wrote to his parents, "Give us your tired, your poor, your huddled masses. . . . It says that at the base of the statue of liberty, yet we're raising hell over those poor people trying to get to our country. I'm never amazed by Americans. I hit a possum the other night and didn't stop to pick him up for stew, so I'm sure this party can hold a few more people."[23] This sympathy for the dispossessed also explains Breece's later interest in writers of the left like Nelson Algren, Tom Kromer, John Steinbeck, Grace Lumpkin, John Dos Passos, Sherwood Anderson, Mike Gold, Jack Conroy, Ernest Hemingway,[24] and James Agee.

Father and son endearingly addressed each other as "Dear Pal" in their letters. C. R. once wrote to Breece, trying to calm his fear of failure at college: "Lathey's boy got his midterms this week. I believe it added up to 1.9 avg. Lathey was a little upset because he was a brain in H.S. But after I talked to him, he understood it better,"[25] and then this note, "Well Pal If I keep this up, you will know everything I know. So I'll cut it off and save some for our walks and talks."[26] C. R. was always in full support of his son and more than once confessed, "You see I consider you my very best friend as well as my son, (whiskers and all)."[27] His father told him, "Just take it easy. It's not worth getting upset over. We all end up old like me anyway."[28] C. R.'s good spirit and willingness to involve his son in his own everyday affairs is evident in the following letter:

> Not much to write about, but I know you must look for mail, so I'll try to update you on any news.
>
> I haven't as yet got back on the regular job. Brown is still working my job. In fact I ain't doing much. Jerry hasn't been getting much FRT from UCC [Union Carbide Chemical] but I'll change that soon. I understand Charley's wife is sick but is improving. We haven't got any mail from the girls latley [sic], but I guess no news is good news, you see it's about the same at home. Hope it's more interisting [sic] with you. I am sure it is, and most thankful you can be exposed to better living.
>
> On the care packages, let me know when you need one. Call when you need to anytime.
>
> Sue[29] is entering a trial Saturday 9/12, the first this season. May or may not place, I'll let you know.[30]

Breece was also endearing to his father. While he was away at school, his father showed the early symptoms of Multiple Sclerosis, and Breece fretfully worried: "Pal, let me know what [Dr.] Miller says and please don't let them operate without telling me. Take those trips a little easier, you old Rat! You aren't 19 and headed for Michigan again—it's time to rest up."[31] In 1971 the disease accelerated, and C. R. struggled to stay working at Union Carbide. His condition inevitably deteriorated, and between 1973 and 1975 he was in and out of the hospital, relegated to using crutches, then a wheelchair. He died from complications of the disease on September 8, 1975. MS can be a slow, progressively debilitating disease, and Breece saw his father lose his pride and dignity in those spring and summer months preceding his death.

After attending his classes at Marshall University, Breece dutifully kept vigil at his father's bedside at the hospital while doing his homework or reading.

In a letter to his mother only two weeks after his father's death, Breece recalled their common interest in boxing, a sport his father introduced him to at the frequent amateur Golden Gloves competitions held throughout West Virginia. "It was the only sport he ever enjoyed and in that respect I'm his son. I find myself becoming more like him. I've been doing it for years and I guess it was what I've always wanted. At least I'm comfortable at it. He was a good old boy and to imitate him wouldn't be a mistake."[32] The loss of his father, if anything, made him focus more intensely on those traits and interests he had inherited from him, as if the search for the lost father could be fulfilled by observing these shared characteristics, and living in accordance with them. After his death, Breece confided to his mother, "We can't keep him, we can only make him over in our own minds."[33]

Three years later, in 1978, Breece was still finding connections with his father. He had been asked to give a reading to the "Creative Righters," a writing workshop organized by Janet (Nutt) Lembke for prisoners at the Staunton Correctional Center in Virginia, and he described his effort this way:

> He [Breece's father] always had a heart for the underdog, like he understood why a fellow would do something wrong to get by—like the war—I'm not sure if he killed anybody, but he was the kind who felt like he'd kill a man just by looking at the body, and God knows he saw the bodies. Anyway, this [reading] is for him; he taught me to give a bum a dime because it might give the bum the last chance he needs to sober-up. So maybe a book, a hillbilly reading a story or just something to break the stay will shake one fellow into thinking it might not be so bad to get by honestly.[34]

Certainly, Breece was searching for connections with his father in his fiction as well. Most of his stories concern fatherless or orphaned characters, isolated and struggling with memory of family or the lack of it. "Trilobites" and "The Honored Dead," in particular, seem to be the most autobiographical attempts to find his father again.

Breece's mother, Helen Frazier Pancake, was a Cub Scout den mother, an upstanding member of the Methodist Church, and the chief story-telling librarian at the local public library. "A reader, bright, infected with the work ethic, a pretty woman," as Sam Harshbarger has described her. "I think an exemplary mother from all I've heard . . . the literary side of the family."[35] She became a working mother when C. R. became ill, which was about the same time Breece started college. She first worked as a salesperson for the Island Creek Coal Company store in Milton. Later, after attending extension courses at Marshall University, she became a librarian at the Milton Public Library. While there, she was more in touch with her own literary inclinations, and her position at the library enabled her to encourage and to support her son's ambition to become a writer. As Olive Steinbeck and Julia Wolfe had done for their sons, she often sent her son news clippings of literary or unusual interest while he was away at school and frequently helped research a story on which he was working at the time. While working on "The Mark," Breece wrote home to his mother, "The story is coming along well, and may mean something after all—many thanks for telling me that weird story this summer. Without you, I might be writing like John Boy Walton—soft soap. If you pick up anything else weird, let me know."[36]

After Breece died in 1979, Helen Pancake, along with John Casey and James Alan McPherson, became the driving force behind the publication of the posthumous collection of his stories, *The Stories of Breece D'J Pancake*, first published by Little, Brown in 1983. She became a tireless campaigner, and her devotion and dedication to her son is reflected in the high degree of intimacy and confidence that characterize her son's letters home. These letters also help chronicle his career and life from his first year at college at West Virginia Wesleyan to his final days in Charlottesville at the University of Virginia. The letters show a relationship between son and mother not unlike the devoted relationship between Breece and his father. It was his mother's influence, Breece recognized, that fomented his interest and desire to be a writer. In one letter he confided to her, "Hope this finds you well and getting out. I enjoy your accounts of the various trips you've taken. That must be where I get my writing."[37] He was also very much aware—and this, too, was reinforced by his mother—of his blood heritage, of his German and Scottish ancestry and where "his people" originated. In another letter he wrote, "[S]o it must be my Scottish blood that makes me like the night so much."[38]

The following letter indicates how intimately Breece could involve his mother in both his ordinary life and his writing:

> Been writing all day, finished first section of "Hollow," and just burned out on second. So I quit for today—with my luck I'll get this done in a week or so. It would have been much harder to write without the visit to Ky. truck mines, and talking with Mr. Caudill. He's a great old salt, and was very nice.
>
> There is, however, one thing I hate worse than shaving—that is a dry county! This, I discovered too late, was the case in Letcher County and Bloody Harlan. No wonder they're so wild. . . .
>
> Not looking forward to getting back to work, but I'm sure nothing short of knocking Webb[39] on his butt could dislodge me now. If they give me any hair shit, I'll quit shaving. Let 'em fire me! Only kidding—I'll be cool.
>
> Anyway, if you want to come over some time, just remember you'll have to entertain yourself during the day. Wd. love to have you.
>
> Keep truckin![40]

Both mother and father instilled the attitudes necessary for hard work and self-reliance in their children. Breece's letters home often repeat, "I don't want any help. If I can't make it on my own then I don't want it."[41] Through his parents, Breece was steeped in the religion of the Great Depression, of making do or doing without, of paying the bills as you go, and he was certainly influenced by the family's memory of hard times during the war years. As a result, Breece was perhaps overly concerned with money and where the next meal was coming from. His letters show a nagging fear of hard times and the suspicion that another Depression was just around the corner, and that hard work and a shrewd wariness were the only things that could stave off economic disaster. While traveling and working out West, he wrote home, "Regardless of what you hear about jobs being plentiful in the west, there is a definite financial borderline—you're either rich or broke. I just keep running back and forth."[42]

Even as a boy, Breece had a strong work ethic, selling garden vegetables in the town and delivering them on his bicycle, and whenever he collected five dollars, he would eagerly deposit the money in the bank. His frugality gave him a sense of pride. In 1974 when he was a teacher at Fork Union Military Academy, he wrote home, "Went to C'ville [Charlottesville] Saturday with another instructor and enjoyed the sights and managed to spend $.69—between the Scots on your side of the family Mom, and Grandad Pancake's saving genes from Pop, I may survive in the world yet."[43] On one hand, this sense of economy and dread of poverty pushed him to work harder, but it caused friction within the family and also added to an almost obsessive fear of failure.

The one time he did "talk back" to his mother was over money—her insistence that he take her financial help while he was in college at Virginia, and his insistence on refusing it. Afterward, feeling guilty and ashamed, he sought advice from a priest about how to make amends. The priest suggested that flowers be sent with an apology. Breece scoffed, "Oh, she would have a fit if I spent money on flowers!"[44] He projected an impoverished image of himself at the University of Virginia, and when his mother discovered that most people thought of him as poor, she objected. He told her, "I am poor. You and Pop have made it. Now I've got to make mine!"[45]

He also had a tremendous desire to please friends and to reconcile with people whom he felt had wronged somehow. He was always a "gift-giver," and sometimes this aspect of his behavior disturbed his parents; he gave favorite record albums and fossils and books to people whom he had just met. "We were shocked, " Helen Pancake recalls, "we didn't scold him because you don't scold a gift-giver."[46] Even stronger was his need to please members of his dearly loved family—his father and mother; his sisters Donnetta and Charlotte, who often read to Breece when he was a boy; his beloved Aunt Julia (Pancake) Ward, who gave him his first typewriter, a 1920 Underwood, which he used throughout his writing career; his "Grandpaw" and "Mammaw" Frazier, whom he often mentions in his correspondence.

His sense of family dictated that loyalty and love of family were the first laws. He could not rest easy over family losses, animosities, and hatreds. While living in Staunton, Virginia, Breece made a concerted effort to make contact with the Romney branch of Pancakes and was rebuffed and shamed by their cool regard.[47] Janet Lembke remembers the dinner party at her mother's house where Breece first met his distant relatives: "Breece was present and so was a member of one of Staunton's Pancake families—Frank Pancake. Frank . . . inhabits the upper echelons of society in the small town of Staunton; he was taught at Mary Baldwin College, served on the City Council, and served on various charitable boards. At the party Breece spoke neutrally, pleasantly, carefully to Frank—and received no response whatsoever. It was as if Frank could not see nor hear him. My own uncorroborated feeling is that Breece represented the countrified have-nots of the family—or worse, its hardscrabble white trash. . . ."[48] There was no further contact after that, but the incident stayed with him and caused him to withdraw from making contact with other people in Staunton. Breece wrote home about it: "The Staunton Pancakes were Romney W.V. branch. No, not as friendly as the Fraziers, and not nearly as good natured. They're very much into tradition of family, etc. It's enough to make you afraid to have a beer because your name's Pancake."[49] He also surmised that his dress and coarse habits offended them because they, he believed, professed gentility and thought themselves more socially removed from the working-class Pancakes of southwestern West Virginia. After his father's death, he wrote to his mother, "I got the money from Pop's policy. It was nice of him to do that. He hated the rag I wore. Besides he wouldn't want me to hob-nob with the Staunton Pancake's in bluejeans."[50]

The pain of losing his father and grandfather and the fear of losing his beloved Aunt Julia (Julia Pancake Ward, 1881–1981) also caused him to "draw up" within himself. The pain of loss could never be relieved, never be replaced by a seasoned peace because he would never be able to please them again, or see them at home in Milton in the rose glow of the past. Three years after the death of his father and during a noticeable deterioration of Aunt Julia's health, Breece wrote to his mother:

> I ain't looking forward to seeing Aunt Julia in such a sad shape. That's pretty selfish of me, I know. That's where your wisdom makes a big difference against my age—I get so tired of thinking that the ones I love draw up like old iris in summer. It seems like it started with Grandad [Robert Pancake] and never has

quit—even with Kat and Granny, and how mean they could be, I still hated to see them go. When I think of how you choke up or Grandpaw cries when you all talk about Grandma and Grandpa Frazier, I know you never stop loving them even when they've been gone a half a hundred years. I try to understand, Mom, I really try, but if I learned anything from my past, it wasn't intellectual understanding of something as deep as love and death, it was the living of love and the living of death, and now that Aunt Jul is in between, I don't know what to do, and I don't think anyone on the face of this earth can tell me. Damn me, I'm awfully depressing. I guess I'm just homesick and tired. I miss you and love you and hope you aren't working too much. Maybe for the Reunion we could have chicken and beans and potato salad for me to step in.[51]

He cherished the gathering of family and longed for time to stand still, just for a moment, without people wanting to be someplace or be somebody else. His eyes never gave up the backward glance toward home and family. Six weeks after his father died and while teaching at Staunton Military Academy in Virginia far away from home, he confessed, in spite of loss and shame, what he had intensely felt throughout his entire life when he wrote, "For now, all I want is to save some money and spend the summer in W.V. with my people. There ain't nothing better nowhere on Earth."[52]

The Pancake home on Route 60 in Milton in the early 1950s. Photo by C. R. Pancake. Courtesy of Pancake Estate.

Covered bridge on the Mud River. This bridge was built after the Civil War not far from the site of the original covered bridge, built in 1834, and mentioned in Pancake's "The Honored Dead." Photo by Tom Douglass.

Front row (left to right): Tom Roach, Breece's grandfather Robert Pancake (1883–1959), and "Sug" Newman. Back row (left to right): Bill Weeks and George McComas. In front of the office of Dr. Morris, now a parking lot for Heck Funeral Parlor, ca. 1910. This group was about to go ice skating. Courtesy of Pancake Estate.

Pete Perry (left) and Gally Pancake, Breece's great uncle, with hunting dogs, ca. 1900. Courtesy of Pancake Estate.

Helen Jean Frazier
Pancake, 1944.
Courtesy of
Pancake Estate.

Clarence Robert
"C. R." Pancake, 1944.
Courtesy of
Pancake Estate.

C. R. and Breece at a cabin in Seneca State Forest, W.Va., 1953. Photo by Helen Pancake. Courtesy of Pancake Estate.

C. R. and Breece, 1957. Photo by Helen Pancake. Courtesy of Pancake Estate.

3

Cadillac Cowboy

To the imaginative man in the modern world something becomes from the
first, sharply defined. Life splits itself into two sections and, no matter how
long one may live or where one may live, the two ends continue to dangle,
fluttering about in the empty air.

To which of the two lives, lived within the one body, are you to give yourself? There is, after all, some little freedom of choice.

—Sherwood Anderson, *A Storyteller's Story*

It is hard to say when a choice of vocation occurs. There are inclinations,
influences, and identifications that seem to shape the choice. Instead of
the stark, sudden vision revealed in a bolt of lightning, a vocation often
forms in the way tree roots grow around a rock, slowly and of a natural necessity. The chemistry of a writer is no secret—a mixture of memory, imagination, and need. For Breece Pancake, the ingredients for becoming a writer
were there from the very beginning. The telling of tales seemed to have been
a natural occupation of the men of the town. Fred Ball, Bill Meadows, Jr.
Blake, Fred Dailey, Shorty Hollandsworth, Pop Amick[1]—each told stories
of one sort or another and in his own way—the way people of a small town
often do, with a sense of surprise, mystery, seriousness, guffaw, and license
to embellish and exaggerate, depending on who is there to listen. From a
very early age, Breece felt the need to practice the art.

His boyhood friend Robert Jackson, now a banker in Milton, recalls,
"When Breece and I were children we would get together after school and on
Saturdays and roam around through the hillsides in this area, and in particular,
we would go up to the Indian mound and he would proceed to tell whatever

story struck him at the time. I never knew if they were real or not. It was never the point. It was just good to sit under a tree and listen to him ramble."[2]

In grade school Pancake loved to tell ghost stories; in junior high he began to write them down. Several stories from his school days have an eerie, ghostlike quality to them—"Keeper of the Flame" and "Rat Boy,"[3] both written in high school, have this tone. The allure of death and the supernatural haunted Pancake's imagination as it does for most young boys. Inspired by the gruesome details of death and war in Remarque's *All Quiet on the Western Front*, he set out to write a war novel using his father's letters and stories as source material. When he was fifteen years old, he spent hours in the cottage behind the house finishing an oil painting which was to be a Father's Day gift—a dark, brooding still-life view of a table before a window. On the table lay a packet of letters, a pair of baby shoes, and a spent hour glass (the sand having run out). Through the window can be seen a snowswept hillside dotted with crosses—a view of the Milton Cemetery.

On his way home from school, Breece routinely passed the front doors of Heck's funeral home where part-time employees Bill Meadows, who was also the milkman, Fred Dailey, who was also the town deputy, and Tom Sovine, who was also Breece's Boy Scout troop leader, often called to him, threatening to throw him into an empty coffin. More thrilled than frightened, he would then hurry home, half-running, half-walking, shouting a defiant remark back over his shoulder. Ten years later, Bill Meadows volunteered to bring Breece's body back home from Charlottesville.

From early boyhood, Pancake seemed to be preoccupied with the macabre and mortality. When he became an undergraduate at Marshall University, he collected oral tales from fellow students, expressly with ghost stories in mind. In an open letter of solicitation he proclaimed: "Ghost stories are the kind we remember, and have a genuine value in research—they speak quicker and more clearly of their culture. The best kind of tale is one you remember from a campfire, relative or friend, and not from books, since this is not in the oral tradition. Any kind of 'spooky' story is O.K., and if it relates to actual events and places, I ask you to change only the names."[4]

Rick Blenko, Breece's best friend at Milton High, describes his storytelling as compelling, demanding the audience's attention. "Breece was always a good storyteller, speaking very precisely, changing his voice to a soft whisper," Blenko recalls, "with small smiles in the sides of his face."[5] He remembers that Breece never talked about his writing. A good storyteller always maintains a bit of secrecy, as if he has been to some mysterious place and has come back to tell of what he has seen, and Breece was no exception. He was a "sort of a loner," Blenko remembers, who kept his emotions to himself and was given to posing or adopting personas.

Standing six feet tall by the time of his high school graduation with blonde hair, blue eyes, and an angular build, his shoulders slightly stooped, and weighing a slight 150 pounds, Breece, dressed in an old green army jacket, often walked the hillsides alone. Robert Jackson recalls: "Where I lived was adjacent to the woods, and I remember sitting in my bedroom on a number of occasions and watching Breece wander the hillside. He had a dog and a red bandanna tied around his head, and a walking stick, which was a pretty avant-garde look for a little boy in Milton, not playing with anyone, just with his own thoughts."[6] Taken with the Clint Eastwood "spaghetti westerns" that were popular at that time, Pancake sometimes wore a cowboy hat with a rawhide drawstring and a Mexican serape draped over his shoulder, smoked thin black cigarillos, and affected a Clint Eastwood drawl.

His ability to create masks made it possible for him to get served in a bar even at the age of sixteen. "He looked older than most kids," Blenko remembers. "He could go buy beer. Breece would stroll up like he owned the place and he got served."[7] At times, Breece also emulated the aristocratic gentleman dandy, smoking an imported German pipe, signing his name Breece Pancake Esq., and emblazoning the Pancake family coat of arms on a wooden chest he had made. In fact, throughout his entire life he was attracted to people and things associated with gentry and class distinction.

His ability to re-create himself, of course, made him popular in some ways; yet, Breece was not the most popular among his classmates. He did not have many girlfriends, and except for a brief experiment with the track team,[8] he did not participate in team sports. Rather, he was the guy who held the towels and carried water for the football squad as team manager for the Milton High Greyhounds. Breece was, however, athletic in his own way. For recreation he liked to go fishing, hunting, and camping, and for exercise he preferred hiking, swimming, and boxing. He also had a good voice and could sing and clog. He taught himself to play the harmonica and, like many young teenage boys, listened to the radio late at night when reception is best for stations as far away as New York, Indiana, and Chicago. Despite his recreational side, he seemed to gravitate toward solitary pursuits.

"We were different," says Robert Jackson. "In this town, growing up in the 60s, in order to be popular, you had to be a jock and neither Breece nor myself was a jock. We were encouraged to read . . . and I think that's what set us apart. We were readers. We saw a world outside of Milton. . . . We were exposed to other influences through books."[9] Although he was exposed to those other "influences" from the outside world, the place for Pancake, the setting for his storytelling, was always his hometown of Milton, imaginatively transformed into the town of Rock Camp in his stories. As a boy, he read John Steinbeck, D. H. Lawrence, Sherwood Anderson, Edgar

Allan Poe, Jack London, Thomas Wolfe, and a writer from West Virginia by the name of Davis Grubb. Reading was as much of a habit for him as hiking or telling stories. Years later, when he became a teacher at Fork Union Military Academy, he noted with surprise that not everybody liked to read. "I like my work and tolerate most of my co-workers, but there's no animosity—we just don't share the same interests. I've discovered that not everybody likes to read a book a week." He was surprised to find out that his teaching colleagues did not read, and, with characteristic wit, he commented: "It was quite a shock at first, but I'll get by."[10]

His other boyhood interests included painting, handicrafts, and the earth sciences—geology, botany, and biology. He painted his version of Steinbeck's Cannery Row and a portrait of D. H. Lawrence. Fred Ball, Pancake's art teacher, recalls that "his art was always different from the rest of the class. It was usually pretty unconventional."[11] Breece, skilled in woodcraft, built model ships, paddleboats, wooden chests, glass bookcases, and shadow boxes in which he displayed his collection of German smoking pipes, some old locks and keys, and the arrowheads and fossils he found while roaming the hills.

After graduating from Milton High School in 1970, he planned to attend college at West Virginia Wesleyan in Buckhannon, a liberal arts institution with a good reputation in the state. There was no question of not going to college; his sister Donnetta had attended Arizona State University and Charlotte the University of Virginia some years before; he would have to complete the family's dream. Instead, it was a question of where to study and what to become. His first intention was to become a biology teacher, but earning a "D" in biology during his first semester at West Virginia Wesleyan convinced him otherwise. He struggled academically at Wesleyan and agonized over his perceived failure. In spite of his dismal beginning, Pancake did discover something wonderful at the school and in himself—his natural inclination toward drama. He studied the subject under the direction of Prof. Charles I. Presar, became involved with the drama club, and earned the only "A" of his Wesleyan career.

While in Buckhannon, he also discovered the songs of Phil Ochs, Gordon Lightfoot, and Woody Guthrie. Breece felt a particular identification with both Lightfoot and Ochs. Lightfoot's many melancholy songs concern the wanderers, the lonely, the broken-hearted in a shiftless world of drunkards, whores, and rough working men. In 1972, while staying with his sister Donnetta in Arizona and working to save money for college, Pancake attended one of Lightfoot's concerts, and he wrote to his parents about the experience: "'In the Early Morning Rain' was played and Gordon's face twisted up like the bum he sang about—that bum had been kicked below the belt by life and Gordon made you feel the pain like no other. . . ."[12] Pancake idolized Lightfoot for what he could emotionally do in a song, and apparently Pancake internalized the theme of loneliness so prevalent in Lightfoot's lyrics. On another occasion, far from home in Virginia, working one of the many jobs he had during his life, Pancake wrote: "A touch of homesickness also came last night. Being away at school, camp, etc. is one thing. But being out on your own—totally alone . . . is quite another. Pop, I told you about going to Richmond to join the union. Well, I've never really understood Gordon Lightfoot's 'Cold Hands from New York' until now. It's an indescribable loneliness that sinks deep in your bones when the sun starts to go down in a city where you know no one and the people could care less."[13] Ochs also sounded similar themes, the bittersweet romantic allure of loneliness and the freedom from loneliness through death, in songs like "Jim Dean of Indiana" and "When I'm Gone." Later, Pancake also became an ardent fan of blues-folksinger Tom Waits and 1970s folk champion Tom Rush. Like many attending college in the early 1970s, Breece Pancake identified with the traveling troubadour and tale-teller—part hobo, part hero of the working class and down-and-out. The full text of the letter cited just above conveys some of his understanding of loneliness and the plight of poorer people—and his gratitude at having close ties with his parents:

> I am now going to attempt to write a letter. Considering that it's 10:30, and I've gotta be up for church tomorrow and I'm dead on my feet, it should be a short one. Really enjoyed talking to you last night and I must say I appreciate your generosity more than ever—now that I have to get out and get my own, I know the economic hell you've been through.
>
> A touch of homesickness also came last night. Being away at school, camp, etc. is one thing. But being out on your own—totally alone (Craig wouldn't do shit even if I asked) is quite another. Pop, I told you about going to Richmond to join the union. Well, I've never really understood Gordon Lightfoot's "Cold Hands from New York" until now. It's an indescribable loneliness that sinks deep in your bones when that sun starts to go down in a city where you know no one and the people could care less. Thank heaven that a guy in the union office felt sorry for me when I asked if I could sleep on a table that night and made a special trip to Mineral just to bring me home. So, I've never spent a night on the road but I came too close that evening to want to chance it again. If I go again I'll have some place to get into when darkness falls, like a camper or a panel truck.
>
> Mom, I can only attribute that 25 dollars in the mail to some sixth sense that seems to come with motherhood. Knowing exactly when and what to do without being asked. I don't understand it but there it is just the same. Many thanks for the cookies, the letter, the money, and knowing what to do when the kid bit off more than he could chew. My greetings to Aunt Julia, I hope she's better, now that she'll have vegetables to give away. Tell Homer that I'll write to him

the first chance I get and that Phyllis' book was just great. I really enjoyed it. Tell Grandpa to take it easy in that sun—I've been living on amonia [*sic*] capsules the past 98 [degree] days and putting up straw, nonstop 6:30 am.–6:30 pm.

I'm working for S. J. Groves and Sons as a laborer—and I must say that I never knew the meaning of the word until now. You break your back for three hours loading a flat bed semi with bails of (sometimes wet) straw 5 layers high, ride for fifteen minutes and then break it again by transfering the hay to a flat car, then you spend the next six hours feeding the spray machines—again nonstop because the train costs the company $100 an hour. This place reminds me of Union Carbide. Yesterday the semi got stuck in the mud so we sent for a grader to pull us out. The grader got stuck so we sent for a dozer which arrived four hours later. I was running around picking up rocks to put under the wheels while the foreman sat under a shade tree. In a little while he yelled: "Flapjack, get your ass over here and set down. I've only got two amonia [*sic*] capsules left!"

Gotta get some sleep now. I love you and miss you both.[14]

In the spring of 1971, after a disappointing first effort at college and on his father's advice, Breece enrolled at Marshall University, which is located in nearby Huntington. There he could be nearer his father, who had become ill with MS, and work toward salvaging his college career. At Marshall he did quite well scholastically, though he still struggled in science courses. Pancake turned to what came naturally: reading and drama. He had decided to become a high school English teacher and studied for his B.A. in English education. He earned excellent marks in "Storytelling and Drama" and in many of his literature and education classes.

Yet, Pancake fretted over his college decisions, very sensitive to the hit-or-miss quality of college courses, degrees, and colleges themselves. He wrote his mother and father, "You can't look forward to anymore of my happy horseshit like taking classes I don't need. I've got to get that English degree and I've got to teach. . . ."[15] He felt, at times, as if he was wasting his parent's money. To him, this was a grievous act of irresponsibility, but the push for a college education was a mandate. What was the choice? His mother describes her son as always having had beautiful, delicate hands, and his father, C. R., once warned him, "Son, you better get an education because those hands will never fit a shovel."[16]

In early 1972, he thought of transferring from Marshall to Arizona State University in Tempe, where his sister Donnetta lived, because of a crushing personal setback: a broken engagement with Suzanne Bloss, the slender, blonde daughter of a doctor from Huntington. Pancake's friend Julia Morgan, then a student at Marshall University, sometimes let Breece and Suzanne have her apartment so they could be alone. She recalls that, although they looked like the perfect couple, "happy and very much in love," there was something strange about their courtship. For some reason, Breece could not write letters to her home but instead wrote to a post office box where she could get them without anyone else knowing about it.[17] Pancake may not have been considered eligible enough to court her. Helen Pancake recalls that all of Breece's girlfriends had belonged to "monied" people—"doctors, brokers, lawyers"—and "they all did him dirty." She guesses that her son may have been "too serious" for them.[18] Nevertheless, there had been an engagement, perhaps a secret one, for March 3, 1972. The break-off was quite sudden and apparently much to Pancake's surprise. They were to attend a New Year's Eve party at the Thunderball Club in Charleston, and, right before he was to pick her up, she called and told him everything was off. He had already picked out an apartment in Huntington, scheduled some remodeling work, and was looking for a job that could support them. He had even applied to the Huntington Police Force but was turned down because he was not yet twenty-one. Pancake took her refusal very hard and dropped out of school that spring term and headed west. A month later, not knowing the circumstances, a friend asked Pancake to bring his girl up to Buckhannon, so he could meet her, Pancake just noted, "Suzanne—Ghosts—I hadn't told him but very calmly set down on paper what had happened."[19]

During his three-month escape to the West, Pancake's identification with the hobo-storyteller and his sympathy for the underclass and dispossessed was confirmed. While using Donnetta's apartment in Phoenix as a base, Pancake explored the surrounding region. He traveled to Mexico, where poverty rivaled and surpassed the kind he had seen at home. He wrote to his parents:

> You should have seen Mexico. I don't think the place has changed in two hundred years. The people are as poor as you could get and still stay alive or so dirty rich that it's ridiculous. . . .
>
> The old cabin (now serving as a dog house) that I had as a child was bigger, better furnished, neater, warmer and by far more comfortable than most Mexican peasant homes. Like much of W. Va. there are old cars sitting dead in the front yard as a testimony to those inside the adobe hut that they had tried and failed to achieve that wispy, illusive [sic] dream of being rich. But in the shiny reflection of that rusting chrome bumper there still remains that faint glimmer of hope that someday, somewhere, someone's bound to drop that million peso's. As long as that chrome shines, as long as that hope glimmers in the heart of a child, socialism will be just another American word that is too big for him to pronounce. . . .
>
> While all of this revolved around me, I was walking about in my fine American clothes with my wallet fat with bills, smiling with my pearly capped teeth, (there's more money invested in my mouth than one of these families sees in a lifetime) feeling guilty of my prosperity and yet glad I was a rich American who could take advantage of the fine Mexican craftsmanship. I'm a Cadillac Cowboy. The West was won for me, the Indians were put down so that I could

camp out without a revolver in my hand. The border was barricaded so I wouldn't have to worry about Comancheros. I am the physical product of two-hundred years of murder, bloodshed, thievery, slavery (white and black) and social degeneration. I was born to sit back and relax because my father and his father worked so hard to give me this chance. Or was I? Hell NO! Who, in his heart, could relax in a plush chair before a fire as long [as] people continue to sell their daughters to the local brothel? And it's no phase either, we get richer, fatter, happier while the rest of the world slides into a cesspool.[20]

Pancake saw the same injustice and disparity in Phoenix as well. He told his father, "Pal, I've walked all over this city—put in a good 15 miles one day going from North to South on the main drag. It's funny how on the northside you see these beautiful houses, big cars, fancy clothes and just 15 miles away the Indians and Mexicans and Negroes are looking for somebody to knock in the head so they can eat. . . ."[21]

The year 1972 marked the beginning of his hobo days, of traveling the West as he did several times in his life, hitchhiking from Flagstaff to Las Vegas, Reno, Sacramento, and San Francisco, then south through Los Angeles and back across the desert to Phoenix, camping out along the side of the road, and exploring the country from Canada to New Orleans. Breece often carried with him a cloth sack in which he kept fossils and arrowheads, and on the sack was traced a map of his travels—from Mazatlan to Vancouver and points east leading home to Milton.

During his travels he worked dozens of odd jobs, which gave him experience that he drew upon in his writing. He worked as a stableboy, construction worker, cab driver, curtain hanger, laborer—anything as long as it paid. Pancake's attitude toward work and jobs had always been "I'd eat dirt if it paid well."[22] Through it all, he maintained a sense of humor. While easing his parents' anxiety over his travels, he often chided them not to worry, that a new opportunity was waiting for him the next day in the next town and, besides, he joked, "Blonde hair and blue eyes should get me some sort of job."[23] He also downplayed the rigors and dangers of the road. Motels, fancy meals, and air-conditioned rides were not for him. "Don't bother yourselves about such trivia as my diet and sleeping accomodations [sic]," he wrote home. "I'll have three hot ones a day and I'll camp in the woods, well away from the road. I'll put my fire out before dusk so nobody will ever know I'm around. If it rains I'll have enough money for a motel but would you please send my plastic parka. . . . I'll stay shy of trouble, keep my mouth shut and I'll stay away from those dirty old roadhouses. Should it come to grips—I've learned to run surprisingly fast in cowboy boots."[24]

His travel out west that spring began as an escape from personal disaster and ended up being the entrance into a vocation. With the songs of

Woody Guthrie and Gordon Lightfoot in his head, he threw himself, at least in a subconscious way, into the role of a writer in the mode of Steinbeck, London, and other writers of the thirties.

Already in the spring of 1972, he was thinking of a novel and writing sketches and notes for a novel called Stuart,[25] about a boy's search for his lost father, which is a consistent scenario in his short stories. Pancake's notes outline the story of a homeless man and a "wobblie"[26] by the name of I. E. Walker who is looking for work during the Depression. By sheer chance, Walker finds himself in Burgess, Virginia, by jumping off a freight train to avoid bodily harm at the hands of a murderous bunch of hoboes with whom he is traveling. The homeless man eventually gets a job at a local farm, marries the farmer's daughter, begets a son, and then leaves all behind to take to the road once more. The heart of the story is the son's search out west for his missing father, his subsequent realization that his quest will be fruitless, his determination "to stop this needless drifting," and, finally, his return home to Burgess. The story as outlined is a mixture of American labor history with union sympathies and a young man's need to establish and maintain a sense of family identity.

Pancake looked back on that experience in the West as a turning point in his life. In a 1977 letter celebrating his first literary success with "Trilobites," he confided to his sister Donnetta: "Those two trips to AZ [1972–73] blossomed the seeds of experience, made me know myself and others more deeply,[27] and gave me a basis to view from. Somehow, you can't look back without having been away. I think Wolfe was right . . . you can't go back expecting the same, but it's the re-evaluation that makes going home a truth. Not like love is a truth—that takes two of one state of mind. Going home is only something that one person can understand, making it presentable to others—trying—is the hardest part of writing. . . ."[28] Breece Pancake, going home to Milton in May of 1972, had a much clearer idea of where he was going and what he wanted to do.

That summer he continued his studies at Marshall and eventually graduated in the spring of 1974. He chose the threads of his education that developed his vocation and his art. In addition to creative writing, he also took courses in drama and the Bible as literature—influences that would later find their way into his writing. At times, he used particular biblical passages to focus the conflict in his stories,[29] and he employed a sense of timing, especially in "Fox Hunters" and "In the Dry," more readily found in playwriting, a rhythm and cadence of delivery that heightens dramatic climax. In "Fox Hunters," the fox suddenly breaks into the camp clearing at the moment when the men have confessed their crimes and "the truth and lies were all told." It is at that climactic moment when young Bo awakens from his stupor and his indecisiveness and declares himself opposed to all that these men have done and will do. He grabs his father's pistol and shoots not at the fox but at the pursuing dogs, slurring, "Try'n save foxie." The rhythmic "show you something" of "In the Dry" builds to the central revelation of the story—the underlying cruelty, insensitivity, and mean-spiritedness of the Gerlock family, which explains the pathos of Ottie's emotional push and pull between the family and home he longs for but can never have. He also studied Appalachian history and culture under the tutelage of Norman O. Simpkins, and this, of course, became another major influence in his work. He began reading the work of H. B. Lee[30] and Depression-era writers like Michael Gold, Nelson Algren, Jack Conroy, and Grace Lumpkin.

In a rough draft of a college essay about the Depression, Breece noted: "The period of American history from 1929 until 1940 has been a subject of fascination for writers, painters, sociologists and countless nostalgia freaks. . . . For my own part, I would like nothing better than to spend two years of my life in a firsthand examination of life in the Depression. I would divide my time, spending one year in Washington among the elite groups of Capitol Hill . . . I would venture off to experiment in misery my final year . . . lose myself in the throng of the unemployed workmen in San Francisco and beg for my meals."[31] In Charlottesville, four years later, Pancake would read, for the first time, the work of Tom Kromer, an author who had experienced the scenario he described. At the time of his discovery, he told his mother, "Please read *Waiting for Nothing* by Tom Kromer. Every word a warning like Pop used to give me."[32]

Kromer was the son of a glass worker in Huntington, and a student at Marshall University, then Marshall College. When he was eighteen years old, his father died of cancer, and, after two years at Marshall—having exhausted the family resources and disillusioned by the firing of two of his favorite professors who protested the removal of Mencken's *American Mercury* from the library shelves[33]—Kromer took leave of college life in 1926 and began teaching in rural schools to save enough money in hopes of someday returning. Two years later Kromer re-entered Marshall, and as part of a writing class he researched a story by posing as a panhandler on the streets of Huntington, just to see how much money he could collect. On March 1, 1929, the Huntington *Herald-Dispatch* published the story under the title, "Pity the Poor Panhandler; 2$ An Hour is All He Gets." Unfortunately, by the spring of 1929, Kromer again had run out of money, and he could not continue his schooling. By the fall, unable to find employment, Kromer hitchhiked west to work the wheat harvest in Kansas, which became his unwitting rendezvous with the Great Depression.

For the next five years Kromer experienced the worst of what it was like to be "on the bum," wandering from city to town looking for "three hots and a flop," barely surviving. *Waiting for Nothing* is a thinly veiled autobiographical account of real life experience during the 1930s when Kromer lived the life of a vagrant and begged for his food in the streets of many western cities including, most likely, San Francisco. It was no surprise that Pancake first chose to study Kromer's work for his graduate thesis at the University of Virginia.

Pancake once remarked that Kromer "had the book world by the ass in a down-hill pull. I guess he had a story, told it and quit,"[34] which in retrospect proved to be an eerie prognosis of Pancake's career. Moreover, Kromer's brief autobiographical sketch describes an understanding of life that could substitute for Pancake's own. "My father never hoped for anything better in this life than a job, and never worried about anything else but losing it," Kromer wrote. "My mother never wanted anything else than that the kids get an education so that they wouldn't have to worry about the factory closing down."[35]

This same kind of life understanding prompted Pancake's ambition and search for vocation. Apparently, Kromer's life reinforced Pancake's idea of what it was to become a writer—how one earned the vocation through experience, how a writer is tested, if not purified, by a life of deprivation and want. So Pancake, to a degree, imagined himself into the role of the starving writer, one who wrote on scraps of anything he could find and who survived in world of poverty and exclusion, a world which by its circumstance would protect him from commercial compromise and material corruption. Kromer explained how "Parts of [*Waiting for Nothing*] were scrawled on Bull Durham papers in box cars, margins of religious tracts in a hundred missions, jails, one prison, railroad sand-houses, flop-houses and on a few memorable occasions actually pecked out with two index fingers on an honest-to-God typewriter."[36] Pancake, too, scribbled notes on Salem and Bull Durham packages, religious programs, store receipts, and other bits of loose paper, and the typewriter Pancake used was an antique, a 1920 Underwood no. 5.

Likely, Kromer's obsession with death and suicide also appealed to Pancake. For the dedication of *Waiting for Nothing*, the twenty-six-year-old Kromer wrote, "To Jolene who turned off the gas," a phrase that refers to Kromer's first suicide attempt. In Kromer's work, suicide lurks in the corners of the many missions and flophouses in which his failed characters find themselves. Kromer's first-person protagonist stoically observes, "After a guy bumps himself off, he don't have any more troubles. Everything is all right with him."[37]

Taken together, the influence of the Depression era and Pancake's understanding of a writer's vocation confirmed by Kromer held a rugged, ascetic appeal for Pancake. To him, being a writer meant being hardened to the demands of everyday life and sacrificing material comforts for the time and effort required to write. After two difficult years in graduate school at the University of Virginia, he wrote to his mother, "It's been a rough two years. Due to be rougher, but happier. Thank God for all those stories about the Depression—

they made me tough."[38] A job was just something that enabled him to buy food and to live bare-bones, so he could do the "real work" of writing.

In an interview with Carlos Santos of the *Richmond Times-Dispatch*, Pancake remarked, "Sometimes I wonder what's more important—writing or eating. I don't know . . . I guess I've got the millstone around my neck."[39] Pancake idealized his vocation as a mission of high order, a single-minded quest dedicated to the perfection of his work. In this way, a writer never compromised himself, never allowed commercial tastes to corrupt or shape his art. And, of course, that is what Pancake wanted to be most of all—an artist.

He was once asked in an interview if a writer needed to "cater" to publishers' interests in order to be successful. He bluntly answered, "I don't cater at all. If they buy my stories fine. If they don't buy them—fine, I don't write to make a living."[40] He knew the difference between the demands of the popular market and the harder thing that art was after. "I don't feel that popular work is a reflection of the literary times," he said. "They [the publishers] are in the business of selling books, not necessarily selling talent. One must separate art from business and decide priorities. Writing, however, endures. The unknown writer that isn't prospering now may well be remembered after he is gone."[41] How art endures regardless of its creator also appears in Pancake's poem "The Carver," written in April 1973:

The Carver

With ancient steel, those horned
Callused hands methodically trim
A piece of maplewood into two
    Balls in a cage.
I kibitz him: "They should roll free."
But his tongue is not as loose as his
Knife. He continues to carve his
    Secure little piece.
The shavings drift in the breeze,
Born to be lost in the grass and dust.
I leave the carver for time and grass
    To cover him.
But shavings cling to my shoes, and love
Of leaves to my mind. Time and grass
Will cover him but not his carvings.

For Pancake, writing wasn't a Bohemian activity; he despised writers of the Beat generation, especially Ginsberg, who appeared to carelessly rattle out words instead of composing them and, in Pancake's view, seemed to espouse perversion. He took to his style of writing with a religious zeal, working long hours in the early mornings or late at night—times of the day when he would be uninterrupted before or after his other "jobs." "In starting out, " he said, "you must do something else. Ideally you would have a job that would allow you to write everyday. To write fiction effectively, it is necessary to arrange your writing around your job."[42] And the ability of a writer to "persevere," according to Pancake, was just pure "bullheadedness."[43] "He worked as hard at his writing as anyone I've known, or known about," John Casey has said. "I've seen the pages of notes, the sketches, the number of drafts, the fierce marginal notes to himself to expand this, to contract that. And of course the final versions, as hard and brilliantly worn as train rails."[44]

Writing also represented a kind of monastic life for Pancake in both its habit of self-denial and moral purpose. He once wrote, "If only one thing is true to being a writer, it is to remain at once the most moral man and most repentant sinner God could want."[45] Writing was art, and all art, in Pancake's mind, if it was any good, was religious, was meant to impart truth, beauty, and morality. His monastic vision of what a writer must be may also explain, in part, his later fervent conversion to Catholicism.

In a way, Pancake had taken a religious vow of poverty when he had decided to become a writer.[46] His nostalgia for the Depression, his training to become a teacher, his West Virginia heritage of making do or doing without, and his moral sense that money and material wealth were the seeds of corruption coalesced in an uneasy compromise. On one hand, Breece Pancake's moral world was not relative; it was bounded by absolutes, and it was the need for purity that compelled him without choice to become a writer and artist, a role that he felt was genuine, because it was the role he had to play in life. Yet, on the other hand, what made this role so complicated for him was the irony of his desire—the tension created by the need to make it on his own materially, to be a financial success, and his career choice that has historically been poorly rewarded. In addition, Pancake obviously inherited the commonly held Appalachian belief that material wealth frustrated spiritual purity and grace, and this complicated his absolute moral sense. Psychologically, he placed himself in the land of the "damned if you do and damned if you don't."

· · · · · · · · · · Toy Soldier: The Beginnings of a Writer

He did not want to wear a uniform today. It hung, a dark green scarecrow, from a nail on the wall. He felt stupid in uniforms. Even the blue jean uniform of college had made him feel stupid. He went to the closet knowing what he wanted, grabbed white corduroy pants, and a blue silk shirt with the two top buttons missing, and began to dress. Over his unmated socks, he wore brown suede cowboy boots, and then he found his faded black raincoat in the corner, and sauntered out to breakfast.[47]

—From "Toy Soldier," an unpublished story by Breece Pancake

In the fall of 1974 Pancake found a job with Fork Union Military Academy through the Southern Teachers Agency in Richmond. Fork Union, Virginia, is located just west of Richmond and is the home of this military prep school for grades five through twelve in the cadet tradition, emphasizing discipline through a strict regimen of study, exercise, and drill. Pancake signed up with the agency and took the job not out of preference, but as a last resort because back home in West Virginia, a teaching position—or any position for that matter—was neither reasonably expected nor easily secured. The economic history of his home state, as a rule, is a history of job scarcity and high unemployment, which caused mass migrations of its citizens to the industrial cities of Detroit, Pittsburgh, and Baltimore during the 1950s and 1960s and to the southern states, North Carolina and Virginia in particular, during the 1970s and 1980s.

According to U.S. Census Bureau estimates, this West Virginia out-migration will continue well into the twenty-first century, eventually reducing the population of the state below what it was in 1974.[48] Pancake was one among many who had to leave to find work, not out of choice but out of necessity, even if the job meant wearing a uniform, adopting the pseudo-rank of captain, and adhering to regulations regarding hair length and facial hair.

Military academies in the mid-1970s suffered from anti–Vietnam War sentiment and an unpopular image, and, as a consequence, enrollments dropped sharply and many schools simply collapsed. He had been hired to teach English in the middle grades amid hard times at the school. In the larger context, Nixon had resigned in August of 1974, and Gerald Ford had taken over the presidency as a caretaker; the country lacked confidence and was headed toward severe recession. Breece feared another depression was imminent and held onto what economic hope the position at Fork Union gave him.

Although the Vietnam War and popular opinion had somewhat tarnished the allure of martial manliness and esprit de corps, military prep schools in the seventies still attracted students. For the failed student, the problem child, the neglected son, military schools have prided themselves on mottoes of obedience and discipline and on promises of improved academic achievement and moral character. Some parents have looked to the schools as a last-ditch hope to instill these virtues in their sons. Breece was aware of the insidious nature of this hope and promise; his understanding of the whole educational transaction was more in keeping with John O'Hara's description of it in his book, *A Rage to Live:* "If I catch you messing around with girls in any way," says a mother to her son, "I'm going to send you to a military school in Virginia. They beat the boys and feed them slop and keep them busy from 6 in the morning to 9 at night."

Pancake found the boys to be desperate and lonely and likened military schools to prisons. "No, private schools aren't the answer either," he told his parents. "The answer, Dear Folks, is that there is none."[49] Of his students he wrote, "My students range from creative to brilliant to leaden slugs, but I'll get by I'm sure. I sort of like working with the little ones, especially the homesick cases—I know just how they feel."[50]

Pancake, too, was desperately homesick at Fork Union. In early September, after his first week at the school he wrote home: "I'm going back to West Virginia when this is over. There's something ancient and deeply rooted in my soul. I like to think that I've left my ghost up one of those hollows and I'll never be able to leave for good until I find it—and I don't want to look for it because I might find it and have to leave."[51] Like many of the boys who went to school there, he had little choice but to stay.

For the most part, he blamed the parents for putting their sons in such a mess in the first place. "So many parents could give a damn if their kids had anything and many give them everything to get them out of their hair," he wrote home.[52] Earlier, he had related:

> To top it off, a fifth grader had a nervous breakdown while I was on duty last night. His parents came down and told him he would just have to stay because they had already payed [sic] for it. I wanted to take both of them by the shoulders and shake the soup out of them. I wanted to say, "Do you know your boy went berserk? Stark-raving mad? That he was willing to take his chances with the wild dogs that hunt in packs in our woods rather than stay here?" I kept my mouth shut. I tried to forget that he nearly dug out my eyes trying to escape. He might have survived the dogs—animals are honest. If they are hungry or afraid, they will kill. It's nothing personal. Humans created the words love and kindness, not wild dogs, yet every evil thing a human does is personal. Man seldom kills his fellow for food, but he is the first to kill for ideas, and will tell all that his ideas were better than those of his dead brother. It makes me sick.[53]

Though he faulted the parents of cadets, he valued his own circumstances and could never bring himself to fault his own parents or to rebel. "These kids are in one hell of a shape," he wrote home to his mother and father, "and if it hadn't been for you two, I'd have been that way too. A long time ago we heard a folk song: 'There but for fortune, go you and I.' I was very fortunate to have you two."[54]

Pancake found himself caught in the emotional crossfire between his compassion for his students and the institution's demand for strict discipline. Captain Pancake marched the cadets to mess in the morning and marched them to class in the afternoon, made sure they heeded regulations, and punished them when they misbehaved, even if it meant having them lose a weekend leave and the chance for a temporary escape. "I know it sounds tough," he said, "but that's the way they want me to do it, so I do it."[55] It didn't sit well with him. He lived in an in-between world of teacher and student, feeling like both the betrayer and the betrayed. On a delinquency report he assigned four demerits to one cadet for failing to hand in assigned work; on the backside of the report he scribbled a note, apparently after observing the parade ground lined with uniformed boys at attention: "Never thought of it as a field of silence, but as a field of empty cries. (lost life—lost youth)."[56]

This long letter to his parents sums up the life at the academy and his ambivalent feelings about it:

> Friday night duty nearly killed me. I "stuck" half the corps for direct disobedience. Getting "stuck" is being put on report. It involves penalty tours (one hour march for each tour), a visit to the commandant's office, and takes my voice. Ordinarily, I don't have problems with the corps. They know I'm fair, and I don't shout to get my point across. But last night I had to get them into formation and take them—all of them—to the infirmary for their flu shots. I couldn't believe they cried, but I suppose I did at that age, too.
>
> Then it happened. Some joker flushed an orange down the commode—stopped it up—then shit in it and flushed it. I not only made him clean it up, but threatened to make him eat the orange. Insted [sic] I put him on report for 25 demerits. 125 more and he goes home for good. A good many lost their leave weekend last night and a good many will lose it tomorrow. I know that sounds tough, but that's the way they want me to do it, so I do it.
>
> Got my first bill from the Agency.[57] Boy, they don't miss a trick—exactly one week before payday. But they know when payday is, and that's when they'll get their money—and not until.
>
> The bill for my uniforms? Two-hundred bucks for stuff the Army didn't want. That's $200.00 over the $100.00 allowance for uniforms under the contract. I'm paying it in monthly installations of $25.00.
>
> Will Blue Cross bill me for the Cabell-Huntington or is it just understood that I'll pay half the bill? If so, please send it back to me.
>
> I'm running two checking accounts—one here and one in Huntington, but both books balance out to perfection.
>
> I called Paula[58] today—I hadn't heard from her for two weeks and I was naturally a little worried. It seems she's received only one or two letters from me. I wrote to her about twice a week—so all that was lost. She said she'd written, but I've gotten nothing. Lousey post offices. I condemn them to sore eyes and addresses without zip codes.
>
> Matt Heard, a fellow instructor, (and a bartender before he came here) and I are taking our leave weekend in Charlottesville. Movies, libraries, and other tours of interest. Don't worry. Matt's driving. He went back to D.C. last weekend—Mindy, his girlfriend came down to pick him up. Matt offered me his car to "run home for a weekend if you want." Later, I found out he bought it

from a friend for $75.00 and the engine mountings are loose. It's a '66 Chevy—just like the monster we used to have, and seems to have the same mechanical problems—like the excellorator [*sic*] sticks—remember, Pop?

So, how much is the plainest Granada? I know it's a good car, but that doesn't tell my check book anything. You won't have to go on my note, even if I do decide to buy one. I've got a job and a decent credit rating. If I finance it through 1st Huntington, I won't need my co-signers. At any rate, I'm not buying anything from anyone but Shorty,[59] and not until '76 at the earliest. Do you know what the insurance would be? Hell, I don't even want to talk about it.

One of the officers offered me a Honda 450 for $200.00 and payments. Great. Then I would get killed. Maybe that's the answer—escape your creditors through death—ought to write a book on it.

Don't worry about Morris or James Ross. Edison said: "Show me a totally satisfied man, and I'll show you an idiot." I'm not satisfied with F.U.M.A. for a life work, so if I go my other place—it has to be up, or I'm a loser. I'm shooting for something better—not necessarily in money. They can take that away in taxes and funeral bills. No, I want peace, and I'll get it yet. You watch me. But once I get it, I can't let myself be satisfied with it—I have to keep getting better. If I don't, I'm just a loser. Might as well bag groceries if I can't better myself in things that can't be taxed.

Freedom of thought is one of the greatest things our nation has given us, and if we refuse—either through laziness or quiet satisfaction—to make use of that freedom, then we may as well chuck it all and give it to Russia or China, or whoever wants it.

Sarge's cooking was devine [*sic*] tonight—steak, cheese casserole, peas, honey-buns and coffee. I ate twice. Mostly it's dogmeat (that accounts for the Richmond Kennels) and rotten eggs—my personal joke to him. Oh well, war is hell.

I'm glad everybody is better, or at least maintaining. Give my love to all. I miss you and love you. Take care. . . .[60]

He wanted to do more than what his duty allowed, yet doggedly resigned himself to the boundaries imposed by his employers. The students responded to him, trusted him, and that made him feel even worse. He wrote:

Enclosed is a note from one of my students. If you look at the grammar, spelling, etc. you may believe he is BSing about my ability as an English teacher, but it will give you some idea of the desperation and loneliness these boys suffer. Fortunately, Ken is one of the quieter students and seldom gets in trouble, but I am convinced that it is the same desperation that drives these boys to a madness beyond knowledge. Of course, I'll meet his family, as it means a good deal to him. The same boy asked me to take him on a day-pass but I had to say no, as the school would call it fraternization—the word means 'brotherhood' which I assume the school is against. Sad isn't it?[61]

Pancake wanted to help them, save them if he could, but felt powerless.

Because he was trying to do what the school wanted him to do down to the smallest contractual details, his sense of betrayal was layered with even more anger when he judged that the school manipulated grades to enhance the students' performance: "I found this place out when I made out my grades," he wrote home. "The quality of the students here is on an over-whelmingly low level," but the school's sliding grading scale, according to Pancake, reported otherwise. "So when a college calls for a grade reading, they get a number and the tough F.U.M.A. scale. The college thinks the kid is brilliant, and accepts him."[62] This was a breach of trust Breece could not abide, and it reminded him of how the world unfairly operates in favor of the economically advantaged.

> In short, Mommy and Daddy are buying Junior a free grade, an easy "in" to a college, and full-time baby-sitters are three grand a year. And for five grand (four after taxes) I have sold my soul to the kind of people I have spent most of my life disliking. Well, I must try to do something about my position, and I will. I may be a lot of rotten things, but I'm basically pretty honest, and I don't agree with what they are doing here. There are too many poor kids who work like hell to get a grade, to try for scales much higher, and make it. But they are ousted from the college doors by kids of the wealthy with their boughten grades.[63]

Pancake needed to escape from the restrictive atmosphere of the school and the jumble of his emotions—anger at the school he felt had betrayed him and at himself for allowing it to happen, compassion for the desperate, homesick boys, and guilt for having to enforce the strict discipline of the school. He always had difficulty controlling his temper. While at Fork Union, he had assured his parents that they need not worry about his rage, that he had it controlled, and that he had also controlled his drinking, some-thing which may have triggered his angry moods. In September he wrote home, "My temper? It's almost gone. I've also discovered that life without beer is not necessarily unbearable."[64] His temper flared most often over per-ceived injustices, or over moral and ethical hypocrisies (the kind he found at Fork Union), and his temper was not always so easily managed.

In October, he had organized a hiking team of sixteen boys, and on weekends they would leave the school compound to go camping. He tried to teach them what his father had taught him about survival in the wild and to help qualify them for their Survival Merit Badges. On one particular weekend, Captain Pancake and his team of boys had inadvertently strayed into a field owned by a cantankerous farmer, which resulted in a minor ter-ritorial dispute. Pancake reported the incident to his parents with some sur-prise about how he had handled himself:

[The farmer] gave me hell for trespassing. Said he was going to report me—oh, just generally made an ass of himself—and I didn't explode back. I hope to God my temper remains in check. I apologized, but he said, "Well, sorry is not enough," and I nearly laughed at him. What did he want me to do? Disappear into thin air? So I very politely informed him of my name and rank, told him exactly who to call to report me, and politely apologized again, took my troop, and left. I hope he does report me. If his land is so important, why doesn't he post it thus: "Shit-Faced-Son-of-a-Bitch—Beware of Bastard."[65]

Pancake was not easy to anger, but once inflamed, his temper took time to cool. His temper often followed a pattern of rage to remorse, a behavior later observed by people who knew him in Charlottesville.[66]

In November of 1974 he decided to leave Fork Union even though to him leaving meant the threat of "poverty." In a rare moment of liberation, he announced, "The thought of being a free man again is enough riches." He resolved: "A lot has happened to me, and I've decided the only dependable thing in my life is my own ambitions. Everything else is here and gone, but a dream is something to make you get up in the mornings. When one has sold one's soul the roof falls in, and one must build the soul again. So I will start now. I will eat the food because I earned it, will teach because they hired me to, and will do the best job I know how because it isn't the kids' fault I have to lie to them."[67] Pancake held fast and always honored his agreements and contracts, both verbal and written, and, for that reason, he could do nothing but plan for and dream of his escape until he had finished the job he was hired to do, so he stayed on at Fork Union until the following spring of 1975. "Better get to what they pay me for," he wrote home. "Like it or not, I'm under contract to do the work, and I will not be dishonest about that."[68]

In the meantime, Pancake experienced some relief from his dilemma at Fork Union Military Academy in the friendship of Matthew Heard, a fellow instructor from Chevy Chase, Maryland. The two were inseparable, and together they often found temporary escape through their "jaunts" to nearby Charlottesville and Washington, D.C., to see the sights and go barhopping. Of course, an automobile made escape more possible, and in January of 1975, Breece, with a "Cadillac Cowboy" irony, bought a blue '64 Cadillac. He named it the "Great Blue Whale," and both car and driver instantly became the envy and scourge of the school.

"The reaction to the car was everything from jealous grunts to exclamations of grandure [sic]," Pancake wrote. "Maj. Clark told me that my dress (jeans) didn't fit my mode of travel."[69] Pancake, dressed in jeans and cowboy boots, must have appeared to be a bemused John Prine alter-ego behind the wheel. Three months later, Pancake remarked, "I am still taking grief—

the upper school has dubbed it a former 'pimp car.' Said I bought it from a whore master who only drove it to work and back."[70]

Pancake also found escape from barracks life in the woods outside of Fork Union. Not long after he arrived, he began taking frequent solitary hikes like he had done when he was a boy, and he found an enclosed space which he could claim as his own to serve as a respite from his homesickness and the military school grind.[71] "The work is hard," he wrote home, "but the long periods of free time on the weekends don't help me much, so I'd rather work. I found a cave, of a sort, in the end of a hollow about four miles from here. That was my first act of colonization. It is a foxden at the present time, but this winter I plan to camp in it on weekends. It's an off grade granite, so there's no danger of a cave-in."[72] Pancake appeared to be surviving emotionally at Fork Union, and he looked optimistically forward to the future.

In the spring of 1975, while teaching his final semester at Fork Union, he was accepted into the graduate school of English at West Virginia University. He had also applied to the law school there. Law schools have long been the avenue for English majors uncertain of a literary or teaching career and desiring success. The road for Pancake became certain that spring when he ventured to Charlottesville and introduced himself to John Casey, then chairman of the creative writing department at the University of Virginia. Breece showed Casey some of his work. He had written "Fox Hunters" and had been working on "The Scrapper." Casey recalls, "Breece showed up in my office . . . one day and asked me to look at some of the things he'd written. The first story I read was pretty good; it turned out to be the best of his old stuff. Possibly he was testing me with something old before showing the pieces he'd just done. He asked me to look at some more, and luckily, I said yes."[73] Through Casey's influence and encouragement, Pancake put off the decision to attend graduate school and continued to write. Also at Casey's urging, he applied to the writer's workshop at University of North Carolina at Greensboro for a chance to write full-time. As for law school, Pancake wrote to Casey, "I took the LSAT, and have little hope of ever joining that learned profession. Veni, sedi, excessi."[74]

While "packing like a rat on a sinking ship" during his final days at Fork Union in the Spring of 1975, he accepted another teaching position at the Staunton Military Academy in the Valley of Virginia near the Blue Ridge Mountains. It was closer to Milton, where his father was slowly dying, and to Charlottesville, where his ambitions lived; but, unknowingly, Pancake had jumped from one sinking ship to another. Staunton Military Academy was doomed to fail within a year. He was a member of the last faculty to teach at the 117-year-old academy, an institution that had graduated Barry Goldwater Sr. and Barry Goldwater Jr., John Dean, numerous professional football players, and Breece's hero Phil Ochs. The school ran aground amid a sea of red ink in July 1976 under the ownership of Layne Leoffler, a self-made millionaire, born-again Christian, and graduate of SMA himself, who, some say, tried to rescue the institution from bankruptcy; others say he fulfilled an oath of revenge upon the school.

In September of 1975, Breece's friend, Matt Heard tried to convince him to stay at Fork Union by driving to Staunton for one last party before the school year began, but he did not succeed. Pancake was glad to put Fork Union behind him and was filled with joyful optimism at the beginning of the new school year at Staunton. "SMA was even better than I anticipated," Pancake wrote home. "Outside of the great pay, the headmaster is a genuine educator, an artist, and easy going as hell."[75] Even though Pancake was still teaching at a military academy, he had hopes that something good could be done at the school. "The job is still as good as it always was, except for the fact that it's military. I guess it beats getting a shiv in the ribs. For the most part I have no complaints. We teach students instead of beating them and that's a relief."[76] He had met the assistant headmaster at nearby Stuart Hall, a prep school for girls also located in Staunton, and together they had planned a cooperative drama department between the two schools. He had been assigned the upper grades, and he was pleased to note that "it looks as if it will be a smooth sail."[77]

His prospects in Charlottesville, too, never seemed better. John Casey wanted him to sit in on his creative writing classes and encouraged him to apply to both the University of Virginia and the University of Iowa writing programs. For the first time in a long while, he was genuinely happy. On September 4, 1975, he told his mother and father, "You may inform all concerned that I'm happy (beardless, but happy) and give them my love."[78]

Life's circumstances, however, allowed him little time to be happy or hopeful. Four days later, on September 8, his father died from complications of multiple sclerosis.

Pancake's next letter to his mother conveys some of his suffering:

> I've been wanting to call you all week, but that probably isn't the best thing since we both have enough Fred[79] in us to waste the time crying.
>
> I worry about you in the house, alone. I hope you are doing O.K. I know people won't leave you alone during the day, but the nights are hard even for me. You haven't said you'd be over, so I don't know what to think. I hope you come. . . .
>
> I'm getting over a very bad cold, and trying to keep up with my work. Things go on the same—it's almost absurd.
>
> Please tell Mammaw and Grandpa how proud I was to have them with us, and I'll try and write them tomorrow. I've written Aunt Julia, but I'm sure you'll hear about that.

You held out so well Mom, but I'm sure the thing has caught up with you now in the same way it has for me. If it helps any, I can assure you that Pop got exactly what he wanted. Many times we talked, and always he realized it could have been a hell of a lot worse. Despite it all, he had a grand sense of humor, and I'll never forget him laughing. I was lucky to have him for my father and friend.

But we have to let him go, Momma. We can't keep him, we can only make him over in our own minds.

I hope I haven't made things worse for you. I'm kind of clumsy that way. Most of all, remember I love you.[80]

In a sympathy note, Breece's friend Matthew Heard had written, "I know you'll miss him alot, Buddy—if it'll make you feel any better you can grab me by the neck and throw me down—which I fully expect."[81] Helen Pancake recalls that "[a]fter his father died, he was expecting Matthew to help him through his bereavement."[82] Then, two weeks later, on September 29, Matthew Heard died in an automobile accident, and Breece's mother bitterly remembers, "that liked to kill that boy."[83] For Pancake, the need for escape and sanctuary returned with a rush.

Weeks after his father's death, Breece wrote to his mother, "Tomorrow I'm going to church. Don't fall over, because I doubt anybody will get near me with any water. I just thought it would beat sitting in my room all morning. . . ."[84] With some reluctance he began attending the First Presbyterian Church in Staunton "to hear the organ preludes," he said, and to "meet people, and comb the cobwebs out of my head. The sermon doesn't make much sense," he insisted, "I think the minister is an agnostic. Everybody's got a freedom to believe,"[85] but there was no doubt he was searching for a haven, some place that could offer peace.

Meanwhile, Pancake somberly noted that the business at Staunton Military Academy "trudges by with the same absurdity."[86] Although the academy focused more on education than on military rigor, there were still moments of excess—rude awakenings at 6 A.M. by screaming cadets, fireworks at all hours, and unreasonable military-like discipline:

While I was on duty Friday, the Real Army Capt. here went nuts, came out of his room with a loaded shotgun shouting that I couldn't control the "men." They had set off some firecrackers—I rather enjoyed the display. At that moment an alumnus came into the compound (looking like a hippie) and the Capt. beat the shit out of him with the butt of the gun because the kid didn't halt when the stupid bastard told him to halt. It was the most disgusting thing I've ever seen. Then the Capt. had the gall to say he did it because he hated to waste (kill) the boy. He also said he'd waste these students before "I'll let them waste this school."[87]

The tension caused by the school's imminent closing created instances of extreme behavior in students and faculty alike and reawakened Pancake's old fear of being unemployed.

He found some emotional refuge by moving out of the barracks and into a cellar apartment on 324 East Beverly Avenue in Staunton. The apartment was owned by Mrs. Sarah Nutt, an elderly widow, who lived upstairs in the main house and who became, for Breece, his "Virginia" mother. Dressed in a blue wool boatman's cap and pea jacket and smoking a pipe, he often raked leaves in the backyard and did other chores around the house. Together, he and Mrs. Nutt sometimes sat around the kitchen table, drank coffee, and talked about a story he was writing. Mrs. Nutt frequently arranged dinners, teas, and other social gatherings at her home, and Pancake always had a standing invitation. Even after he had left for Charlottesville the following year, he stayed in close touch with Sarah Nutt until his death. She remembers that "he was most generous in bringing . . . gifts, many from the glass factory in his home town. He was proud and did not want to be 'beholden' to anyone." She also remembers that "he liked to play music on a record player and, having trouble getting to sleep, consumed some beer which aided that problem. Also, he had a tendency to sleep walk which I only discovered one time when he had ended up in another room."[88]

Tall, aged trees line Beverly Avenue where many of the large, three-story houses of Staunton overlook the town. Compared to barracks life, the cellar apartment was quite spacious, with two bedrooms, a dining room, a sitting room, a garage and kitchen privileges in the upstairs part of the house. "My sanity was ready for this apt.," he wrote home to his mother.[89] He could now breathe easier in a place "furnished with antiques, . . . a fireplace," and "back yard complete with squirrel." Two months later, Mrs. Nutt invited him to live upstairs in the main house for less rent and also offered him the use of "Faraway," a small hunting cabin on the family farm in Middlebrook, Virginia, where he could fish in a stocked pond and roam the woods. The cabin also served as an escape for him while he attended the University of Virginia.

"You don't know what a relief it is to get out of the barracks," he told his mother. "I must be asocial, but I can't exist in these conditions. I haven't told anybody about it, and plan to keep this room as a sort of stop-over when I pull duty. I'm moving in a little at a time so no one will notice. Don't worry about it jeopardizing my job. Preston [Preston Doyle, headmaster at SMA] won't give a good damn whether I'm here or not, as long as I do my job."[90] The house on Beverly Street , his friendship with Sarah Nutt, and attending church on Sundays provided some brief refuge from the harsh emotional climate of life at a military school and from the deathblows of his father and best friend.

His developing relationship with John Casey and his writing, however, became the path for his most immediate and long-lasting emotional escape. Casey became for him both mentor and, at least for a short while, father figure. Pancake needfully invested Casey with the trust and confidence he would have otherwise held back, and he engaged Casey in activities that he and his father had shared—watching boxing matches on TV, fishing, playing pool—he even asked Casey to go hunting with him, though Casey declined. In a letter to Casey weeks before his death, Pancake recounted their early relationship:

> Remember May 1975? "God, why didn't you tell me . . . if I'd known you were this good, I'd have offered you a fellowship." I hadn't told you because I knew I wasn't. Then the summer of bad times when I pounded on doors, got fed-up, went fishing, and bingo they offered me a job sight unseen from Staunton, and bingo my father and my best friend croaked within a week of each other, and bingo I held on for dear life. I held on because of me, but I held on with the help of you. The night we went to see Ali murder Frazier in Manila, that night I nearly knocked your brains out with my driving into the parking-lot abutement [sic]. I was trying to think of some way to thank you for going with me to the fights, and I forgot to hit the breaks [sic].[91]

Casey was also a writer, something more than his father could ever be and something Pancake wanted to become.

Pancake's experience at Fork Union and Staunton Military academies encouraged a strict daily regimen of diet, exercise, and work, and he borrowed those Spartan habits for his life as a writer. As a result, the two years from 1974 to 1976 at Fork Union and Staunton Military Academies proved to be his most prolific. Pancake had already completed "Fox Hunters" in the spring of 1975. In September, weeks before the Ali–Frazier fight, Casey had used "The Scrapper" in one of his classes at the University of Virginia, and he agreed to write "a facing letter for the story to the 'Atlantic.'"[92] In October Pancake began work on "The Mark," then quickly followed with a story called "Cowboys and Girls" (which was to become "The Way It Has to Be") and then wrote the story "Hollow." In the spring during his last months at Staunton, Pancake began writing "The Salvation of Me," "Trilobites," (originally titled "Will o' the Wisp"), "Time and Again," and "The Honored Dead." All totaled, nine of his twelve published stories had either been completely written, shaped, or conceived before the fall of 1976.

In February of 1976, Virginia's literary magazine, the *Rivanna*, published "The Mark," and Vance Bourjaily recruited Pancake for the University of Iowa's graduate writing program. John Casey and Peter Taylor wanted him at Virginia. Exhilarated by the attention and his success, but still swamped with work at failing SMA, Pancake didn't quite know what to do.

On March 3, 1976, he wrote his mother: "The fellowship at U.Va. is at least 2,000–2,500, only lasts a year to confer an M.A., and both Casey . . . and Mr. Taylor . . . really want me here. Casey, however, is asking me to wait because he feels the prestige of U.Va. offer may prompt Iowa to try to beat the offer. Mr. Bourjaily (Iowa) is pretty impressed, and wants me there. Honestly I don't know what to do. Va. is third in the U.S. and Iowa is #1, but there's a gossamer entanglement of things. You are wise to await my decision, as I am still not sure what's going on."[93]

It seemed that after his father's death, Pancake never really accepted the good things that came to him. His reality was always shaded with suspicion and the expectation of loss; he seemed to believe that the good things would never last too long. In the same letter home that announced his successes, he still looked back with a gloomy paraphrase from Steinbeck's 1961 *The Winter of Our Discontent*: "Last Spring I drove whale back, and Matt had a great time riding around the back seat drinking beer. Well, the spring is coming, and then it all goes away—this winter of our discontent."[94]

In April 1976 he began making plans to move from Staunton to Charlottesville. "More than likely be at U.Va this fall—no need to carry stuff back—will store at Casey's house. Iowa accepted, but no promise of money—therefore U.Va."[95] He shed his skin by exchanging "The Blue Whale" for "The Bluegill," a 1964 blue Volkswagen convertible. That spring Staunton Military Academy closed its doors for the last time, and Pancake "turned back into his room and looked beyond it, beyond the bed of restless sleep and the desk clutter of seventh grade compositions."[95] He was looking toward the green lawns and white columns of the University of Virginia, seeking his ambition.

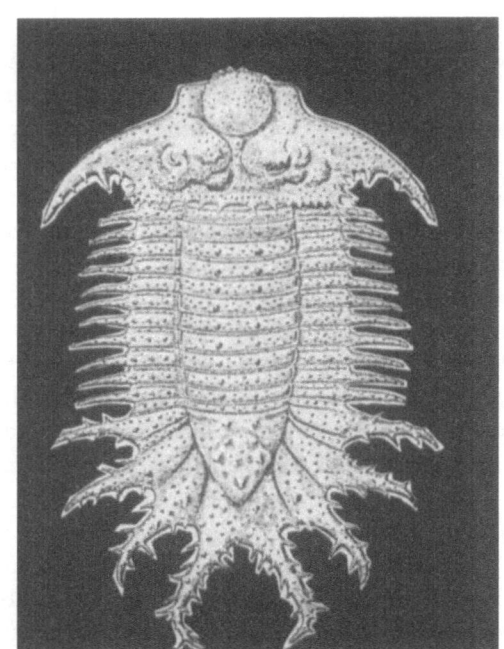

Fossil of a Trilobite. Pancake kept this print framed on the wall of his room at Charlottesville. Courtesy of Pancake Estate.

Milton High School graduation, 1970. Milton High Yearbook. Courtesy of Pancake Estate.

Breece Pancake, self-portrait, 1970. Courtesy of Pancake Estate.

The 1920 Underwood no. 5 typewriter that Aunt Julia Pancake
Ward gave to Breece in 1974. Photo by Helen Pancake.
Courtesy of Pancake Estate.

Breece and C. R., Christmas 1971. Photo by Helen Pancake. Courtesy of Pancake Estate.

Capt. Breece Pancake,
Fork Union Military
Academy, 1974–75.
Courtesy of Pancake Estate.

Breece's Father's Day Gift, June 1967. Oil painting by Breece Pancake.
Courtesy of Pancake Estate.

4

Aristocrat in Blue Jeans

I look inside. It is a classy joint . . . I cannot go in there. It is too classy, and besides there are too many people. They will laugh at my seedy clothes, and my shoes without soles.

—Tom Kromer, *Waiting for Nothing*

In September 1976 Breece Pancake wrote home to his mother, "Tell everybody it's confirmed I'm crazy for doing this!!"[1] He had enrolled in the graduate school of English at the University of Virginia in Charlottesville, feeling untested and inferior in the larger literary world that the university represented. He was driven to succeed, to prove himself, if not by writing fiction, then at least through his teaching. To be admitted to an English program of high reputation and to be tutored and judged by such renowned writers as John Casey, Peter Taylor, James Alan McPherson, and Richard Jones would be a step toward recognition and a boost to his literary ambition. To complete a graduate degree, Pancake reasoned further, also would allow him to qualify for something more than a secondary teaching post at a military school. However, his graduate career, more realistically, became both the opportunity that he sought and a treadmill that wore him down.

In the spring of 1976 Pancake had been accepted to both the University of Iowa and the University of Virginia. Pancake had submitted several of his stories as part of his application to graduate school; Peter Taylor reviewed his application, read "The Mark," and wrote a quick note on the manuscript to Casey, who was then head of the Creative Writing Program at Virginia: "This man is very good. I'm all for him!" Virginia awarded him the Emily Balch Fellowship in creative writing, and he began to pack his bags for Charlottesville. Almost at the same time, the *Rivanna*, a literary review of the University of Virginia published "The Mark." To Breece, his first published story and his acceptance into graduate school proved that he could measure up to and exceed the expectations of the folks back home. He wrote to his mother, "Nonetheless Pop was right about success being the sweetest revenge. Helen Blake [his high school English teacher] never thought I'd be worth a lick."[2] Pancake's own expectations were much higher. He not only wanted to be accepted and to perform up to the task, but he also wanted to excel. "If the best I can do is B work," he told his mother, "there isn't much point in doing anything but writing."[3]

Graduate school, for him it seems, affirmed his legitimacy as a writer and a teacher, and a graduate degree was the necessary union card. The quest to go on for a Ph.D., however, didn't make any practical sense to him. "I've decided not to go on for a PhD and Peter [Taylor] agrees that it's a pretty hopeless route. I'd much rather work and write as write a dissertation (not stories) on some unknown fact."[4] In another letter he explained, "So many of these turkey-students are staying in for Ph.D.'s, but the whole orientation theme was telling them they couldn't get work with twelve Ph.D.'s from Harvard. I guess there comes a time when you decide the sky isn't the limit and the road doesn't go on forever, and that's where you stop. And I guess I prefer the real world to these ivory towers of learning."[5] For Pancake, graduate school was an "oh well" proposition, a grueling but necessary detour from real life and work.

He was already familiar with the university and the town; Breece and Matt Heard had often taken the forty-minute drive northwest from Fork Union to "C'Ville" to watch rugby games and to have their fun in pool halls and bars, and during the spring of 1976 he had been driving east on Route 64 from Staunton (west of Charlottesville) over Massanutten and Afton Mountains to attend one of John Casey's writing classes. He had become acquainted with many of the faculty at parties John Casey had for his students. He met fellow West Virginian Mary Lee Settle, an accomplished author and member of the university faculty, and was a little embarrassed at not having known of her work beforehand. Breece eventually took a part-time job tutoring her grandchildren and helped provide some of the research for her book *The Scapegoat*. Although Breece was just another graduate student, just one among the competitive best in the nation, he tried quickly to break down formal student-teacher relationships:

> Caseys' have invited me up to R.I. for some fishing, etc. this summer, but I doubt I'll have the time for it. John just bought a canoe, and if he finishes his novel[6] by the end of the week, we're going to try it out. He's been writing like

a whirlwind to finish this one before his leave. I don't know if he's sold it or not—he doesn't say much except, "I'm on page 650," and you'd better remember the last time to mark whether he's made any progress.

I have to go to a small coal camp[7] the first day I'm on break—please suggest one, should be deserted or near it. If I can't pass it coming through, we'll take a day, o.k.? My regards to all, and, mostly, my love to you. Look forward to seeing you and home quite soon.[8]

In particular, he became good friends with McPherson, Jones, and Casey and tried to get close to the more formal Peter Taylor. After the deaths of his father and of his good friend Matthew Heard, Breece leaned heavily on his relationship with John Casey, who gave him the necessary opportunity and encouragement to become the writer and artist he dreamed of becoming. Casey recalls their relationship as gradually becoming like that of two brothers, Breece being the older brother.[9] Richard Jones, one of Breece's neighbors, enjoyed an easy friendship with him, marked by casual visits to each other's homes on their way to and from the university; Breece often brought by a string of fish or a bag of small game.

Jim McPherson and Pancake also experienced a special friendship; they fished together a few times, and occasionally they caroused in the local pool and beer halls. They shared an almost immediate bond because they both felt emotionally distant from Charlottesville, both feeling like "outsiders," but for different reasons. McPherson recalls, "I didn't have to explain certain things to Breece as a white person. Those things were understood. And that's the most comforting thing in the world when you can say, instead of saying 'you know,' the person does know."[10] In the spring of 1977, Pancake gave McPherson a shotgun for helping him get published in the *Atlantic,* and he hoped they might go hunting together in the fall. Pancake joked to his sister, "I'm hoping he's quieter in the woods than in the pool halls, or we'll never see anything. He brandished the damn thing in the parking lot and said—'I want all you white people to be in Cleveland by midnight.' Told him I'd rather be in Milton. 'O.K. all you white people go to Ohio and Pancake can stay here and be my slave.'"[11] McPherson has said that he and Pancake shared a kind of "secret country" in Charlottesville "that had to do with 'recognition,' or with 'spirit,' or with a shared . . . view of the implicit irony in the public image of reality during the middle 1970s in contrast with the complexity of the private realities." McPherson said, "The two of us laughed a lot over jokes that we could not share with other people."[12]

Pancake did make many friends among the faculty and students—Rod Kilpatrick, Mike Jennings, David Field, T. B. Shutt, Chuck Perdue, Carl Beckman, Nancy Ramsey, Raymond Nelson, Libby Wilson, Kathleen Devereux—but from the first day he had left Milton, left West Virginia, he felt homesick and out of place. This feeling was made worse by his solitary nature, which kept him isolated and haunted. In addition, the feeling of the town and the university that came from the well-boundaried landscape, the colonial style houses, and the provincial people reminded him of an alien country which emphasized a more genteel tradition than the one in which he had been reared. The old historical perceptions of class division and condescension that have existed between Virginia and West Virginia, between landed gentry and backwoods hillbilly, aroused feelings of inferiority and resentment in Pancake, though he attempted to shrug them off with humor.

Eleanor Ross Taylor recalls a graduate student party at her home, where her husband, Peter Taylor, served as host. "There was a gathering of writing students at our house," she remembers, "amid the UVa style of that era—jacket and tie. [Breece] went up to another newcomer in shirtsleeves and said merrily, 'Jim, you'll have to buy a jacket!' As he himself was in shirtsleeves, he had evidently appraised the social scene and made his own decision."[13] To Pancake, Charlottesville represented a land of refined manners, wealth, property, bloodlines, and exclusion, and he found himself a stranger in it.

From the outset, he rebelled against that feeling. He rented a small apartment located on the "well-to-do" Farmington Estates, a collection of large manor homes neatly tucked around the tidy, manicured fairways and greens of the Penn Park Golf Course, a few miles from the university. Actually, the apartment was a small room in the east wing of a large home, formerly servant's quarters for the family maid and nanny. The large brick house, painted white, with a black roof and black shutters also had a landscaped, circular driveway, swimming pool, and an apple tree in the backyard. About his new home Pancake remarked, "I plan to gig frogs in their pond, and hope to be thrown out about January. Don't worry, by then I'll have friends."[14]

He called his new home a "phone booth," and told his mother, "You couldn't sleep there—even on the floor!"[15] The twelve-by-twelve-foot room had a small shower and toilet alcove, a stacked stove/refrigerator unit, one door, and one window and it rented for fifty-five dollars a month. He slept on a cot and kept his makeshift desk of plywood in front of the window. Pancake observed that "even a fox has his den." Though he was only planning on staying in graduate school for one year, the apartment at One Blue Ridge Lane was his home for the next three, and from this address he could see the Blue Ridge Mountains rising in the west above the Shenandoah Valley. The following letter provides an insightful view of Pancake's new situation—and the pull he felt toward Milton and his old ties:

I don't know when you'll get this, but I may as well write now, as time is coming I'll be going nuts again.

Today, the first day of small game season, I listened as the rats with bushy tails laughed at me from just out of range. And with deer season only one week away, a four point buck walked within ten yards of me, stopped, stared, walked off. Tell Glenn and Jr., because I won't see another one, I'm sure. There I sat with the shotgun, no slugs, and the season a week away. I could cry rivers. I have been tracking this fellow for a week, but never saw him in that part of the woods, so I'm not as smart as I thought. But it was a nice sight, and I thought of Dad, sitting there in his hunting clothes.

Peter Taylor is starting another magazine, and has invited me to help edit it, but that remains in the shadows, as P. T. is often other-worldly about plans. He wants it to be a mag. for regional stories like my own and others. I think he is rebelling against the so-called new story, and trying to get a clique of southern writers together again—much like it was when he was young. I asked him how much he was going to pay me. There will be money, says he. Sure. In the words of Sally in "Hollow," They's always gonna, but they ain't never any.

Richard Jones asked me if he could buy some of the game I get this fall, but in England, they do that. I told them they throw the key away if you do that here, and he said that it was "barbaric" to do such a thing to a man.

Many thanks for the check. It's in the tobacco can if I need it. The thing is, you don't have any money if this keeps up. Granted, I left two C-notes with you, but as I recall, it was because you were short. I don't want this becoming a habit because I don't want to get used to the extra income, and two, I don't want you counting your pennies. Right, you do have bread in the bank, but that's a cow of different color. You are working for what you live on, and you had better keep it. When Carter gets through, they may close the country down.

Well, I've been up since four, and I'm going tomorrow. Somewhere there is a critter with my name on him, just waiting to become pot-meat.[16]

All around this "foxden" in Albemarle County were reminders of what he had grown to abhor. "I am sick to my stomach of people who drive fine cars, live alone in big apts., never worked a day in their lives and bellyache 60% of the time. This county is 2nd in the country for millionaires—L.A. County being first. It do get to be hard to swallow."[17] His landlady, Mrs. Virginia Meade, lived up to Pancake's suspicion of the class exclusion that existed in Charlottesville. He wrote to his mother, "Mrs. Meade is throwing a party for the Eng. dept. and had the gall to ask me to tend bar. Said if I didn't, she'd have to hire a colored, and they don't mix a good drink. That tells me where I stand as a Hillbilly—one notch above the colored—only because I can mix a good drink. If Mrs. Meade forgets herself and invites me, I'll decline on the basis of not having any shoes, and having to tend my still and welfare check."[18] "Mrs. Meade absolutely got up his nose," Richard Jones remembers. "She was a very modish, worldly lady. She would give a cocktail party and emerge in silks and satins from New York. She brushed Breece the wrong way. . . ."[19] At the Meades, he seemed to be constantly reminded of the social and economic differences that separated him from the well-to-do. While researching the history of Milton for story background, he wrote, "I kept looking . . . for some mention of the Pancakes, then I realized we were just poor buckra compared to the land owners." He joked, "We had the second flush toilet in town, and that's some kind of fame. If it hadn't been for Rob [his grandfather], we would still be poor buckra. Probably still have an outhouse."[20]

If his suspicions of condescension and exclusion had been confirmed in the Charlottesville community, they may have been further heightened at the university. McPherson has characterized the halls of the University of Virginia as "an environment reeking with condescension."[21] In a fanciful elegiac of Pancake, T. B. Shutt, a former colleague of Pancake's, confirms this impression. "The University cultivates detachment like an orchid," Shutt wrote. "An epiphyte, and stemless, straining color from mid-air. The serpentine walls and the oxford-cloth shirts all starched just so—they're hanging gardens. Rich, well-cared-for—an exhibition, and the point of it is waste. The wealth to spend where there's no need. And even we, who participate, know that it's more than half of it done for show. A ceremony, something to enact, to don like choir robes and then take off after services." Shutt describes the university as "a living diorama to the Sage. Mr. Jefferson himself still half alive and half invented and bought into."[22] Pancake, in spite of himself, was more than a little awed by this impression of the University of Virginia.

On campus Pancake provided a startling contrast. Among his fellow students Breece stood out because of his cowboy boots, his large U.S. Army brass belt buckle and blue jeans, and the hill twang in his voice. His friend and classmate Nancy Ramsey recalls, "He was so different from all these mealy-mouthed little English graduate students. There was Breece, coming down the hall with his cowboy boots clicking and stomping."[23] According to Chuck Perdue, Pancake was thought of "as some sort of Appalachian primitive. Some were both attracted and repelled by that perception." Once he told a group of graduate students about how he had stopped along the highway to pick up a freshly killed rabbit and took it home, skinned it out, and cooked it. "They were rather negatively impressed and talked about it with considerable disgust," says Perdue, and adds, "Breece enjoyed their reaction."[24] Raymond Nelson, who shared an office with him in Wilson Hall, has described Pancake as having a physical presence that no one could ignore: "He's a big brash guy, powerful, but he felt very often uneasy in a place like this or felt he should be uneasy. So he asserted himself that way, and of course one of the things he learned here—God knows how well he learned it—is that he could survive. He could function, he could triumph even, in a place like this. But there was always that—I think it's real—that 'I'm just a hillbilly from West Virginia. To hell with you'—that kind of thing as a way of putting his own defenses up, and establishing who he was and his own integrity and so on."[25]

In her book *The Clamshell*, Mary Lee Settle has portrayed the predicament of the West Virginia mountaineer coming to Virginia, which produces a kind of defensive shyness created by a sense of history and cultural perception. Speaking through a character, she suggests that many West Virginians have "a familiarity with Virginia, which means more to us than simply another place. Physically, it is only a barrier of mountains away, across the Allegheny Divide, but to us Virginia is our Europe, hated and loved, before we are shy, as Americans are shy in Europe."[26] Pancake had not only crossed the Allegheny Divide into his sister state, he had also come to Jefferson's university to pursue a career that would make him an anomaly back home. "Wanting to be a writer as a West Virginian is sort of like wanting to be an actor, or an astronaut, or President of the United States," according to West Virginia writer Lee Maynard. "These were all fantasies and that was okay, but in reality you had to go out and do some real work."[27] For these reasons, the differences, the feelings of alienation, the unnerving newness Pancake felt were accentuated. Settle also noticed something ironic in Pancake's image, his appearance, his persona at Virginia: "He had a totally aristocratic, Anglo-Saxon face" and that sometimes he played the hillbilly role to repress any class distinction he may have felt in himself. "His judgments were almost naive judgments. You know if your clothes fit you were the enemy, and this was ridiculous because Breece's clothes always fit."[28]

In reality, Pancake was different than many at the university because he came from the mountains and because he had access to something that many no longer had—a rural woodsman's experience. He also had worked dozens of jobs before entering graduate school, and Pancake found that many of his fellow students had not worked at all. This was incomprehensible to someone who had been taught to work hard, to pay as you go, and to make it on your own. Concerning his fellow students, he raged, "What the hell do those people know about getting by? What the hell good is knowing books if you haven't had a life?"[29]

He chafed against the values held by the more affluent students, values that seemed to ignore self-sacrifice and overlooked the importance of family. "I don't want to be like them. They're in the money, but they haven't got enough heart to fill a thimble. They don't want kids because kids cost time and money and they are too selfish to take either away from themselves."[30] In fact, Pancake found a whole range of political, social, and artistic values espoused at the university difficult to accept. About a writing class Pancake complained, "We just had a story where a guy rents a hotel room, sets up a movie camera, and proceeds to cut off pieces of his body while talking about art. Trish got up and walked out. I should have."[31]

McPherson's first impression was that Breece supported the candidacy of Jimmy Carter and had the raised expectations of the lower middle-class southerners whom Carter represented and perhaps would redefine. In 1976 McPherson, like Pancake, had just begun his work at the University of Virginia, and in his first few days there in Wilson Hall, McPherson recalls:

> [T]he sound of a voice [Breece's] . . . It was in the hall outside my office door and it was saying, "I'm Jimmy Carter and I'm running for President, I'm Jimmy Carter and I'm running for President." The pitch and rhythms of the voice conveyed the necessary messages: the rhythm and intonation were southern, the kind that instantly calls to mind the word cracker. Its loudness, in the genteel buzz and hum of Wilson Hall, suggested either extreme arrogance or a certain insecurity. Why the voice repeated Carter's campaign slogan was obvious to anyone: the expectations of the South, especially of the lower-class and middle-class South, were with Carter. He was one of them.[32]

Breece's political attitudes were more complex than McPherson's first assessment. Pancake certainly felt "alienated . . . in the hushed gentility of Wilson Hall," and he rebelled against class exclusion, perhaps in a self-conscious way, as Richard Jones has pointed out. He was always playing down his intelligence to fit the stereotype. "He was always trying to disguise from people how clever and perceptive he was."[33] Politically, however, Pancake did not see any hope or promise in what he considered free-spending Democratic social programs. He distrusted Democratic governor Jay Rockefeller, was suspicious of his motives and his family history, and overall he did not think Carter would be good for the country. Just before the 1976 election he told his mother, "Well, tighten your belt. Carter's the one. I guess Grandpa is happy, anyway. I'd better learn to hunt well. May have to eat once in a while,"[34] and after the election he told her, "When Carter gets through, they may close the country down."[35]

Though Breece, like his father, championed the underdog, he was by no means a believer in privilege, egalitarianism, or a free handout. He had the political and social instincts characteristic of many Appalachian people: "Let everybody have a fair shake, but each must do as best as they can on their own." In political terms he could perhaps be described as a conservative Democrat with more than a pinch of anarchy and libertarianism. This philosophy is carried over in social attitudes about life, death, and survival—a no-nonsense approach to working, making a living, or putting food on the table. "Mom, I don't understand these students, or the faculty or darn near anybody," Pancake confessed. "They just don't operate on the same logic I do. Met a girl the other day who was talking about her abortion, and she shit a brick when I said I hunted—'You kill the little animals?' I should have said, 'Yes, and I understand you do too.' Better enjoy Aunt Julia while you can—at this rate people are next in line. One lass in my writing class quit an $18,000 a year job to come down here to graduate school—I've had it—nothing makes sense."[36] He could not always make sense of the university or Charlottesville, and he always felt like a misfit there, an outsider, sometimes lonely and afraid.

That fall Pancake had never been so busy. If hard work was what he was after, he certainly found it in graduate school—teaching classes, attending his own, and writing. "I swear to God this is killing me,"[37] he wrote home. But the social isolation, he believed, made "good work time,"[38] and he made use of his Spartan work habits and frugal sense of economy. "I've not been this busy in years," he told his mother.[39] "I've been up since 3 am writing long hand on this teaching paper, and I'm done for. It is now 5 pm. You see, I go to bed before the news goes off, and I'm up in the wee hours. This because I can get nothing on the radio, have to leave the stereo off, not tempted to beer since I just got up, can't look at the window since it's dark—nothing else to do, may as well study. That's discipline for a chicken fried rat—which is what I am."[40]

In this new environment and during this period of adjustment to graduate school life, Breece was still grieving for his father. A week after the anniversary of his father's death in September, he wrote to his mother: "Sounds like you spent the Eighth O.K. I went plowing around town that night looking for somebody to talk to about anything. Just didn't want to be alone. Nobody. Not a single soul I knew was home. It was very frustrating, then I remembered how Pop watched life go on around him for three years, and couldn't be a part of it. Somehow I couldn't feel sorry for myself." Then bitterly, he confessed, "I'm doing my best Mom, but it's a son of a bitch. As the old man in *Tattoo* always said 'Goddam such a Goddam way of doing.' It makes more sense than anything else I could say."[41] His grief and confusion deepened his longing for home and the identification with "his" people. "In some ways I miss Milton," Pancake wrote to his mother. "I bet it's all based on people. The place isn't much, granted, but Jr., Bliss, Claude, Fred Ball, Dude, they're all so important to me as friends. Lots of times I wish you could just tell me a tale about something that happened in Frazier's Bottom. And Mary Jane, Shorty, Glenn, the people who make a town live down in its roots . . . they all stay in my mind. I reckon that Dad and Duck aren't dead, but maybe I'm them and they are me."[42] This letter sheds some light on his solitary existence and his struggle to adapt to the demands of graduate school life:

I did get some therapy today. It was pouring rain, so I soaped the can, and let the rain rinse it. Saved fifty cents. Roof leaks so I'll have to waterproof it soon. Did I tell you I fixed the electrical problem with 13 cents? A fuse. Wish it was all like that.

Enclosed are copies of the Declaration.[43] At this time, I can't say how "Cowboys and Girls" will look, but Chris told me a picture went with the story, which is O.K. There are also some back issues with "Hollow", but it's an old version, still the girls haven't read either one, and if you want to send them a copy, that's O.K. too. I just can't afford the postage.

Peter Taylor is driving me nuts with "Will-o-the-Wisp."[44] He wants a D. H. Lawrence story, and that ain't what she's about. I don't know what the hell to do . . .

I wish the hell I'd taken John's [John Casey] advice and just taken the money to write. As is, I'm so busy reading and writing papers for class I haven't got time to write stories. I was so burned out Monday, that I took rod in hand, and kept everything I caught. Ate it too. And the fact that it was under limit size did not give me heartburn.

As far as I know ——— is still feeling sorry for herself about not getting more money from her daddy. She called, oddly, at midnight to say hello. She knows my pattern of study, and knows I'm asleep, but that makes no difference. Next time ——— talks about suicide, I'm going to offer her my pistol, gratis. May we both get some rest. Jesus, but that shit makes me heave a gut. What the hell do those people know about getting by? What the hell good is knowing books if you haven't had a life? *Tattoo and Garden of Sand*[45] ought to be required reading to get in this place.

Well, better go. Miss you much, and reckon I'll see you before long. Love you.[46]

Although it was a distraction from grief, school drained him and allowed little time for writing new fiction. But Pancake believed in what he had written in one of his stories: "quits ain't the answer." Once the job or game began, he wanted to "stick," no matter the outcome or consequence.[47] Regardless of the frustration, Pancake somehow did keep up with his writing. He regularly charted deadlines for himself in two-week intervals, requiring the completion of projects or story drafts, and he was unusually productive compared to most other graduate students. Pancake fine-tuned "Hollow" and "The Way It Has to Be," stories he had written while living in Staunton, and the university publication, the *Declaration*, published both in the early fall. He had already finished "Fox Hunters," "The Scrapper," and "The Mark" the year before,[48] and he was now working on "The Salvation of Me" and a story called "Will o' the Wisp," which would eventually be titled "Trilobites." In all, nine of the twelve stories posthumously collected and published in *The Stories of the Breece D'J Pancake* bore a Milton or Staunton address on the original manuscript. Only three of the stories, "First Day of Winter," "In the Dry," and "A Room Forever" were probably begun and written at One Blue Ridge Lane in Charlottesville. The exhausting work schedule demanded by graduate school provided little time for the creation of new work, and Breece directed most of his writing effort to reworking and rewriting previously conceived stories.

In an interview with Carlos Santos of the *Richmond Times-Dispatch*, Pancake described his work routine—writing forty or more hours a week, four drafts of story in longhand, ten drafts on the typewriter. "I want to make sure what I've said is what I've said," Pancake told Santos. "It's a risky business. You put one month of your life in a story and you've got it where you want it and then they say, 'We don't get it.' . . . I'd hate to count my rejection slips."[49]

Rewriting was something the university taught well, and writing at least ten drafts was the treatment he wanted to give each of his stories, but which only a few received—"Trilobites," "The Honored Dead," "In the Dry," and probably "Hollow." On a draft of "The Honored Dead," Breece wrote a hurried note to Peter Taylor: "Mr. Taylor, Yes, you have seen this before. Yes, I've changed it quite a bit. Yes, this is the 8th draft. Breece."[50] He worked with both Peter Taylor and John Casey on "Trilobites," a story begun in 1976 but not finished until the following year. Pancake also argued for the necessity of rewriting in the fiction classes he taught at the university. He told his students to "look upon your stories as a fine wine, one aged and well made, and not as a cup of instant coffee. Rewriting is the key to refined fiction . . ."[51]

His theory of "refined fiction" was further defined by physical and emotional exhaustion. "I have sweat and bled over a new story until it is finally taking some shape. P. Taylor has it now, and I won't be able to get it back until I've heard his comments. One thing I have not done is cried over it, which I believe is an absolute to any story told well. Maybe that will come toward the end."[52] He expected the same commitment from his students: "[W]hile you should not expect the O. Henry Award this year," he told them, "I expect you to write as if you did, [and] . . . short of a death in the family or your own suicide, non-academic functions will not be entertained as excuses to miss class or be late with assignments."[53] His students admired him for his integrity. "They knew that Breece was rough on himself, on his own writing, as he was with them, and that made it okay."[54] Sometimes the students copied his dress—the blue jeans, flannel shirt, cowboy boots, and the blue jean jacket—and once they teased him, "See Mr. Pancake we're just like you." Pancake laughed and said, "Yes, but you are not authentic like me."[55]

One letter to his mother presents a fair picture of his daily life as a writer while he was at Virginia:

The latest plight of this poor machine is that big chunks are falling out of the roller, so if some letters don't print out, that's why. The man said it would cost a fortune to fix it, but I'm going to do it when I get a job. I like this type-writer.[56] We've seen lots.

MLS [Mary Lee Settle] said she was going to write to thank you for Miner.[57] It was nice of you to go to all that trouble, and thank you for the check. Some-day I'll get around to cashing them. I'm too busy. I'm still eating pretty well, but I have to force myself to eat anything. I'm really off my feed when I write, and these people are turning my stomach, too. New paragraph for that. . . .

I'm interested in this story I'm writing—wrote it in a week as a "credit" piece and sort of like the way it could work if I had the time to fix it up right. I don't know why I started this M.A. nonsense. I'd be better off punching tick-ets at Camden Park.[58] MLS went out to Iowa to read last week, and I'm afraid mucked my chances by nagging Bourjaily on a decision which he never gave. Of course she thinks she helped me, but Bourjaily is so touchy since his last novel bottomed—"I can't understand why he (meaning me) didn't come last year. After all, we accepted him." Stuffy, huh? Well, I can always live in Milton.[59]

His was a rigorous, nose-to-the-grindstone theory of work, one that guided him through the first to last draft. "The only thing about writing first drafts is that it's just as much a drain as Basic Training. I've been at it since seven this morning, and at two-thirty, I feel whipped. Wrote seven pages— I know that doesn't sound like much, but I assure you I bleed with every word."[60] The blood came from his life experience, something else he con-sidered an absolute before a story could be told well. "All I have to sell is my experience," was his maxim,[61] and for Breece, experiencing something firsthand was the best kind of research.

This experience, of course, came as a natural consequence of his own life in West Virginia and Virginia, but some of that experience was consciously sought for the sole purpose of a story he wanted to write and consciously embellished. James Alan McPherson remembers that Pancake "liked to im-press people with tall tales," exaggerations of his experience. "He would get into fights in lower-class bars on the outskirts of Charlottesville, then return to the city to show off his scars. 'These are stories,' he would say."[62] Yet, with Pancake there were always conscious exaggerations, mysteries, deceptions; his mother, for example, never knew him to be in a fight in his life.

To gather material, Pancake explored out-of-the-way haunts of small towns, roadhouses, and coffee shops, and he had always sought out the older people of any town to hear them tell stories of their experience; they were what he called "walking encyclopedias." He had researched "Hollow," for instance, by traveling to a coal camp in Harlan, Kentucky, where he met and spoke with that "great old salt," Harry Caudill.[63] For other story ideas, he and Collie Dudley, author of the *History of Milton* and one of the patriarchs of his hometown, had plans to attend local Klan meetings for literary and historical research. They also had plans to attend a "Glory" meeting of snake handlers near his mother's homeplace of Frazier's Bottom, West Virginia, for a story called "Shouting Victory." Neither of these plans were realized because of Collie Dudley's death in September of 1976 at the age of seventy-three. However, Pancake had read Weston La Barre's classic study of southern snake handlers, *They Shall Take Up Serpents,* and a sketch of the snake handler story (included in this volume) exists.[64] Pancake's unpublished story, "A Loss of Tone" (probably written sometime in 1976 or 1977), shows his interest in the destructive Klan attitudes prevalent in the Kanawha Valley.

In addition to his fiction writing, Pancake also found time in Charlottesville to begin an oral tale project with folklorist Chuck Perdue, with whom Breece had a special relationship. Their rural backgrounds and knowledge of hunting helped establish a bond that was immediately understood by both of them.[65] Pancake had always been interested in oral tales, and as an undergraduate at Marshall, he solicited audio recordings of local stories with this open letter:

> To the Tale-Teller:
> Sadly, at a time when it is most needed to rebuild the Mountianeer [*sic*] Spirit, the oral tradition of the Appalachian Region is all but buried. What with television and the printed word invading our homes by the hour, and the extinction of the extended family (grandparents living in the home with children and grandchildren), we cannot expect the art of telling tales to last much longer. This, then, is why I've asked you here to spin yarn.[66]

In Charlottesville, he transcribed the tales he had collected and wrote an essay on oral narrative with the help of Perdue, an essay he planned to deliver at the fall meeting of the Virginia Folklore Society in 1978.

Pancake also began compiling the unpublished manuscripts of Tom Kromer, whose writing he had discovered in the fall 1976 and which now deeply influenced his own. He had planned several trips to West Virginia University in Morgantown where Kromer's manuscripts are collected, and he had contacted the Kromer family. After Pancake's death Arthur Casciato, one of Breece's classmates, and James L. West continued and completed the project, which was published by the University of Georgia Press in 1986.

Maintaining a rigorous schedule of exercise and hard work obviously paid off. In the spring of 1977, still his first year of graduate school, the *Atlantic Monthly* accepted Pancake's story, "Trilobites"—a remarkable accomplishment for a young writer still in school. "Made it! Atlantic bought 'Trilobites' for $750. Don't know when they'll print it, but [Robert] Manning wrote personal congrats and said they'd have some editorial comments at a later date (?). This has really set fire to Wilson Hall and the (Cross yourself) English Department. Poor second rate citizen Pancake who can't speak the King's English, who lost the Balsch [*sic*] prize by one, who just never was good enough for Peter Taylor to take seriously, who (God forbid) went to work when the money ran out—that turkey made it."[67] He temporarily felt vindicated. The *Atlantic* published the story in the December 1977 issue, the first of four of his stories the magazine would eventually publish.

By the end of his first year of graduate school, it seems that what he hoped for had happened. Edward Weeks of the Atlantic Monthly Press had written and asked him to put together a collection of stories. Excited and elated, he wrote home, "Got a letter from Little-Brown The Atlantic Press, and Mr. Weeks wants me to get a collection together for him. This would mean the book I've worked on five years to put out. There is no promise or advance money, but it's a chance, which is more than I've gotten before. He was all-praise over 'Trilobites,' and loved my 'muscular economy of style.' Tom Kromer is turning in his grave—at least I'm not E. L. Doctorow—I didn't steal the story, just the way of writing it. Don't call Ms. Kromer, O.K.?"[68] Pancake had planned a collection of short stories or a story cycle, much like Anderson's *Winesburg, Ohio* or Joyce's *Dubliners*, that would be unified by one setting, the fictional recreation of Milton called "Rock Camp." Helen Pancake's pride is evident in her next letter to her son:

> Your letter arrived today and I can see your typewriter may not look so hot but it types great. Yes, there is a lot of difference between 20 dollars and 250 and a heck of a lot easier to pay.
>
> I have been working out this morning—just worked too hard and now my writing arm, is nervous, so excuse the messy script.
>
> Mr. Weeks seems anxious—I haven't the slightest idea as to what your muscular economy of style is or what "Trilobites" is about but I certainly wish you luck. Hon. you done gone and run off from your old Moma in writing and reading—but I do want to read everything you write and I am mighty proud of you. I certainly [will] not mention anything to the town folks or the Kromer's. No, I don't think Tom will turn over in his grave—he would be very proud to know someone was carrying thru his ideas. Just look what we would have been stuck with if someone hadn't picked up where the Wright Bros. left off. And perhaps someone will follow you—you aren't stealing or copying. You are improving and that's what it's all about.
>
> Hon, I cried when you asked me not to send you anymore checks. Yes, you are a gentleman to make that request and I shall obey but gifts for [a] special day must be accepted—okay! You are trying and as I always said if and when you want to come home to stay for any reason you are always welcome. But you do things the way you want to—if you think you can't work and write at the same time—pack your car and come on in. You can always mow the lawn and do as you please and I like your company.[69]

Yet, his success with *Trilobites* caused only a ripple in the deep waves of the University of Virginia English Department. He continued to feel largely unnoticed and unrecognized. He had submitted "Trilobites" to the *Virginia Quarterly Review* fiction contest in the spring of 1977, only to lose out, in his mind, to the effort and reputation of Ward Just.[70] "For my April Fool, I lost the VQR contest," Pancake wrote, "make it up to the odds, and then lose. Man, it was tough to hear that, then I was told Ward Just was getting a second crack at his story. Name. Big Name, big money. Forget it I'm looking for a job."[71] A year later he would try again for recognition at the university. After having a second story, "In the Dry," accepted by Robert Manning of the *Atlantic* in the spring of 1978, Pancake submitted another story to the Jefferson Society fiction contest, only to receive second prize, an eight-dollar Jefferson cup. He rationalized the outcome: "The Jefferson Society gave me a Jefferson Cup for second place in their fiction contest—nice of them. I didn't read my best story, but tried to keep within the page limit. As it turned out, I was the only one who did. But the first prize story was really very good, and I've got much more going with the Atlantic than an eight dollar cup."[72]

By the end of the spring semester of 1977, he was still far away from earning an M.A. degree and achieving any kind of recognition from the English department. He anxiously awaited news of a teaching assignment for the fall, and in the meantime he took a job as a short-order cook at the "19th Hole" of the Penn Park Golf Course to support himself during the rest of the semester and through the summer. He bridled at being called "boy" by the golfing clientele, and the old fears returned. "The weeks roll by on this job, the rent gets paid, and I'm waiting for July when I'll get my car in top shape. Yesterday I could see daylight peeking around the edge of the back floor, so I'm not going all out as planned. I'll drive this one until it wears out, then walk or ride a bike. No need to get a new one, as we won't need them in ten years. What we may need is a good stallion and a gun just to stay alive. When that happens, I'm going to a monastery. All Hail Dark Ages."[73]

Only a week away from the new fall semester, the idea of a graduate degree seemed as impractical as ever and the success of the previous spring forgotten. "All week I have been looking for loopholes to avoid paying tuition this fall, thereby collecting more of my salary. This is a 'company store'—you never see what you earn, just work, starve, and don't make waves. Since that part of the system can't be beaten, I may as well make use of it and finish the degree. I found a way around two classes I don't want, and actually will learn more my way. I'm creating two courses before 1800 for myself, will be my own boss, do my own research, etc. It's much harder this way, as there is nobody to tell you how to think, but in the long run, much more interesting. So it looks as if I'm after just one more useless degree." He told his mother, "You can be proud of me the rest of my life while I stay home looking for work."[74]

It seems that Breece could feel success and reward only for a moment. Casey surmises it may have been that "the rhythm of his work didn't let him glory or even bask. He had expected a great deal from his work, and I think he began to feel its power, but he also felt he was still far from what he wanted."[75] Now again in his mind, he was living the life of the starving writer with a long way to go, a role complicated by the strains of graduate school. As solace, Breece regularly attended Mass at the Catholic Church of St. Thomas Hall and became a communicant around the same time "Trilobites" was accepted by the *Atlantic*. Characteristically, as a token of his new faith, he gave the $750 fee to the church to feed the poor.

More problematic, the additional approval and acceptance he apparently needed were never forthcoming, and in the context of the university and Charlottesville, the perception of being the inferior outsider and shy misfit never left him. His literary ambition still drove him, but his goals in graduate school became murky. In some respects, his last two years of graduate school dissipated his energy and distracted him from his talent. To work so hard for so little reward was disheartening. "Just a short note," Pancake wrote his mother in the fall of 1977, "Things have gone badly the last couple of days—my proposal for independent study was turned down. The director didn't think it was worthy. I wouldn't have minded that so much. It's just that he dislikes writers and took the opportunity of having me down to give me a few swift kicks in the ribs: 'You haven't done much worth doing' . . . or 'I can't see anything you've done as solid evidence of scholastics' and on and on. I kept my mouth shut—more hurt than angry. As a result, writing has gone poorly."[76]

In the three years that Pancake attended the University of Virginia, he accomplished an incredible amount. He published six stories—two in the *Atlantic Monthly*, three in the *Declaration*, and one in *Nightwork*, a literary magazine in Richmond—and was working toward a collection of the "Rock Camp" stories for Edward Weeks. In the fall of 1978, Wendy Jacobson of Doubleday solicited a novel, which he began soon thereafter.[77] In addition to his writing efforts, he often taught two or more classes a semester, read for the *Virginia Quarterly Review*, and attended courses required for the M.A., but at the time of his death in the spring of 1979, he was still six hours short of completing a degree.

He returned to his father's grave and stood for a moment perplexed and scowling at the fresh earth.

Listen here now—he began clumsily, and then abandoned it because it was just a pile of dirt and he had been foolish enough for a moment to think that it was really him there and that maybe he could have made his Dad say that it didn't really matter—that it was all right to tell them after all because it was more than he would be able to endure: holding it all inside. Then suddenly he could not believe that anyone alive or dead could be there no matter what the older people said or that any of it had any reality at all: the square eroded slabs with the little names, the numbers, the pictures of the sad, smiling ladies and the little dimpled stone babies. These were the great stone toys of a giant who had grown weary of his play and wandered away long ago. It was a joke of some kind. It was just letters—like the letters on Preacher's fingers.

—Davis Grubb, *The Night of the Hunter*

On a sheet of notebook paper, tucked in between the pages of the manuscript of "Trilobites," Breece Pancake wrote down a list of the real things that inspired certain details of the story—Milton's Company Hill as the basis for Rock Camp, for instance, and the ancient geology of the Teays Valley and the difficult search for a trilobite. The list also explains that the line about China near the end of the story, "I've got eyes to shut in Michigan—maybe even China or Germany. . . " comes from what his father said to friend Wyatt "Duck" Gay after C. R.'s last operation, and that the cups hanging on hooks "are for real in the West Virginia Restaurant." In this list, Pancake also noted that "Turkles really do go for roots," "the 'Will O' the Wisp' is really a weird, weird light," the C & O depot is indeed "boarded up," and that "For me at least, we are suckers for the roots that hold us."[78] He felt compelled to leave a trail, maybe for the same reasons he had written and rewritten his last will while he was in Charlottesville and jotted notes on the back of things he owned, instructing his mother or someone to "dispose" or to "keep." On the back of a print of George Bellows's "Dempsey and Firpo," he had written "Keep the frame, throw away the picture." He was making arrangements, putting things in order, as if he were going away.

Ever since he left West Virginia in 1974, he had dreams of escape, and they still came to him, but in Charlottesville they came less often. Like the flight of Tom Wingfield's father in Williams's *The Glass Menagerie*, Breece sometimes fantasized about Mazatlan and the coast of Mexico (a place he had visited years before during his trips out west), contemplating a postcard consisting of two words, "hello—goodbye." In Staunton he had written: "The coast of Mexico has never looked better in my mind, but I'd feel as if I was letting you and Pop down if I flew the coop."[79] In Charlottesville, it appeared that he was trying to make a final stand against flight: "[W]ish there was some way around all this, but I guess not. Sooner or later I've got to make my own way. . . ."[80]

Above the title of "Trilobites," Pancake had typed: "Death-Bed Edition." In an adjacent handwritten note to his sister Charlotte, he explained: "This because Mr. Taylor drove me nuts with this story. When he asked why I put this here—I told him: 'It's your death bed or mine.'" Pancake often expressed a hangman's sense of humor, which is funny so long as one stands on the scaffold while the trap door is shut. He filled his letters with macabre jokes and references to the notion that "this life is short, and the next one long."[81] Just for fun, he wrote letters home on an insurance company's letterhead. At the top of letterhead was the company's question, "Where Will You Be at 65?" and Breece playfully answered, "On food stamps you turkey?" On another letter he answered, "In one hell of a shape," playful, but always with an undercurrent of tragedy or disaster. On yet another he answered, "Pushing up daisies."

He joked about his work at the university: "This is the fifth ribbon since I came to UVA, so the grades didn't come cheap."[82] Sometimes he illustrated his letters with crazy cartoons, or wrote notes to Postmaster "Bob" on the envelope.

He had decorated the walls of his apartment at One Blue Ridge Lane and his office in Wilson Hall with the usual kind and amount of pin-up pictures and announcements common to college life. He detailed an eclectic calendar of art, concerts, books, free lectures, and films. On the walls he thumbtacked magazine cut-outs of Edward Hopper's *Nighthawks*, Wyndham Lewis's portrait of T. S. Eliot, Thomas Hart Benton's *July Hay*, Ivan Albright's *Room 203*, and an anonymous face view of a human skull. Posters like "Tom Rush in Concert" and "The West Virginian is proud to present The Charlottesville Blues All-Stars" marked events of the times as did posters announcing a Bayley Art Museum author luncheon with Burke Davis, Mary Lee Settle, and James Alan McPherson, an upcoming free lecture by Ralph Ellison, and a University Union Cinematheque presentation of Vittorio de Sica's *Garden of the Finzi Continis*. Breece also had cut out a reproduction of a still photograph from *Casablanca*, the scene at the airport where Rick Blaine is holding Captain Renault at bay while Ilsa and Victor Laslo anxiously look on. Breece had captioned the photo: "What did you say your name was, Pancake?" and tacked that to the wall as well.

The free play of college life, what little there was for Pancake, also included bars and girls. "But it isn't all work. I went fishing for six hours yesterday then took a girl to a 11 p.m. movie. I know I said I'd probably not leave grad school without a wife but I just don't have time for that. I'm up at five, and hitting the books, by noon I'm in classes, and until 9 pm I write. Then I have a few beers, and bang, it's five. Besides, most of the girls here are into getting their own jobs and being independent of anybody. Most of them never worked, too, and that is a problem."[83] He dated many girls and had many female friends while he was in Charlottesville. He played the courtly gentleman, properly shy and reserved, presenting them gifts of record albums, flowers, or books on the first date. One of the women, who still has the Joan Baez album Breece gave her, remembers: "Upon first meeting Breece I kept thinking why is he so shy, why so afraid when someone else would talk. To me Breece seemed to surrender."[84]

Pancake did not believe in the fledgling women's liberation movement. He once wrote, "[I]f they want equality, they get equality. I think women ought to be drafted and placed in the Service just as men are. That would shut up Women's Lib in a big hurry."[85] His relationship with women seems to have been circumscribed by an older generation's sense of what the roles for men and women should be, particularly when it came to conventional morality. His newfound faith in the Catholic Church reinforced his "old-fashioned" ideas about family and sexuality, and his enthusiasm for the opposite sex seems to have played against his religious fervor. "Last night, I met the most terrific girl—a writer who isn't going to school, but working in the business lib. and studying under Taylor much the same as I worked under Casey. She's 25, Catholic, 5'2", blond, brilliant, and built. My priorities are in order. Mom, I named her age and religion before her physical attributes. . . . I had a habit of calling her Liz, and it stuck. We struck it off really well, and talked all night over Bass Ale."[86]

At times he joked about sex in a coarse way, parodying a line by his new folk-blues hero Tom Waits: "If the 'girls' there want to meet me," he wrote to his sister Donnetta, "you might warn them that I'm so horney the crack of dawn has to be careful around me. Or, as was said of old, I'd take a naked leap at a rolling doughnut. I'm dating, but these children don't do much for me—takes a thirty year-old woman to even get a good conversation going."[87] Yet, he had an older generation's sense of what the proper conduct between a man and a woman should be, and even his own sexuality was subject to the most profound moral self-scrutiny.

He despised the idea of casual sex, "sex for sale," and easy divorce. After receiving a disturbing news column about "Dial-a-Doll" nightclubs in Charleston, Pancake wrote:

> I was disturbed by the culture change in the area. I'm talking about the dial-a-doll services, and was grossed out to the max by the club in Charleston boasting a phone at every table (you see a girl you like, just call her table—if she turns you down, you don't have to walk back feeling like a fool.) I guess

I really expected West Virginia to keep her virginity (so to speak) when it came to things like that, but the Magic Fingers should have told me long ago how wrong I was. When I got out—to Frisco and Phoenix—I saw how horribly alone people are when they have to resort to call-a-doll. Even the dolls are alone. The saddest part, to me, is that it is a despair created out of loneliness, and the whole thing just snowballs all to hell and back. As long as [someone] can go to phone-bar, he can be sure of only one thing—he will always go, in the end, home alone.[88]

It seems that Pancake wanted to believe that the verities and moralities of an older generation still held true in West Virginia, and he was very moral about sexuality. He wanted to believe that sex was not something consumed but was rather the physical expression of a deeply humane and spiritual bond which was most properly confined to marriage or, at the very least, to a man and woman intending to marry. Consequently—and much like Flannery O'Connor—Pancake screened the world in search of moral purity, and he regarded both West Virginia and the Catholic Church as two of the last remaining moral sanctuaries surrounded by a banal and permissive society.

Brought up in a Methodist family, he rejected what he saw as a weak and relativist faith. "By the way, the Methodists have come up with a liturgy for divorce—a rite similar to the marriage vows, only in reverse! You each agree to give the other freedom, then switch rings to the right hand. This is not Vatican propaganda—I read it in Newsweek. As an up and coming Ro Cat, I find this appalling. . . ."[89] He preferred the world of absolutes that Catholic morality offered him and even thought of becoming a "padre" himself.[90]

In the late winter of 1977, just a few months before his confirmation as a Roman Catholic at St. Thomas Hall, Pancake wrote, "I still haven't met a girl worth her salt in this place yet,"[91] but he did meet someone later that year—a pretty girl with brown hair and blue eyes, Emily Miller, born in Richmond and reared in Virginia society. She, too, was a graduate student in the English department at the University of Virginia, but Emily was "staying on" for a Ph.D. She was of a different world than Breece, more accustomed to teas and recitals than to riding in a pickup truck or eating a pawpaw in the woods. Breece delighted in taking her to Staunton to meet Mrs. Nutt and to explore the fall woods on the Blue Ridge. They fell in love. From the fall of 1977 until his death, she nursed him through minor aches and illnesses, argued with him, supported him, and helped crack his "hard shell."

Never one to show his emotions easily, Breece held his strong feelings inside until they sometimes boiled over in a noticeable display of bad temper or remorse. From the beginning, he was known in Charlottesville as someone who was "slightly difficult."[92] His relationship with Emily had a moderating and healing effect, and because of this, the sad memory of his dead father came easier. "The early part of the month was tough. One of my students wrote a sad piece about an old man in a wheelchair giving a kid a peppermint in return for a handful of dandelions. Fortunately I had time to get it out of my system before class. Em is to blame for a lot of that. Before I met her, I had a good hard shell built up which she set to dissolving."[93]

One of Pancake's letters to his mother captures his domestic life shortly after he and Emily began dating:

> Just a note to thank you for my socks—they are truly warm, and very comfortable. I should imagine they'd be good to hunt in—should I ever get time to hunt.
>
> I'm happy to report a woodpecker busily at work on the wooden part of One Blue Ridge Lane. He's got a hole about the size of a baseball and improving on it daily. While I have no objection to either him making merry with Meade property, or his noise, I find myself getting rudely called from bed just before dawn everyday. The problem is that with all this work, I'm not getting to bed soon enough to co-habit with this red-head.
>
> But all this aside. I'm doing well enough considering—and although I have gotten no word on the new job, I feel sure they hired another. No job teaching is ideal, but this would have been better than most and I'm sorry I lost out. Don't mention it to Homer, please, as that would only embarrass me.
>
> After shivering through Mass, I attended Em's church. The heat was on high, and they were begging for money. Just like the good old days at Milton Methodist. Em's church is undergoing too quick a change in attitude and threatens to fall apart. If I could find a nice old fashioned Catholic Church, I might convert her, but she doesn't go for new outlooks. I believe I told you, she's Episcopalian. (I'll strangle the first one who says they are "just like Catholics.")
>
> Peter Taylor is ill, and not of much help. He's got diabetes and still fighting over the recent death of his closest friend, Robert Lowell. While I try to be patient with him, I wish he would be the same with me and think about my story[94] before judging it.
>
> Unfortunately, Casey is the same way. His father is dying of cancer (82?), but I think he's got some hatchets yet to bury, some peace he finds hard to make with his old man. Of course, he is taking the crazy attitude—thinking of quitting U.Va. and moving to New England. I don't think he has any money or work, but if there's a free lunch handy, John would screw it up.
>
> Only McPherson is his usual hidden self.
>
> Em and I will be in Milton someday. T-giving is out since her major papers are due thereafter. Christmas is out because she has to hold two jobs to make ends meet. I would imagine I'd be home Christmas—but I can't see much sense in a $40.00 train ride for three days. That leaves us somewhere between Jan. and Easter—I might even get brave and drive her over. Anyway, barring flood and the A-Bomb, I'll be home in a few days and remain approx. 10 days—so bake a ham. I might seek rides and therefore arrive earlier—around Dec. 20.?[95]

Emily Miller was also someone who fit into Pancake's moral vision of family. "Did you see Awakening Land? I watched one episode with Em and when that guy grabbed Elizabeth Montgomery's tit on national T.V., I swore off the Tube for life. I guess I'm thinking of children growing up with that in their living room. Somehow learning the facts of life from Steve Spence behind a backstreet church seems right and fair now."[96] The purity of marriage and family, especially in keeping with Catholicism, did not include what he saw as the pervasive back-alley morality of the times. In early 1978, Pancake had planned a story called "Of Time and Virgins" that describes a young man trying "to make a decision whether he should propose to a virgin he just met. He reviews the four great loves of his life, sees how each falls prey to sexual promiscuity in a different way, and eventually decides he is tainted, but not beyond help. Since he has been with this girl more than a year without bedding her, he decides she is more to him than the others and decides to 'propose' tomorrow."[97]

In spite of falling in love, his hopes for happiness and marriage were also tainted with the suspicion that they would soon disappear. He told his mother, "Falling in love is disastrous to ambition! But she and I will go our own way, I'm sure."[98] The summer of 1978 confirmed his suspicion. After Breece proposed marriage, Emily Miller's parents had successfully discouraged the match for reasons with which Breece was all too familiar.

> Her parents have decided I'm not good enough for her and they've been after her to give me the boot and look for more promising material among her own kind. What "her own kind" means is a good Southern Virginia family. People around here really are snobs, especially if you get seriously involved with their only daughter. While Emily is above the age of consent, she also has strong ties to that sort of life—you can't (nor can I) blame her for being reared a Virginian. I think that sort of prejudice is pretty funny until it becomes real. I'm convinced Emily loves me, but much of her heart is with her family as well. . . . (I know I'm as good as they are), and if I got angry it wouldn't hurt anyone but Emily. . . .[99]

He bottled his anger.

About the formalities and rules of Virginia society, Emily had been a reluctant disciple, but a disciple nonetheless. When she was invited to be a member of a wedding in Richmond, Pancake complained of the time she spent making her dress and buying gifts for the shower and of her mother's domineering influence: "She resigns herself to the idea that it's proper to do such things," Pancake wrote. "It puts a strain on what little her parents have left us in that I say 'to hell with such things,' and she gets upset because her Virginian sense of what is proper has been violated."[100] Although Breece and Emily did not stop seeing each other after the ill-fated proposal, Breece seems to have retreated into himself and the specters of fear and loss returned.

In a letter he wrote to Emily but never sent, he asked, "Is your papa right to ask you to re-consider? He wants his boat-dream for you—what chance can a pen-pusher provide for?"[101] He concluded that the status of a writer could never be worthy—"my profession bears the nasty condition of perpetual poverty in this life and riches for my heirs: I chose it, and I should live with it"[102]—and for such a condition, he saw no one to blame but himself. It was a sense of things that had always plagued him. After a reading he gave in the spring of 1978 at Randolph Macon College, he noticed the irony of a writer's success. "The reading went well—standing ovation—and I got the royal treatment of coffee on a silver tray and suit of rooms reserved for special guests. Somehow though, it's very strange to step off a Trailways Bus into the royal treatment, then back to the bus!"[103] In addition to what he had accomplished during his first year at the University of Virginia, it was "strange" to have another story, "In the Dry" accepted by the *Atlantic*, "Time and Again" accepted by *Nightwork*, to be awarded the University of Virginia Jefferson Society Prize for fiction and a Hoyns Fellowship, to have a novel solicited by Doubleday, and to be accepted by the North Carolina Arts Council Visiting Artists Program, and yet still feel as if he hadn't made any progress toward recognition or status. He felt that the bus would always be waiting. He questioned why he became a writer in the first place. "Thomas Wolfe— 'the great' writer—died in a cab in New York, and Hemingway blew his brains out. Maybe I'd been better off a lawyer."[104] As for the rewards of graduate school, he just shook his head. "Believe me, it isn't worth the trouble."[105]

By the spring of 1979, Breece's list of accomplishments and prospects had grown enormously, but apparently it was not enough to offset nagging psychological defeat and the pressing weight of memory. The loss of his father and best friend and his longing for home had always been just under the surface. "[Y]ou can't leave sorrow behind," he wrote. "The hell of it is that it goes wherever you go, and leaves you a part of nothing."[106] Since the day he had mixed the mortar and set his father's gravestone, he had not been able to talk about his grief for his father or about the death of Matthew Heard. He had always been very private about these feelings.

Breece also felt that he was "frozen in time writing,"[107] and home, the place he knew, had been forever changed and lost to him. "I am homesick as I can be," he told his mother. "From the papers you've sent, I see such a change in thinking, that I'm afraid people won't be the same when I come back. I feel as if I've been hit from behind."[108] He also was grieved to learn that his Aunt Julia had been taken to a nursing home to live her last days. "Damn me, I'm awful depressing. I guess I'm just homesick and tired," but still trying to maintain some sense of humor, he added, "Tell Jr. I've tied my cat to the top of the fence-post."[109]

Though things seemed to be closing down on him, Breece tried to remain upbeat, as can be seen in the following letter to his mother:

> Many thanks for the candy and brownies—they came a little worse for wear, but fresh, and they're both delicious (a little too much so, I've rationed myself). It was good talking to you the other night—although I must say I forgot to ask why you sent me two blank calendar pages of November in December??
>
> The news here isn't all that great—I'm still waiting for word on an interview and imagine that most schools call two days before the convention—it's really a buyer's market. They'll invite five people for interviews & four of them always go home empty-handed. Really not very considerate of our future bosses to spend our money for nothing.
>
> On the cover you see Papa Hemingway.[110] Since nobody will be around to tune his guitar or feed him, I told Em I'd ask you if Papa might spend Christmas with us—Actually, it all depends on how well Papa makes a trial trip in the car.
>
> Everything else is the same old 6 & 7. I'm booking for my last exam, trying to read students' work, read for VQR, make out grades, etc. Emily is in the same boat, only she's finished her course work and is doing French for her upcoming exam (you never seem to finish "exams" and graduate).
>
> I'll leave here early the 19th & will probably take my old route through Buffalo Gap & etc. Will call you if I get snowed in at Rainell [sic].[111]

In the fall of 1978, he and Emily had found a stray tom cat underneath his car, hungry and cold and scarred from too many cat fights. They named him "Papa" because his gray, tufted whiskers reminded them of Hemingway. For five months, he and Emily cared for him and nursed him back to health, but then, in the small memo diary Breece kept for appointments and addresses, there appears this brief note for March 29, 1979—"Papa Died."—put to sleep by a veterinarian after being hit by a car.[112]

Heavy snows fell in Charlottesville that winter, and the spring of 1979 came later than usual. Breece had been frantically looking for a job, knowing full well that the university had denied the transfer of the six foreign language credit hours from Marshall University required for the M.A.; undaunted, he still planned to retake German and graduate that summer. For his master's thesis, instead of the Kromer project, he submitted "Two Original Stories: 'Trilobites' and 'In the Dry.'" Trying to return home, he had been applying for teaching jobs with high schools and colleges mainly located in West Virginia. He was looking for anything he might be qualified for and that would pay a wage—teaching, newspaper writing, or advertising work. He even thought of getting a boatman's job on the Ohio River or a job as a handyman for the Virginia Center for Creative Arts. He had also applied for internships at writers' workshops—the Provincetown Fine Arts Workshop, the Millay Colony, the North Carolina Arts Council, and the Kentucky Arts Commission.

John Casey remembers that Pancake was deeply depressed over not finding a job and that he and Breece had drifted apart a little, due, in part, to Pancake's deepening religious faith and insistence that Casey follow suit. "He was zealous," Casey has said, "Knocking on my door and dragging me to Ash Wednesday, getting the ashes on me, and getting me to confession. It was completely a topsy-turvy thing and in a way we did have a topsy-turvy. I started out as his teacher and he was my student, but he knew a lot of stuff that I didn't and he did a lot of stuff that I couldn't."[113] Pancake, who felt indebted to Casey, tried to bridge the distance. He dedicated a reading of "The Honored Dead" to Casey, and in his speech to the audience at the Methodist Student Center he hinted of the turmoil he felt, of "ghosts [that] cannot be put down." "Tonight I must read 'The Honored Dead,'" he told the crowd:

> [A]n unpleasant story, unpleasing because memories of war, of love, of lust, of misunderstanding can never be pleasing. In 1968 L.B.J. launched an offensive which later became known as Tet. History records the disaster in two ways—a paragraph in books and thousands of stoney [sic] inscriptions. In that brief battle one Eddie Grass of Milton, West Virginia, served as a naval attachment to the U.S.M.C. and was charged to the duty of radio operator on field patrol. He lasted thirty minutes on the job, several grenades having dispatched him homeward. I wanted to say that this reading was for Eddie, but ghosts cannot be put down. I ask instead that you consider this reading thanks to the living, specifically to the one who chanced I could write. This one is for John.[114]

But the dedications and gifts and gestures never bridged the distance for very long, or made him feel the debt was paid. That spring Richard Jones had gone back to England, McPherson to New Haven for the year, Perdue was on sabbatical, and Casey was looking forward to a two-week stay in Ireland during the summer. Everyone seemed to be going away.

Though by April he still hadn't found a full-time job, his prospects were good, and his letters home filled with news of Emily and his usual sense of humor. He threatened to model the underwear his mother had just sent him for the Women's Club of Milton. Although he had been pessimistic about finding work, claiming that "[p]retty soon, we're going to be singing, 'Buddy Can You Spare a Dime' again,"[115] he joked about his job search. "I'm now getting ready to attack the Jr. College job market. I have often thought of creating an opening for myself—I'll find a place I like, simply murder the current job-holder, then apply. All things considered, it makes more sense than robbing a bank (my second calling). But don't worry until a large bundle of cash arrives in the mail—actually, don't worry until you get a sudden postcard from Mexico."[116] Dreams of escape were returning, but his dreams had also grown darker.

In his notebook, he recorded a dream filled with supernatural images of life, death, redemption—and violence.

Then winter came with heavy powder-snow, and big deer, horses, goats and buffaloes—all white—snorted, tossed their heads, and I lay down with an Army blanket, made my bed in the snow, then dreamed within a dream. I dreamed I was at Fleety's,[117] and she told me the bones were poor people killed by bandits, and she took me back to the place, and under a huge rock where no light should have shown, a cave almost, was a dogwood tree. It glowed the kind of red those trees get at sundown, the buds were purple in that weird light, and a madman came out with an axe and chopped at the skulls, trying to make them human-looking. Then I went back to the other side of both dreams. . . .[118]

For months he had been preparing to leave Charlottesville. Emily was staying on to finish her Ph.D., but he was setting things in order, giving things away—a normal routine for students preparing to leave a university town. He had always given gifts and tokens of friendship and his gift giving that spring did not seem out of character. He informed Mrs. Meade that he would be leaving One Blue Ridge Lane at the end of May, visited teachers and friends to tell them of his plans, and gave most of his guns away—except for one.

Breece's daily list of things to do for Saturday April 7 appeared ordinary. "To Barracks Road, Movie, A&P—Beer/Milk, To Carl's [Carl Beckman], To Emily's & Wash [Washington, D.C.], To Home."[119] On Saturday evening he had taken Emily out to see a movie, *The Deer Hunter*, which includes scenes of horrific violence and graphically portrays several games of forced and voluntary Russian roulette. That evening, he had also called his mother and strangely repeated "I love you" three times.

The next day, Palm Sunday, he did not attend church with Emily in the morning because he was sick, complaining of a headache and a cold. Rather, he stopped off to see her in the afternoon on his way to three o'clock Mass. She asked him to stay and eat, but he declined, reminding her that he would be by in the morning to pick her up so that they could drive to Winchester, Virginia, together. Breece had scheduled an interview for a reporter's job with the *Winchester Evening Star*. His friend Kathleen Devereux had arranged it. "I think in many ways you would enjoy this job," Devereux told him, but also advised, "Breece, I think you are a much maligned person . . . anyone that suffers the way you do with those headaches should look into it. . . . I know how much religion plays in your life, but it does not seem to be blessing you with joy or happiness, in fact, your last letter was a subtle example of a rather depressed and fatalistic attitude. . . ."[120]

After Mass, he went back to his apartment at One Blue Ridge Lane and drank a few beers. Around 6 P.M., he wandered dreamily into the yard where the dogwoods and apple trees were in bloom, then through a thick planting of bamboo into the nearby cottage of Mrs. Meade's other tenant, a golfer, who often shared the Meades' small shedlike cottage with his girlfriend. This apartment was not more than a dozen yards from Pancake's own. For a few minutes, Pancake sat inside the half-dark apartment, and then, fatefully, the girlfriend arrived, walking up the Meades' driveway with a sack of groceries. Opening the door she saw a dark shadow of a man sitting in a chair, and she screamed, dropping the groceries on the floor. Breece snapped out of his trance and started up out of the chair. He tried to reassure her, telling her his name, that he would not harm her. He turned to go back to his own apartment, muttering something about walking in his sleep. According to the sheriff's report the girlfriend had clearly been frightened: "The complainant [the golfer's girlfriend] stated that Mr. Pancake *cornered her* and explained that he had a drinking problem and had a tendency to wander around."[121]

Ignoring Pancake's reassurances, she called the police anyway and then informed Mrs. Meade about the intrusion. Aroused by the scream and the neighbor's complaint, Mrs. Meade, who was disturbed by Pancake's behavior, knocked on his door, telling him through the door that the police were coming "looking for a Breece Pancake."[122] Calling out from his room, muffled behind the door, Breece replied, "Yes, I'm sorry."

A few minutes later Breece emerged from his closed "foxden" carrying his last remaining gun, a Savage Arms over-under shotgun, from its place of safekeeping. He then walked into the backyard and sat down in a folding chair underneath the Meades' apple tree. He did this quickly. Placing the gun stock on the ground, he put the muzzle into his mouth and pulled the trigger. In his last moment, Richard Jones surmises that he could have heard the siren.[123]

After the gun shot, Mrs. Meade immediately telephoned her daughter's house, where her husband was dining with Peter Taylor. Mrs. Meade informed her daughter that Breece had been shooting his gun in the backyard, and that her father should come home immediately. "I came back and my wife said that there had been, that Breece was missing," Mr. Meade recalled.

> And I said I'd go look for him, and unfortunately I found him. We never did find out what happened, but we have a guest cottage, and there was a girl out there who was waiting for the person to whom we rented the cottage, and Breece, who was probably a friend of his as far as I know, went to the cottage. And she thought it was the other boy. And it was just getting dark, and he's a big, tall, bearded guy and she scared him, I mean he scared her, and we don't know if that's what triggered it or not, but she was running over to Mrs. Meade because she was frightened. And the next thing Mrs. Meade said she heard a shot.[124]

Mr. Meade found Pancake in the chair, a pool of blood at his feet, the gun cradled in his right arm. The police arrived just then.

At midnight, a Milton policeman came to the door of his mother's home with the news. Helen Pancake had been ill that day; she had been taking medicine, nursing a cold, and had been asleep for some time. Her daughter Donnetta answered the door, then walked upstairs and woke her, saying, "Breece is dead, Mama." Helen responded, "He can't be. He's such a good boy."[125] The word got out through town by CB radio and telephone, and the people of Milton came pouring in. Helen Pancake did not sleep again that night or that morning; indeed, not until the next afternoon. Several months would pass before anyone in Milton would learn the actual circumstances of his death. McPherson, the next day, telegrammed Pancake's mother from New Haven: "I am grieved to learn of Breece's death. He was one of the most humane people I've ever known. I offer my deepest sympathies."[126]

Just that previous summer, Pancake had told his mother to cash in his life insurance policy and promised "not to die for at least twenty years,"[127] and he had joked about death with Emily after she helped him through one of his many colds and headaches: "I keep telling her I'm going to die on her just to spite her."[128] Who could have known that he may have been more serious than joking? The clues that now seem so obvious were hidden in the affairs of everyday life and in his own nature that everyone had come to know, but some friends had a feeling that something was wrong. "When I visited his small room at the Meade's, I felt that he was always yearning for another life," Laura Keene has said. "It was like he really didn't know why he was in Charlottesville." She remembers that "he was wonderful, generous and kind and . . . [e]veryone that I knew that met him wanted to ease his burden."[129] But it seemed no one knew how. At the time of his death, he had a thousand dollars in the bank, two stamped letters on his typewriter ready to post, a grocery list taped to the dash of his car.

His mother has said, "I think he was startled, he was frightened, he was confused, he was pushed, he was . . . sick. . . . I know he loved me. He wouldn't have put me through this. That's why he couldn't have done it in his right mind. . . . He was somewhere between fear and frustration and his mind just snapped."[130]

In letters written that spring to McPherson, Casey, and others, Pancake enclosed his gratitude and cryptic farewells. "Everybody had a kind of suicide note from Breece from a couple of weeks ago or a couple of months ago," Raymond Nelson has said. "But none of them seemed that way. . . . They all had other kinds of explanations when you got them."[131] It appeared that Pancake was just saying good-bye to Charlottesville and the people he had known there, but then he ended his last letter to Casey this way: "Short time gone, long time coming. Come hook in the gills, come bullet between does shoulders, come long cold and the Cross, come time to lay down, come time to get awake, I'll remember you with love."[132]

In his last letters to Casey and McPherson, Pancake wrote of noblesse oblige, an aristocratic code of noble obligation that made things perplexing because Pancake wanted to believe in it and adopt it, but he also experienced its self-defeating reality. Pancake understood noblesse oblige to mean that whatever you request must never put anyone under any obligation, and that whatever you are lacking is assumed by everyone, including yourself, as something you already have. However blatant the hints and "cries for help" may have been, Pancake was apparently too proud to be helped by his friends' concern, even if they had noticed.

Furthermore, his own ideas about suicide, reinforced by his strong Catholic faith, denied the possibility of suicide. He abhorred incidents of self-destruction and could not understand what would bring someone to that point. "This guy I knew chose to leave this world in a very foul manner, so I'm not in much of a mood to say great happy things," he once wrote. "I just don't understand that sort of despair—I always fought back."[133]

Pancake's final letter to Casey, which has been referred to several times before, is worth citing in full:

> Ms. Casey: Please do not give this letter to Mr. Casey until he is in Ireland this summer. I promise it isn't a bomb.

> Dear John,
>   In this country those who have have all, and the have-nots have the bones. When I came to you in 1975 the two met, and I am grateful for your sense of noblesse oblige. In this country about all a have-not can ask for is a chance to be a have; you gave me that chance, and I thank you; now I'll blame myself if I fail.
>   I could never (even when I tried) tell you how much you, Jane and the girls have meant to me. I only regret that I never made a larger effort to become a part of your lives, but my own sense of privacy tells me not to do such things— even when I'm far away, it would be hurtful for us to miss one another.
>   Short time gone, long time coming. Come hook in the gills, come bullet between does shoulders, come long cold and the Cross, come time to lay down, come time to get awake, I'll remember you with love.[134]

Pancake's story "A Room Forever" is one of the strongest indications of how he must have been struggling. The story, probably completed during the last year of his life, is about a young girl who attempts suicide and is narrated by a young man who has been contemplating the same possibility ever since he stepped into town off the deck of a tug, the *Delmar*. It is set in a town very much like Huntington, West Virginia, an Ohio river town, and the place of the climax, the room where the young man awkwardly and bitterly attempts to reach out to the lost girl, is similar to the kind of third-floor apartment on the corner of First and Second Avenues where Pancake lived while he was a student at Marshall, an apartment that was "[b]are, Spartan but neat" his mother remembers. From this apartment window in Huntington, Pancake watched the bums gather near the warehouses, and he would go down and take them food and listen to their stories about life on the tugs that pushed the coal barges up and down the river.

In the story the narrator describes his own reflection and that of the lost girl together as "ghosts against the black gloss of glass"; they are united in their predicament and in spirit. In the story she becomes nervous by the way he looks at her—"like you seen something awful was going to happen to me." Their meeting is a mutual struggle of spirit, of sizing up reality, of alternating between giving up and deciding "quits ain't the answer." Then the young man looks "for her in the mirror but she is gone," and the girl's spirit does quit, cutting her wrists "down to the leaders." At story's end, the young man turns away and walks down to the river to see if the *Delmar* has put in early; he has made the decision to live. On the cover of the manuscript, Pancake wrote a brief explanation: "This story is about learning how to fight fate." Whether suicide is indeed a matter of fate or a result of a conflicted psyche, surely Pancake struggled to overcome it.

Many people linked his suicide to the occasional episodes of sleep walking (a phenomenon usually associated with physical or psychological trauma), to his frequent headaches, or to his drinking. To the people who had shared a drink with him, he was more of an "outbreak drinker," who would occasionally go on binges, rather than a habitual "problem drinker,"[135] but his drinking led him to moments of excess and depression, which were complicated by his hypoglycemia, a low blood sugar condition diagnosed while he was at Marshall University. "I think it's true that Breece, on some days, could drink a six pack and it would have very little effect on him," said Casey. "Other days he would have two beers and he would be loaded."[136] While drinking, his mood leapt from somber reticence to unchecked expansiveness. "Two drinks and you couldn't shut him up for two days," remembers Mary Lee Settle.[137] His mother, too, was aware of the negative effect that alcohol had on Breece. She remembers, "[H]e did drink, like all the boys do. But I think drinking made him remorseful and sad."[138]

In the weeks that followed his death, Breece's job prospects came through, intensifying the sense of loss for those who received his calls and mail. Both the Fine Arts Work Center in Provincetown and the Millay Colony for the Arts had accepted him as a Writing Fellow for the upcoming year. He received two interviews for academic teaching posts, and the North Carolina Arts Council had invited him to become one of its visiting artists.

In Charlottesville, John Casey and Pancake's older sister, Donnetta, had begun the difficult task of sifting through boxes of papers and personal belongings at One Blue Ridge Lane. After the boxes had been transported back home to Milton, many of his papers and letters were burned or thrown away by his mother and sister in the confusion of sorrow, some because Breece's familiar scent could be detected; others because of the intimate nature of their content; all because of raging grief, the stigma of his suicide, and the intuition that there would be a paparazzi interest to know more about him.

A few days after the tragedy at One Blue Ridge Lane, Mrs. Meade hired a local laborer to dig up the soil stained with Pancake's blood and replace it. A month later, Mrs. Meade wrote her condolences to Breece's mother: "It was a great shock to us all at this turn of events. We never knew he walked in his sleep, in fact, we never saw a great deal of Breece—he was a very hard worker. Sometimes he'd be typing at dawn or late at night and his dedication to his writing certainly had wonderful results. . . . It seems hard to believe but I didn't even know the town in West Virginia where Breece came from, he only said, 'It was a long drive almost in Ohio. . . .'"[139]

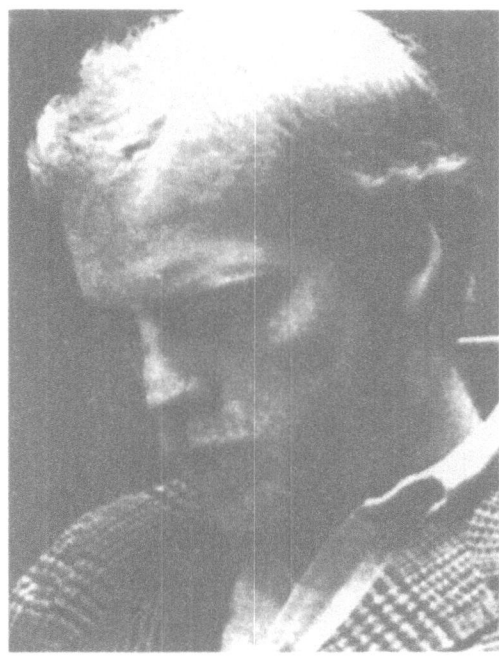

Breece Pancake, portrait taken for an interview with the University of Virginia's *Declaration*, Dec. 1977. Photographer unknown. Courtesy of the Pancake Estate.

Portrait of Pancake by Carlos Santos for the *Richmond-Times Dispatch*, January 1979. Santos wrote to Helen Pancake: "I still remember trying to convince him to let me take that picture—he didn't want me to and I think that's why he looks so stern" (July 19, 1990). Courtesy of Carlos Santos.

Breece and Emily Miller in Washington, D.C., 1978. Donnetta Pancake wrote to Helen Pancake: "This was taken the day B & Em came to D.C. . . . . Breece had just remarked 'Can you believe *they charge* .87 for water?' I told him the really amazing fact was that *he paid* .87 for water and we were all laughing" (November 1978). Photo by Donnetta Pancake. Courtesy of Pancake Estate.

"Faraway" hunting cabin in Middlebrook, Va. Sarah Nutt gave Breece free use of the cabin from 1976 to 1979. Drawing by Joe Nutt. Courtesy of Sarah Nutt and Janet (Nutt) Lembke.

Sarah Nutt's house at 324 E. Beverly Street, Staunton, Va. Pancake rented the cellar apartment from Sarah Nutt and then moved upstairs to share the house with Nutt, his "Virginia mother." After he moved to Charlottesville, Pancake continued to visit this house until his death. Drawing by Joe Nutt. Courtesy of Sarah Nutt and Janet (Nutt) Lembke.

Breece with "Papa," winter 1979. Photo by Emily Miller. Courtesy of Pancake Estate.

Pancake's grave at Milton Cemetery. Photo by Tom Douglass.

5

A Room Forever

Declaration: Getting started, to what extent does the writer as an artist pander to publishers in order to satisfy popular demands?

Pancake: If that is the type of writing one cares to do, you can go to Hollywood—they use writers like kleenex out there. I don't cater at all. If they buy my stories—fine. If they don't buy them—fine. I don't write to make a living.

—Interview with the *Declaration* of the University of Virginia, 1977

"When promising authors die at a young age," Robert Merritt wrote for the *Richmond Times-Dispatch*, "there is a tendency to remove them from the mainstream and look upon their work with the new purity of a small but completed oeuvre. When the young author takes his own life, a morbid cloud passes over that purity and often causes readers to seek signs of imminent disaster and doom. There is, however, no sense of doom in the stories of the late Breece D'J Pancake. If anything, these dozen works are about people coming to terms with their own fate in life."[1]

In the months following Pancake's suicide, John Casey, whom Breece had named literary executor in his last will, and Helen Pancake had focused the energy of their grief on fulfilling a graveside promise—to see a book of his stories posthumously published. Little did they know how remarkable and unusual the critical reception would be. At first, they began collecting his papers, some in Milton, some at Beverly Avenue in Staunton, and some at Blue Ridge Lane. They found dozens of letters, poems, story fragments, beginnings of novels, and thirteen completed short stories, two of which Casey had never seen before. They rediscovered some previously unpublished work—"The Honored Dead" and "Fox Hunters," which he had written and reworked for his writing courses, and a few of his earlier stories written in Staunton and Milton, "The Scrapper," "A Loss of Tone," and "The Salvation of Me." Casey and Helen Pancake also found "First Day of Winter" and "A Room Forever," stories they had never seen before that probably had been completed in the year before his death.

Since many publishing houses wait for an author to be published five or six times in literary magazines before considering publishing a book, Casey packed a few of Breece's stories under his arm in the summer of 1979, and approached various editors of literary magazines with the idea of getting them published individually, thereby working toward a posthumous publication of a collection of stories. The editors of the *Atlantic* accepted "The Honored Dead" for the January 1981 issue and then "Hollow" for the October 1982 issue. The editors of *Antaeus* included "A Room Forever" for their December 1981 issue. By early 1982, John Casey and Helen Pancake were closer to their goal of proposing a book with realistic hopes of getting it published, since six of Breece's stories had been accepted by literary magazines.

Random House and Doubleday showed interest, and the editors and staff at the Atlantic Monthly Press had consistently been enthusiastic about Pancake's work. *Atlantic* editor Robert Manning, who earlier in his career as correspondent for *Time* had landed one of the first interviews with Ernest Hemingway, had published "Trilobites" and "In the Dry." In a letter to Pancake, Manning had written, "It is always a special pleasure to come across a fresh new talent. I congratulate you, and look forward to more of your work."[2] Senior editor Edward Weeks, who had solicited stories from Hemingway in the 1940s, admired Pancake's "muscular economy" of style and asked him for more stories, possibly a collection.[3] In 1982, poet and editor Peter Davison, one-time associate of Sylvia Plath, accepted "Hollow" and pushed for posthumous publication of a book of Pancake's stories.[4] Phoebe-Lou Adams, a member of the *Atlantic* editorial staff since 1945, was also impressed with his talent and began an encouraging personal correspondence with Pancake in 1977 that continued until his death. In her frequent letters, she lightly joked with him about colloquialisms, about "turkles" (turtles), and etymology. She responded to his stories and nurtured his talent. "Don't lose patience," she once wrote him, "your stories are being read with interest by the whole outfit. Word anon."[5]

So it was only natural that Helen Pancake would enlist Adams's help in bringing Pancake's collection of stories to press:

> It is my understanding that John Casey has been to see you with several of Breece Pancake's stories. In going through some of Breece's papers I noticed your personal notes on letters you had written to him. Thus I feel free to write to you regarding his work. Assuming you have seen his stories, we would like

very much your comments. In the event you have not seen them, I enclose a copy of "The Honored Dead," with the suggestion that it would be a fine story for your May issue—Memorial Day.

Your encouragement to Breece while he was alive meant a great deal to him. As Thomas Wolfe wrote in "You Can't Go Home Again," "If a man wanted to live in this world without getting his pockets picked, he had better learn how to use his eyes and ears on what was going on around him. But if he wanted to live in this world without getting hit over the head, and without all the useless pain, grief, terror, and bitterness that mortify human flesh, he had also better learn how *not* to use his eyes and ears." Breece saw too much. I hope you can help us with this unpublished work. It seems a shame to cast it aside.[6]

In May of 1982 the Atlantic Monthly Press, in association with Little, Brown and Company, proceeded with plans to publish a collection of twelve stories. This book would include a foreword by McPherson, who at the time was also member of the *Atlantic* editorial board, and an afterword by Casey concerning the author. The book was unique; it had a plain front cover that included the title and name of the author at the top in large, royal blue letters and the prominently printed names of Casey and McPherson near the bottom in brown letters. In between, near the middle of the gold cover, a small, black illustration of a fossilized trilobite divided the name of the student from those of his former teachers. On the back cover was a haunting, grainy photograph of a downward-looking, bearded Pancake with shadows on his face in a seemingly introspective moment—an old photograph taken by University of Virginia's student newspaper the *Declaration* in November of 1977.

In answer to Helen Pancake's letter, Phoebe-Lou Adams confessed how special Pancake's work was regarded:

> Thank you very much indeed for the photograph of Breece. Both John Casey and James Alan McPherson have tried to describe him to me, and despite their verbal skills and affectionate regard for him, neither thought to mention that he was an exceptionally handsome young man. Perhaps men don't see each other on those terms.
>
> I am enclosing a letter which you may wish to answer. I've been slow to forward it because I wanted to give the writer plenty of time to object if she had any reservations about my sending it to you. I have not heard from her, so here it is. You know, we have seldom published a new writer whose work aroused interest and enthusiasm in such a variety of people as Breece's has done. Much of it came in conversation and could not be handed on to him in solid form, but how I wish, now that I, or somebody here, had reported to him. We had no idea that he was unhappy, much less that he was sitting on stories we are delighted to publish.
>
> Please forgive me for my delay in thanking you for the picture and your note. . . .[7]

In the summer of 1982 advance proofs were sent out to a variety of writers for comment, among them Margaret Atwood and West Virginia author Jayne Anne Phillips. Both responded with unequivocal praise. For the book jacket, Atwood wrote: "This is an exceptional voice; gritty, mordant, invested with the texture of stroked reality; urgent and haunting." In answer to Casey's inquiry about reviewing the manuscript, Phillips told Casey that she had already seen one of Pancake's stories in the *Atlantic*. "I'd be quite willing to read Pancake's Little/Brown collection," Phillips said, "in fact, I'd be grateful if you'd send me a copy of the book. I was so disappointed to hear about his death; he was to be at the Provincetown workshop the same year I was there. I didn't realize he was from West Virginia, though I recognized something quite familiar in the spirit of the one story I've seen. The story was wonderful."[8] For the book jacket, Phillips wrote: "Breece Pancake's stories comprise no less than an American *Dubliners*. We find here a landscape preserved in rich sadness because it is forgotten, a people whose lives are informed by loss, wrenching cruelty, and the luminous dignity which marks the endurance of all that is most human." Though some critics disagreed with Phillips's comparison to Joyce,[9] she began the long list of weighty comparisons that would follow after the book was published in February of 1983. Both Atwood and Phillips also began naming the most repeatedly noticed qualities of his work—the unique, hard-edged, powerful voice, and the depiction of a sad, unforgiving world.

Gratified, but still somewhat surprised by Little, Brown's commitment to publish, Casey remarked to a reporter, "It's pretty rare that a publishing house will publish a book of short stories as a first book. It's also very rare that they'll publish when there's not going to be a follow-up. That's some indication of just how good the book is."[10] However, in the way the book was conceived and marketed, there seems to have been a unanimous, though unstated, notion that Breece's stories and his own story were so tightly intertwined that both his biography and his fiction would have to be read and considered together; that each could not stand alone without the other. Hence, two eloquent and poignant biographical reminiscences by Casey and McPherson served as bookends to the twelve stories, beginning with "Trilobites"—the story of Colly, a young man who struggles to escape—and ending with "First Day of Winter"—the story of middle-aged Hollis, who resignedly accepts his confinement. This arrangement presented problems for the reviewers and the critics, who had the task of determining the literary value of Pancake's fiction while having foreknowledge of his suicide.

Three years earlier, in 1980, the literary work of another suicide had also been posthumously published—John Kennedy Toole's *A Confederacy of Dunces*. This further complicated the critical milieu. Toole's suicide in 1969, which had been attributed to his despair at not having found a publisher for his book, along with the notable support of Walker Percy, who wrote the foreword to *A Confederacy of Dunces*, created a wave of critical notice that culminated in the Pulitzer Prize for Toole in 1981. The circumstances surrounding *The Stories of Breece D'J Pancake* seemed to make up a similar critical scenario; Randy Hogan, for example, writing for the *Village Voice*, first thought Pancake's book was a "literary hoax" based on "the unfortunate saga" of Toole.[11] Nevertheless, Peter Davison could not help but push the comparison in a letter seeking support for the book to Barbara Bannon of *Publisher's Weekly:* "I'm writing you because you know how hellishly difficult it is to launch a book like this—no matter how excellent. No author to generate publicity. No glamour to excite adulation. . . . There is something here, Barbara, which makes me think that we may have another CONFEDERACY OF DUNCES on our hands. I wish to God that Breece Pancake were here to see his stories published. I wish I could have met him. . . ."[12]

The reviewers had seen this kind of thing before, and many of them were wary of giving unwarranted praise to a work of fiction merely based on the sensational circumstances of an author's early death. Yet, the book received an enormous amount of attention, especially for a first collection of stories by a relatively unknown author (the book was reviewed in over one hundred newspapers and magazines), and critics echoed the pre-publication endorsements by editor Ronald Sharp of the *Kenyon Review* and writer Andre Dubus. "Thanks for passing along these stories, " Sharp wrote Casey. "Pancake was clearly a writer of genuine talent. The stories remind me of Harry Crews's work, which isn't exactly my cup of tea (or moonshine), but there's no denying that they're powerful and skillfully wrought. The best of them seems to be 'The Foxhunters' [*sic*]."[13] Dubus, solicited by Richard Todd for a book jacket blurb, responded, "My God what a story 'Hollow' is. Please have someone [send?] me a note or announcement of the title of the collection, and its publication date. Please don't send me a copy. This man's stories ought to be paid for. . . . I read excellent stories all the time, all over the place, and this one ranks with them all. . . . I wish someone could have saved him, since being a wonderful writer isn't enough."[14]

Reviewers uniformly praised Pancake for his artistry, his ability to unify sharply honed sensory detail, his talent for making sound and meaning converge, his imagery, dialogue, and his fine sense for drama. They noted the tremendous emotional compression in his stories and the minimalist style which begged comparison with Raymond Carver, a writer who gained eminent stature as master of the short story during the 1980s. More accurately, however, Pancake's style came from an older tradition in American literature, particularly from writers of the thirties.

Stylistically, Pancake borrowed heavily from West Virginia writer Tom Kromer and the early work of Ernest Hemingway. Pancake's tough, bare language, his use of regional idiom, his "heat" and "chippies," and his simple, direct sentence structure demand comparison with Kromer's Depression-era classic *Waiting for Nothing* and Hemingway's story collections *Winner Take Nothing*,[15] *Men Without Women*, and *In Our Time*. Joyce Carol Oates was the first to note the comparison with Hemingway in her influential review appearing in the *New York Times*: "Twelve stories, set in an impoverished region of West Virginia, by a young writer of such extraordinary gifts that one is tempted to compare his debut to Hemingway's, when the interrelated stories and prose pieces of 'In Our Time' were published in 1924. . . ."[16] Like Hemingway, Pancake created a realistic surface in relatively few words, where underneath lurks a much larger emotional and psychological reality. Like Kromer, Pancake exploited the dramatic effects of first-person, present-tense terse narration, which created "an atmosphere of extreme tension in his readers as well as in his protagonists."[17]

In addition, some critics, particularly after having read the foreword by McPherson, guessed that Pancake realistically captured a part of the texture and mood of the Appalachian experience. Inhabited by waitresses, miners, people on welfare, prostitutes, tugboat men, ex-convicts, highway maintenance workers, hardscrabble hillside farmers, garage mechanics, truck drivers, and the unemployed, Pancake's fictional characters exist on the periphery of the American mainstream. These were Pancake's forgotten mountaineers, whom Robert Towers described as "trapped, crippled, or obsolete,"[18] and struggle to escape or merely survive. Critics chose to recognize these characters as representatives of an unfortunate socioeconomic inheritance, a legacy which has earned people from the region a number of dubious labels, among them "hillbillies," "ridge runners," or the more current cultural distinction as the "ultimate others" in contemporary America. Albert Wilhelm rightly observed that the collection introduced the American reading public to a "sensitive treatment of a region and a social stratum typically ignored in literature."[19]

For most critics, however, Pancake's work reminded them of an earlier tradition in American literature as it had been defined by Jack London, Stephen Crane, Sherwood Anderson, William Faulkner, Ernest Hemingway, Flannery O'Connor, Carson McCullers, Erskine Caldwell, and John Steinbeck.[20] "The subject matter smacks of Flannery O'Connor," one reviewer wrote, "her half-mad families trapped by the ultimatums of time, place, and morality."[21] Another described Pancake as "a Southern writer, telling tales of pure Americana, and [who] makes no bones about his debts to certain ancestors (Faulkner, Hemingway, and in his matter of fact meanness, Flannery O'Connor)."[22] But the reviewers also noticed the setting for these stories represented a region of the South, a region of the Border States, "never quite penetrated and laid bare in American literature as skillfully, honestly, and hopelessly as it had been in *The Stories of Breece D'J Pancake*."[23]

Critics recognized a regional quality that made Pancake's work easily distinctive. Some ten years after the book's initial publication, Eileen Battersby, reviewing the British edition of Pancake's stories for the *Irish Times*, noted the same distinction:

> Writers from the Southern United States are a bit like Kenyan middle-distance runners; their consistently high standards result in individual excellence being expected as generically standard behaviour instead of gathering de- served plaudits. As U.S. writers maintain their stranglehold on international fiction, all the while protesting that there is such a thing as literary regional- ism in the U.S., the emphasis has become increasingly placed on New York or the small towns and farms of the Mid West. Shopping malls and streets and suburban kitchens—in addition to the time-honoured university cam- pus—have begun providing the setting for most of the current American fiction, which now inhabits a largely urban world devoid of trees or animals or mountains. But in spite of this national trend, the Southern writers have rarely lost touch with their native, natural landscape. Nature has always had a powerful role in their fictions which continue to be inhabited by haunted individuals who are burdened by dark family histories and private fears of failure. The oddly named Breece D'J Pancake is the latest of a long line of remarkable writers from the South.[24]

Pancake's fictional town of Rock Camp is a kind of southern Winesburg, a coming-of-age wishing well gone dry where characters struggle in terms of "the human heart in conflict with itself" and "grace under pressure," American literature clichés that represent the hard-to-achieve qualities in fiction that writers and readers still seek. His depictions of violent misfits, the misfortunes of rural poverty, along with his use of biblical allusion, natu- ral imagery, and animal metaphor align him with an earlier American tra- dition in writing. His use of symbol and color hints of the naturalism reminiscent of Crane, London, and Steinbeck; his hollows and wrecked au- tomobiles fight against freedom;[25] his blues and dark grays overcome the hope of green.

To the mind of the critic, Pancake's fiction seemed to fit the intellectual frame of Leslie Fiedler's *Love and Death in the American Novel*—"the dark vision of the American—his obsession with violence and embarrassment before love."[26] Pancake's characters routinely search in vain for love and goodness in a negative and loveless world, compulsively and unconsciously seeking a moral standard. They live on Fiedler's "last horizon," where innocence is in retreat, a physical and psychological "frontier" (in this case, Pancake's Appalachia)—"the region where the theory of original goodness and the fact of original sin come face to face."[27] As a result, critics were quick to label Pancake's work as southern gothic in the sense that "gothic fiction," in the Fiedler conception, is "nonrealistic and negative, sadist and melodramatic—a literature of darkness and the grotesque in a land of light and affirmation."[28]

The reviewer's job, of course, is to categorize, compare, locate, distinguish, and judge, and Pancake's work drew a remarkable list of comparisons from Beckett to Joyce, Caldwell to Faulkner. "With an obsessiveness reminiscent of Beckett," David Bosworth wrote for the *Boston Globe*, "Pancake dramatizes characters who are trapped by the land and their past, who long for escape yet don't know how. Often young, always poor, usually haunted by some tragedy in their recent past, a dead parent or a maimed friend, they (Breece Pancake) test the boundaries of their imprisonment for a secret passage, a way out."[29] According to Robert Monroe and others, Pancake evoked "on a smaller scale, a local world as nuanced and distinctive as the Dublin of Joyce's *Dubliners;* the region itself, with its hills, rivers, fogs, and wildlife, is a vital presence. Pancake constantly includes owls, opossums, and snakes, ironweed and sycamores, even buried bones and fossils in describing the lives he portrays. The situation of his strong, reticent, and trapped characters embody the unique milieu, but the problems they struggle with transcend it to reach universality."[30]

Nevertheless, reviewers also knew that the sensation of a suicide by a literary figure invites the making of a myth, a larger-than-life imaginative ideal of the young artist who chooses "to cease upon the midnight with no pain . . . while still young and beautiful and full of promise," as Samuel Hazo noted in his *Pittsburgh Press* review. "The fact that he eventually did effect such a divorce by his own hand lends a kind of darkness and mystery to the end of his life," wrote Hazo, "and it's easy to fall into a Keatsian reverie because of it ('What might he have written if he had lived, etc.'). Such reveries are the stuff of myth, not fact."[31] Critics were aware that the suicide of an artist inevitably invites conclusions about the painful and demon-ridden world of the artist, a world generally defined by a romantic (yet possibly fallacious) view of suicide that "the passion for destruction is also a creative passion."[32] Obviously, the way the book was packaged encouraged such mythic conclusions and corrupted a clear judgment.

A fact not known by most reviewers was that Pancake's work had invited praise and critical respect before his death. His stories had already elicited a huge response from readers while he was alive, readers who were ignorant of the author's personal life and who admired and praised his work because of its own merit. "In thirty-some years at The Atlantic," Phoebe-Lou Adams remarked, "I cannot recall a response to a new author like the response to this one. Letters drifted in for months, obviously from people who knew nothing about him, asking for more stories, inquiring for collected stories, or simply expressing admiration and gratitude. Whatever it is that truly commands reader attention, he had it."[33] Still, the unique manner in which the book was produced made it impossible for reviewers to read and judge his stories without knowing that Pancake had committed suicide at the beginning of a promising writing career.

What also hampered a clear critical judgment was the knowledge that this was a posthumous collection of stories put together by people who did not write them. Although six of the stories had been published during the author's lifetime, the other six stories of the collection may not have met the author's own critical standards. The critics noticed a lack of uniform quality. "An uneven gathering," Joyce Carol Oates called them, "But even the weak stories, 'Time and Again' for instance which has a sort of comic Gothicism—are nonetheless compelling. . . ."[34] John Casey, too, admits that only four of the stories were probably up to Pancake's own standard: "The Mark," "In the Dry," "Trilobites," and "Hollow"—four stories the author himself had seen in print. Regardless, reviewers generally praised the artistry evident even in the stories of lesser quality. This was a typical judgment: "A few of the stories are weak, understandably given the brevity of the author's creative life. But even the less effective selections are interesting, and the artistry of most of this work makes an evocative elegy for a darkly beautiful region, and for the haunting struggles of the lives which unfold there."[35]

It is also interesting to note that, although critics agreed on the uneven quality among the stories, curiously they did not agree on which stories were of higher or lesser quality. "Fox Hunters," "Time and Again," "A Room Forever," "The Mark," "The Way It Has to Be," and "The First Day of Winter" were the most controversial; yet, there were also critics who named these stories as the best in the collection. "Trilobites," "The Honored Dead," "Hollow," and "In the Dry" were unanimous favorites, but there was no critical consensus as to where the "uneven" quality exists.

In addition to the posthumous circumstances under which the stories were compiled and arranged, the biographical facts surrounding the publication of *The Stories of Breece D'J Pancake* explain some of the hostility the book received, most notably from Daphne Merkin, writing for the *New Republic*. "It is certainly evident that literary suicides succeed in doing themselves out of a genuinely critical appreciation," wrote Merkin. "What they get instead is the most uneasy kind of praise. . . . There is only the critic, properly elegiac or improperly picking at bones."[36] As Merkin suggests, the book did receive several "properly elegiac" responses. Note this review from the *West Virginia Hillbilly*: "Apparently fame came too late for Pancake. Whatever dark troubles he harbored were of such magnitude that he chose to drop the curtain before he had played out his creative life, and left a stunned audience to speculate on just how great a voice Breece D'J Pancake would have become,"[37] and this from *The Virginia-Pilot Ledger Star*: "[T]he stories that we have are a moving brilliant artistic testament to a writer who gave voice to lives heretofore unchronicled. What could he have done in his maturity?"[38] These were only a few out of over one hundred reviews that qualified as pure elegy.

Specifically, Merkin built her negative opinion of the book on a more cynical impression that the publisher may have intended to squeeze more commercial mileage from the suicide of a young man just emerging as a writer rather than from a writer's genuine talent made manifest in the stories. "The depressive in literature," Merkin wrote, "has acquired, these past decades, an unimpeachable stature; we respond to it with automatic seriousness. . . ." And because of this, she concluded, "I doubt that many readers will be moved to go back to any of these stories a second time . . . a distinctly minor collection with glints of a larger gift. To elevate these modest offerings by hailing them more than they are is to honor neither the reality of the writer's talent nor of his pain."[39]

No doubt many reviewers had difficulty overcoming the romantic inclination to regard Pancake's suicide as a literary act in itself. "Tennessee Williams died last month, strangled on a bottle cap at 71," began Bud Foote's review for the *Detroit News*. "He would have made something fine and ironic out of such a death. Thank God that he could write, when you consider his fierce and troubled trajectory through this life. At least he could make something out of his pain, and without that he would have been dead long ago. It is the sort of death one might find in a story by Breece D'J Pancake."[40]

Merkin's hostility and negativism, I think, centered on the possibility of this kind of mythmaking, but her view did not reflect the majority opinion, though many reviewers honestly noted the same uneasy reservations. Many reviewers, instead, overcame their own individual suspicions of tampered objectivity in favor of the subjectivity impressed upon them by the stories tucked between two views of the author's life. According to M. K. Dieckman: "Breece D'J Pancake is the perfect target for that peculiar and irresistible practice of literary romanticization. . . . How is one to separate out the hype and hyperbole to determine what is of interest and value in these stories?"[41] It was a question that somehow had to be answered, and the reviewers almost universally found a way to praise Pancake's work apart from the details of the author's life. Ever wary, Dieckman answered her own question by differentiating Pancake's talent from Merkin's fear of the fashionably tragic in literature and affirming the quality of his work: "Gradually, perhaps only with re-reading, one comes to recognize the essential difference between Pancake and other practitioners of the icons of the hip."[42] Bolton Davis, in his review for *San Francisco Review of Books*, also considered, then dismissed, the confusing shadow of suicide: "Though Breece's suicide casts a shadow over these stories, I think it is paying him the ultimate compliment to say that it really doesn't matter here. Like fossils formed over millions of years by enormous pressures in a single place, these stories have the polished, purged, hardwon qualities that will insure that they last far longer than the flesh that once inhabited them."[43]

Reviewers surmised that the "facts of biography are likely to dominate responses to his work," but they also insisted that the enduring quality of his writing would prevail. "The linked mysteries of creativity and death," wrote Raymond Nelson in the *Virginia Quarterly Review*, "may initially heighten the appeal of Pancake's pages, but readers will return to them for their sureness and variety of character, their clarity of life imagined and made known."[44] The "linked mysteries of creativity and death" apparently did heighten interest in the book's debut; it went through three printings its first year. The book tempted readers to search for clues to Breece's suicide, a tragedy that subsequently imbued the stories with authenticity and authority.

"Suicide, especially a young man's suicide, cannot be brushed away as easily as jacket copy or an author's suspect praise," wrote Bosworth. "The sacrilegious act haunts our reading habits. We cannot help but place the book into a new and disturbing category, a sort of Literature of Last Words, wherein the text acquires an added, deathbed gravity. We search its pages for a life's summation and yet hope to find, too, an explanation, a reason for the tragedy. . . . No explanation ever truly satisfies, of course, but the stories in this book are worthy of that deeper search."[45]

Reviewers attempting to overlook "that deeper search" generally agreed that the collection of stories was brilliant, regardless of the mystery of Pancake's suicide. "This knowledge, naturally, will color any reader's response to his stories," wrote Martin Kirby in the *Philadelphia Inquirer*, "but fortunately they are excellent and would hold interest without the opportunity for amateur psychoanalysis that their author's suicide offers."[46]

Some reviewers found it difficult to resist those amateur attempts at psychoanalysis and confessed that the normal impulse of any reader would be to look for clues. "I would rather not know that," Foote wrote:

It makes it hard to be fair to his stories. I keep reading them as symptoms rather than as works of art. . . . Further, I find myself looking at the stories as fossils, like the trilobites in the lead story, remnants of life now dead, creatures with no successors. And so, instead of reading the stories as stories, I think grim and maudlin thoughts about the pain of creation, wondering whether the agony makes the art or the art makes the agony, and why some of the gifted and sensitive live to be old and crusty, like Robert Frost and Louis Armstrong, while others take themselves out in mid-course like Phil Ochs, Sylvia Plath, and Breece Pancake. But in spite of the tragedy of his life, in spite of the loving, moving tributes of McPherson and John Casey, the stories deserved to be read standing on their own feet. Pancake was one splendid writer.[47]

Balancing the question of life and art, death and creativity, critics found a common theme between Pancake's life and work. They tended to look upon his life and death as compelling evidence of the forces that drove him, forces which naturally influenced but did not dominate his work. "Genuine" was a word often used by the critics; if anything, it appeared that his suicide underscored the word's meaning. In the *Charleston Gazette* Jim Dent wrote, "Whatever the reason for his death it deprived us of a genuine talent."[48] This sense of the "genuine" caused some to observe that the "enormous emotional power" of Pancake's writing must have originated from the author's own struggle: "Pancake's stories do not constitute a cheerful invitation to beautiful West Virginia," Martin Kirby wrote. "Even so, I would not want to influence anyone to avoid reading the stories out of fear of being depressed. Pancake was a genuine tragic artist. Aristotle would have approved of him, because his stories do stir up the emotions and a sympathetic reader would emerge feeling better than before."[49] In the mind of the critics, Pancake's fiction and his biography were inextricably tied together in a way that neither overshadowed the other. In fact, some reviewers could not even begin to separate them.

To Mike Ritchey of the *Fort Worth Star Telegram*, Pancake's real life story and his fictional stories were one and the same, and this led to some unfortunate, though eloquent, conjecture as to the circumstances of his life.

Pancake's song was hard and fast. He hit a few impressive high notes which, while they all ring true, add nevertheless to a monotone. The devil of it is, Pancake thought there was something unalterably wrong with that. He knew almost everything about very little and he regretted it. Fearing he might never rise from the ashes of what he saw as being a disagreeable birthright and believing finally that he had said all he had to say—or wanted to say—he folded his tent. The truth is, of course, that he was blessed with an enormous talent and, too, fiction's bona fide bluebloods—both ambulatory and fossilized—have merely understood a few verities about their narrow stomping grounds. Being his own worst critic, Pancake was simply too hard to please.[50]

What Ritchey thought he read in the stories was a profile of the author. So, too, Alan Cheuse writing for the *Los Angeles Herald* could only understand Pancake's work through the lens of his suicide: "There's mature craft abounding in these pages but also great despair, so much so that you wonder as you read not that Pancake lived long enough to write these fine stories, but he lived long enough to write anything at all."[51]

The book posed an aesthetic problem; whether to judge the object of art on its own merits, to judge it in relation to its creator, or both. Carolyn Wilkerson Bell outlined the problem this way: "The two elegiac essays and the twelve stories they frame, raise many questions not only about Pancake's fiction but also about the connections between the work and the life. More than most books, *The Stories of Breece D'J Pancake* invites the reader to reflect on the complicated relation between an author's emotional realities and the fiction he creates."[52]

Here it seemed there was a merging of life and art, where the artist's life and the object of his art converged, so much so that Sharon Barrett of the *Chicago Sun-Times* was more taken with the quality and interest of the biographical essays by Casey and McPherson than with Pancake's stories. "This slender volume is both a first collection and a posthumous collection," she wrote. "Perhaps that is why, despite the power and quality of the stories, two of the most interesting pieces in the book are those about rather than by the author."[53]

The "power and quality" of the stories apparently did come from the "emotional realities" of the author, and, as a consequence, reviewers placed Pancake's stories far above those routinely manufactured for the fiction market. These emotional realities distinguished his writing from most other books which came across a reviewer's desk. Here is an example of how one reviewer writing for the *Nation* explained the difference, distinguishing Pancake's collection from another collection appearing that same year:

> Bobbie Ann Mason's book of sixteen short stories has been treated to a remarkable amount of favorable critical attention for a first collection, and indeed her appeal is undeniable. . . . When you turn the page, however, her people vanish because their stories have no emotional gravity. . . . This aimlessness is not unique to Mason, of course. It characterizes much of what passes as good fiction right now—but it disappoints all the same. It's all the more exciting, therefore, to turn to *The Stories of Breece D'J Pancake*, for here is fiction that offers the deep pleasure of art created out of the need to transform suffering. . . . These twelve stories are all we will ever have from him, but they may well be read for generations to come. While Mason's characters are sociological types, Pancake's are individuals who act out of kinds of necessity present in our own lives. We are not tourists in his fiction, but residents. . . .[54]

Pancake was described by McPherson as an "empopath"[55]—a person with the obsessive and extraordinary ability to closely empathize with other people and with the characters he created. As a result, many critics were overwhelmed by the moving and often "embarrassing" emotional power evident in the stories. "What stands out in all of these stories is the sheer pain of this life," wrote Gregory Morris for the *Prairie Schooner*. "Characters walk about with their hearts torn out, bare gaping wounds like the yawning mouths of mines. So much emotion is expended, and ex-pended wastefully, as bodies heave down on bodies, forcing their pain upon others, that we can almost understand the inward intensity of feel-ing Pancake himself understood and, tragically, never seem to outlive."[56] Critics were praising Pancake's ability to write about his characters from the inside, not from an observable, safe distance. "Author and reader are inside the characters, not outside seeing them as picturesque, humorous, pathetic or symbolic."[57] "Breece D'J Pancake never, as he says of one of his characters, talked through his beak. His voice came instead from 'some-where deep' in his chest."[58]

It is important to note that the biographical details of Pancake's life did not exactly parallel those of the characters he created. He never was a coal-miner, or a pick-up boxer, or a truck driver; but he did have the ability to project his own emotional realities upon his characters, most of whom were adolescent males or men in their early manhood. This ability disturbed some critics. A few critics winced at the adolescent emotional quality in some of the stories, "a quality of late-adolescent Weltschmerz that verges on the maudlin," complained Robert Towers.[59] Yet, wrote Carolyn Wilkerson Bell, "At his best, Pancake writes about these subjects with so much energy and intensity that it saddens even embarrasses the reader to come upon the stories in the collection. . . ."[60] To most critics, these were not just individual emotional realities; they were feelings shared by many people who find themselves in "the conflict between who we want to be and where we find ourselves."[61] This was that rare quality, as many observed, that made his stories "ring true."

By the end of 1983 *The Stories of Breece D'J Pancake* had been reviewed in over one hundred national and regional publications. Among the other books competing for the reviewers' attention that year were Bobbie Ann Mason's *Shiloh*, William Kennedy's *Ironweed*, Mark Helprin's *Winter's Tale*, Andre Dubus's *The Times Are Never So Bad*, *The Stories of Bernard Malamud*, William Least Heat Moon's *Blue Highways*, Gabriel García Márquez's *Chronicle of a Death Foretold*, and Raymond Carver's collection of short sto-ries, *Cathedral*. Amid this competition *The Stories of Breece D' J Pancake* re-ceived overwhelming praise and critical attention resulting in a nomination for the Pulitzer Prize, a nomination for the Weatherford award representing the best in Appalachian fiction, and a place among the American Library Association's "Notable Books of 1983."

In 1984 the book became available to a wider audience through a reissue in paperback by Holt, Rinehart and Winston, and since then, Pancake's stories have been read in college literature courses and college writing workshops across the nation, most notably at the Iowa Writer's Workshop.

Ten years after its initial publication, the reputation of the book and its author still attracted interest. In 1992 Neuer Verlag purchased rights for a German translation, and in 1994 Bertrand Brasil published a Portuguese translation by Jose J. Veiga entitled *Contos Cortantes* ("Stories of the Heart"). Also in 1994 the London publishing house Secker and Warburg published a British edition under the title *Trilobites and Other Stories*. This paperback edition featured a front cover photograph by Walker Evans, and the same grainy 1977 photograph of Pancake on the back that Little, Brown had used for the original book jacket.

Surprisingly, the book's critical reception in Great Britain was consistent with what American reviewers had written a decade earlier. Tony Tanner writing for the *Manchester Guardian* made some of the same comparisons. "This is the world of these stories by Breece D'J. Pancake, and even his bizarre and hardly credible name seems to come from that world of the weird, the grotesque, the malformed, the mean and the violent, which has been depicted for us by Flannery O'Connor, Carson McCullers, even Faulkner himself."[62] David Montrose of the *Times Literary Supplement* wrote that "several of the stories show the influence of other writers—not the minimalists who were then becoming fashionable, [i.e. 1970's–80's], but traditional, altogether more robust writers: Sherwood Anderson, Hemingway, Faulkner, Steinbeck."[63] And Eileen Battersby, writing for Dublin's *Irish Times*, noted, "[T]here is a curiously remote and timeless quality about Pancake's world just as there is about Faulkner's or Flannery O'Connor's."[64]

Reviews from the British Isles also echoed many of the same critical suspicions surrounding his suicide that were previously sounded by American reviewers. "Thirteen years ago, aged 26, Breece Pancake pulled the trigger on the shotgun he had put in his mouth. It's therefore more than likely that Trilobites will be his only published collection," read one review in the *Glasgow Herald*, "but that's not the only reason it ought to be read."[65] British critics grappled with the same uneasy connection between the facts of the author's life and his fiction, but could not fail to notice the power of Pancake's fiction perhaps because of it. "The writing has an enormous unforced power. . . . It's amazing that someone can depict so much pain in life and it having nothing to do with self-indulgence," noted Tom Butterworth of London's *City Limits.* "I suppose it all boils down to that slightly troubling notion of 'literary authenticity,' that extra added power which has as much to do with biographical circumstance as actual product. The fact of Pancake's suicide can't help but weld these stories together with an idea of death. It's an unreasonable, macabre 'authenticity' but, as with Sylvia Plath, it's just there."[66] Most often, British critics chanted the same haunting praise for what might have been. "These are finely-built, savage tales," wrote Erica Wagner in the *London Times,* "poignant in their vast potential."[67]

Though only two unpublished stories, fragments, and unfinished pieces by Pancake remain, the "potential" of the published stories still exists in the many dramatic and film treatments that have been written based on the book and the author's life.[68] Paul Hendrickson declared: "Now, the legend of Breece D'J Pancake glimmers and spreads like fox fire"[69]—a legend that Pancake himself, perhaps unlike Hemingway, had unconsciously promulgated. In a 1977 interview Pancake was asked: "[D]o you feel a sense of injustice that very talented writers are not tremendously successful (in a monetary sense), while other junk writers are?" Pancake responded: "I don't feel that popular work is a reflection of the literary times. They are in the business of selling books, not necessarily selling talent. One must separate art from business and decide priorities. Writing, however, endures. The unknown writer that isn't prospering now may well be remembered after he is gone."[70]

This slim book of stories and the story of its author have inspired a generation of readers and writers, and that phenomenon, in itself, has become a part of the literary legend. His admirers have included some of the best American writers: Raymond Carver, Andre Dubus, Sam Shepard, Carolyn Forché, Peter Davison, Jayne Anne Phillips, Margaret Atwood, and Joyce Carol Oates. His influence has been felt by his former teachers, James Alan McPherson and John Casey, who are often questioned by their students wanting to know more about him. An accomplished writer himself, Casey thinks that Pancake's stories are "one of the real nodes of artistic energy in the last twenty years."[71] Remarkably, Casey's novel *Spartina,* which won the National Book Award in 1990, strongly captures the spirit and sympathy of his former friend and student. The legend has also become a kind of touchstone for aspiring writers. Emerging novelist Cynthia Kadohata's essay "Breece Pancake" chronicles a journey in search of the spirit of the author, and West Virginia writer Pinckney Benedict's "Recalling Breece Pancake" acknowledges his literary debt to the writer who showed him a style, a method, and a subject to write about—his home state.

Critically, the legend of the author and reputation of the book continue to grow, and Pancake has come to be considered "a master" of the short story form.[72] His stories have been anthologized in *Stories of the Modern South*, edited by Ben Forkner and Patrick Samway, *Soldiers and Civilians*, edited by Tom Jenks, and *Appalachia Inside Out: A Sequel to The Voices from the Hills*, edited by Robert J. Higgs, Ambrose N. Manning, and Jim Wayne Miller.

Appalachian scholar Bob Snyder, noting his personal obsession with the stories, declared that Pancake was "certainly the best of the new generation of Appalachian writers."[73] Regionally, his work reminds us, after all, that "stories should be studied not because they manage to escape the limitations of their particular time and place, but because they offer powerful examples of the way a culture thinks about itself, articulating and proposing solutions for the problems that shape a particular historical moment,"[74] and for this reason Pancake's work has come to be regarded as central to contemporary Appalachian fiction.[75]

After *The Stories of Breece D'J Pancake* was published, Helen Pancake sold the house in Milton and moved to the west coast of Florida, where the family had often vacationed. The last time the entire family had been there was 1957, when Breece was five years old.

6

"The Only Value":
Pancake's Moral Vision

Had I lived some years ago, I think I would have been a moralist, i.e., one who lays down, so to speak, rules of behavior with no small amount of self-satisfaction. But the writer isn't allowed that function anymore, or no man can take the job on very happily, being aware (as he must be) of what precisely that will make him.

So there is left this other area, still the short story or really the tale, and all that can be made of it. Whereas the novel is a continuum, of necessity, chapter to chapter, the story can escape some of that obligation, and function exactly in terms of whatever emotion best can serve it. . . .

The only possible reason for its [the short story's] existence is that it has, in itself, the fact of reality and the pressure. There, in short, is its form—no matter how random and broken that will seem. The old assumptions of beginning and end—those very neat assertions—have fallen away completely in a place where the only actuality is life, the only end (never realized) death, and the only value, what love one can manage. . . .

—Robert Creeley, Introduction to *The Gold Diggers*

The legend of Breece Pancake has made it difficult to read his short stories with an objective eye. The fact of suicide has been carved into his fiction. Furthermore, Pancake's suicide, like those of many other literary figures, has been misunderstood because of the James Dean aura that surrounds him. In effect he has been granted a marble-like stature that has been deemed off limits to those who cannot claim a common regional heritage. Even a hint of judgment or criticism has been regarded as an attempt to disturb a hallowed grave, as if so soon someone were to forget the circumstances of his short, tragic literary career. While critics found reasons to value the work apart from the biography when the collection first appeared, these reasons have been largely ignored in the romanticizing of Pancake in subsequent years. Distracted by the legend, we lose sight of what Pancake tried to do in his fiction, what his stories were about, and where they came from in his imagination.

The confusion arises from the very region that has so fervently claimed him—his sense of place. As Leonard Lutwack has pointed out in *The Role of Place in Literature*,[1] "Places may have a significant influence on a writer," and certainly the West Virginia Breece Pancake knew deeply influenced his imagination. This was something British novelist Richard Jones realized more fully about his friend and former student only after visiting the state in 1987, eight years after Pancake's death. "There was this incredible feeling for the lives of the people who had gone before him and the traditions that had formed him," Jones remarked, "which is perhaps not so uncommon in say an old established nation like Scotland or Ireland where the past lives on in a really vital and sometimes constricting way. But this was a very powerful force in Breece, and it was only when I came to West Virginia that I appreciated that this was also something that this state, his society, had given him."[2] "West Virginia was the subject for him,"[3] John Casey has noted, not only in its present condition but also its past.

His was the kind of fiction of place rooted in the past that prompted comparisons with an earlier generation of American writers, a generation to which Pancake's mentor, Peter Taylor, belonged. Robert Wilson, a classmate of Pancake's at the University of Virginia remembered the lesson Taylor had to teach his students, but it was one which Pancake already knew: "[A] writer must, to be more than a journeyman, have a subject—that is, a world all his own, a world he knows better than anyone else, knows so well in fact the he can extract from it what meaning there is. This was not something Breece needed to learn."[4]

Pancake, like Taylor, set his fiction in the time and place of his birthright with painstaking care, but the subject was always something more than just local color and nuance of place. The subject of Pancake's fiction concerned the people in that place and the "rules of behavior," something which also concerned Taylor. I think what Shelby Foote has observed about his friend Taylor can also be said of Pancake: "If you'll keep your eyes open," Foote has said, "you'll see he never wanders. He stays right on the subject. He was very concerned about what went on inside people. And their reaction to what was expected of them. . . . That was a big thing and one of the most southern aspects of his writing. All of Peter's characters are thoroughly aware that what is expected of them has to be paid attention to."[5]

In Taylor's *A Woman of Means*, for example, a young man named Quint learns what is expected of him and how the lessons of behavior are made sacred because of their connection to time and place. Quint recalls:

> On my grandmother's farm there was only one white oak. . . . Every summer . . . Grandma used to take the other children and me down in the field and point out the white oak to us. We always went by way of the Indian graveyard which made the whole west side of her shady lawn uneven, but she never allowed the children to walk on the graves; and all the children following after her would reverently put their feet down like hers between the grass-covered mounds. Yet when Grandma had gone back into the house, I would watch Rob and Jeff running helter-skelter over the graves, and even digging into them for arrowheads and skinning knives. It was only upon the graves of the two Indian children that they would not walk or play. For Grandma said the graves contained children of peaceful Indians who fell victim to the more barbarous nations. Once when I stepped on one of the graves by mistake, Rob threatened to lock me away in the cellar. And Jeff agreed that was their rule.[6]

Appearing at the beginning of "The Honored Dead," Pancake's young protagonist narrates a similar scenario: "I keep thinking back to the summer me and my buddy Eddie tore that burial mound apart for arrowheads and copper beads gone green with rot. We were getting down to the good stuff, coming up with skulls galore, when of a sudden Grandad showed out of thin air and yelled, 'Wah-pah-nah-te-he.' He was waving his arms around, and I could see Eddie was about to shit the nest. I knew it was all part of the old man's Injun act, so I stayed put, but Eddie sat down like he was ready to surrender." The grandfather warns the boys: "Now put the goddamned bones back or I'll take a switch to your young asses. . . ." Although the grandfather makes it clear that the Indian grave, a symbol of blood, land, and the past, is sacred and not to be violated, the young narrator remains skeptical: "Wah-pah-nah-te-he—the fat of my ass."[7]

Taylor's characters often recognize the rules of blood, the land, and the past as solid moral parameters, but Pancake's characters stare blankly at something they cannot recognize or even see; for them there is only an absence of tradition and belief. The lessons, time-honored recitations in Taylor's Tennessee, have been forgotten in Pancake's West Virginia, and if remembered, they are not to be believed. Pancake's uncertain young men and women seem to tread a more ambivalent ground, and many of them "count the pass-at-your-own-risk marks on the road" as a way of determining their own direction in life.

Like Taylor, Pancake "never wanders" from the rules of behavior, but the rules of Taylor's past and place, as Pancake guessed, had changed. Pancake's approach, though connected to an earlier tradition, captured the confusing tenor of the sixties and seventies. As Casey has observed: "It seemed he'd taken in an older generation's experience along with (not in place of his own)."[8] Pancake's characters are, in some ways, similar to those found in the work of Peter Taylor, Walker Percy, and Faulkner, set adrift in the "plastic present,"[9] cut off from the past; but whereas Taylor's characters can still find a firm, yet unsettling, footing in their recollections of family and place, Pancake's characters sink into even more uncertainty and misdirection. Behavior still has its gatekeepers in Taylor's fiction, but in Pancake, the gates have been left unguarded for too long and moral passage has been entirely left up to the individual arbiter of conscience.

Pancake's fiction, filtered through his own experience and memory, grappled with the moral perplexities of his generation, a generation that frequently lost its balance trying to keep up with a disorienting pace of change. Edward Fox, writing for the *Charleston Gazette*, observed:

> Pancake's career was in many ways like that of many West Virginians who leave country towns like Milton in search of better opportunities in bigger cities in other states. But Pancake, an artist, perhaps felt more acutely the sense of dislocation that transplanted Mountaineers feel in cities like Detroit and Chicago, and which leads some of them to return. At the time of his death, he was by all accounts troubled by somber preoccupations. His imagination was rooted in West Virginia, especially Milton, yet he could not live here and succeed as a writer at the same time.[10]

This "sense of dislocation" is and was a part of the predicament of the region, but during the 1960s and 1970s, it also applied to the nation as a whole. Michiko Kakutani, writing for the *New York Times*, noticed that Pancake's fiction "creates a powerful, elegiac portrait of an America reeling from the dislocations of recent history."[11] The effect of dislocation and the migration out of Appalachia is not new to Appalachian literature; from Arnow's *The Dollmaker* to Smith's *Oral History*, the struggle for identity without a sense of place has been the region's central theme. But since 1952, the year he was born, Breece Pancake's America had become even more mobile, more transient, and more fluid than ever before and, because of this, also more disconnected from the America of the past. Post–World War II and post-industrial, technological America experienced massive shifts in employment and population, and a new generation of youth represented the first in their families to attend colleges and universities in record numbers. It was a time when "everybody's going to college to be something better," and it was an uncertain time of confused direction, as Pancake's fictional father in "The Honored Dead" reflects, "Well, when everybody's going this way, it's time to turn around and go that way, you know?" The Vietnam War, equal rights for women, the civil rights movement, and the "generation gap" revealed an America off-balance and in transition. These uncertainties and upheavals, in addition to Pancake's personal anxieties, became conscious reflections in his art, made even more salient because West Virginia in many ways is more transitional than any other state in the nation, both well connected still to America's rural past and painfully industrialized.

A feeling of dislocation and rootlessness, of course, has been the point of departure for many southern writers, and in particular the Agrarians, for they understood that dislocation meant disintegrating families and communities along with the attendant lack of expectation, continuity, and moral sense. This theme fills the pages of their fiction. In *A Summons to Memphis* Taylor's protagonist reflects, "It may be that by that time—1931—the family in our sort of world and in our part of the country, without any real economic function or any relation to the old earth it had been formed by or any significance in the heavens above, was now such a frail and fractious thing. . . ."[12] What Taylor's protagonist describes is part of the Agrarian premise and the same moral assumption from which Pancake's stories emerge.

Pancake felt the absences of his time (which in part explains his world of negation), a time out of touch with past and place; his fiction laments how "frail and fractious" the family had become, but, unlike Taylor—whose characters can still remember a time "forgotten almost"[13]—Pancake presents characters who have lost their memory. Pancake's stories reveal characters suffering a Percy-like "moral amnesia" where they cannot find a place that will either physically or spiritually sustain them; they cannot find a family who knows "their relation to the old earth it had been formed by or any significance in the heavens above." In life Pancake had wished that West Virginia would resist the disorienting changes of the times,[14] but the West Virginia of his fiction shows that his sense of his place was not immune to what the Agrarians had known decades earlier.

Pancake's work continues and intensifies what an earlier generation of southern writers set out to do, without being "heavy" in the contemporary sense—that is, gruesomely violent—and without being cynically flippant. His stories often concern a protagonist, like Faulkner's Quentin Compson, or Percy's Will Barrett, who longs to escape the suffocating realities of home, family, and the past, and who, at the same time, fervently desires to maintain a vital connection to all that has formed him.

In Pancake' s most critically recognized story, "Trilobites," Colly is a young man of college age caught between the pull to keep the family farm and the desire to escape the futility of trying to do "something you're no good at." Pancake at his best intensifies the predicament of his protagonists by surrounding them with rings of emotional and psychological conflict. In "Trilobites" Pancake carefully layers the tension: Colly's inability as a farmer is exacerbated by a blighted, dry, and infertile landscape; he is haunted by memories of the lost father, the good farmer, appearing as a "khaki cloud in the canebrakes"; he is insulted by the imminent sale of the family farm to an outsider, a much despised double-knit flatlander from Ohio whose "voice sounds like a damn TV"; and he is frightened by the uncertain and undesirable future far away from the homeplace in Akron.

Colly's impotent rage and rebellion further complicates his dilemma. He talks back to his mother, defies her, resists the sale of the farm. "I talked back. I've never talked back. I'm scared, but I stop shaking. Ginny can't see me shaking." His rebellion ends in self-condemnation and fear. Pancake's assault on Colly's sense of well-being is relentless, for Colly's love for Ginny, the beautiful but unattainable college girl, is also frustrated and denied. When she returns home during a brief break from a distant college in Florida, Colly realizes yet another side of his impotence—she will again leave without him.

The emotional descent of his characters is like a deep echo and each echo suggests a farther fall. College and all the economic and social-climbing hopes for the future that college inspires is yet something else out of reach for Colly. Colly's impotence rings even deeper in the final moments of the story when, ironically, Colly and Ginny's rough sexual encounter on the floor of an abandoned train station among shards of broken glass doesn't bring them together but separates them forever.

A Pancake protagonist does not have much of chance; he or she lives in a world of closed and closing doors. Conflicts of family, identity, class, the past, homeplace, love, and sex are heaped upon them, almost as if to see just what it is they can and will do. They are always under pressure to see what "rules of behavior" will emerge, or what moral last stand they will make in a disintegrating world. These layers of pressure are often suggested in a few well-compressed paragraphs near the beginning of each story. In "Trilobites" many of Colly's troubles are outlined in the opening paragraphs neatly tucked between the simple action of Colly opening a truck door and going into the local cafe.

> I open the truck's door, step onto the brick side street. I look at Company Hill again, all sort of worn down and round. A long time ago it was real craggy and stood like an island in the Teays River. It took over a million years to make that smooth little hill, and I've looked all over it for trilobites. I think how it has always been there and always will be, at least for as long as it matters. The air is smoky with summertime. A bunch of starlings swim over me. I was born in this country and I have never very much wanted to leave. I remember Pop's dead eyes looking at me. They were real dry, and that took something out of me. I shut the door, head for the cafe.

I see a concrete patch in the street. It's shaped like Florida, and I recollect what I wrote in Ginny's yearbook: "We will live on mangoes and love." And she up and left without me—two years she's been down there we without me. She sends me postcards with alligator wrestlers and flamingos on the front. She never asks me any questions. I feel like a real fool for what I wrote, and go into the cafe.[15]

His stories have been characterized as possessing "deep time and narrow space,"[16] a description founded on Pancake's "worn down" landscapes, which do not have much practical use, but rather contain more of a past than a future. These landscapes represent the homeplace his protagonists "never much wanted to leave." The narrow emotional and psychological space of home offers no opportunities for the future, but many compelling incentives for escape. Characters are held tightly in place, haunted by the ghosts of the father and/or other ancestors, which in this instance irrevocably chain Colly to family and the past where he cannot escape the "dead eyes" that remind him of guilt, grief, and his own futile mortality. Finally, Colly's frustrated desire for love, hinted at here in these beginning paragraphs, comes under pressure as the story develops and explodes into violence, a pattern repeated in Pancake's "Hollow," "A Room Forever," "Fox Hunters," "The Mark," and "The Way It Has to Be."

"What is it Colly? Why can't we have any fun?" asks Ginny. Colly tries to explain his dilemma to her, but inevitably fails.

> "When I was a young punk, I tried to run away from home. I was walking through this meadow on the other side of the Hill, and this shadow passed over me. I honest to god thought it was a pterodactyl. It was damned airplane. I was so damn mad, I came home." I peel chips of paint from the window frame, wait for her to talk. She leans against me, and I kiss her real deep. Her waist bunches in my hands. The skin of her neck is almost too white in the faded evening. I know she doesn't understand.[17]

His stories often turn on moments of violence, which serve as a predictable and dramatic result of language failing—something also found in the work of Raymond Carver. But unlike the sensational and nonsensible variety of violence found so often in contemporary fiction, violence in Pancake's fiction helps focus the conflict at the precise moment when the main character can no longer emotionally or psychologically move. In "Trilobites" Colly's last-ditch effort to make positive human contact ends in a sexual act devoid of any feeling other than lust, resentment, and guilt: "I slide her to the floor. Her scent rises to me, and I shove crates aside to make room. I don't wait. She isn't making love, she's getting laid. All right, I think, all right. Get laid. I pull her pants around her ankles, rut her. I think of Tinker's sister. Ginny isn't here. Tinker's sister is under me. A wash of blue light passes over me. I open my eyes to the floor, smell that tang of rain-wet wood. Black snakes. It was the only time he had to whip me."[18]

When love is unavailable in stories like "Trilobites," "The Mark," and "Hollow," relationships become sexually lurid, forbidden, animalistic, driven by physical domination and/or possession and reduced to appetite. In this moment Ginny becomes the underage and taboo Tinker's sister, "her scent" triggering the animal impulse to copulate while a memory of the father and black snakes sits in judgment.

His stories end ambiguously with muted epiphanies that suggest either hope, more of the same impasse, or further violence. In "Trilobites" Colly violently "ruts" the woman he would rather love and drifts into a reverie of a mythic past, of home and father, and sees and hears in the now passing "highballin" train, a direction of hope, one he must pursue to alleviate his fear.

> I watch her beat by. A worn-out tie belches mud with her weight. She's just too fast to jump. Plain and simple.
>   I get up. I'll spend tonight at home. I've got eyes to shut in Michigan— maybe even Germany or China, I don't yet. I walk, but I'm not scared. I feel my fear moving away in rings through time for a million years.[19]

These are intended, of course, to be stories of small degrees, where large movements are neither made nor expected. In Pancake's more open-ended stories, like "Trilobites," "In the Dry," "The Scrapper," and "Fox Hunters," the protagonist claims some small degree of freedom from the incessant, claustrophobic pressure. Whether a protagonist like Colly will find what he is looking for or whether he resolves his many conflicts is beyond the pages of Pancake's short fiction; but this technique demands an imaginative search for some sort of resolution that promises either escape or moral affirmation. In more closed-ended stories like "A Room Forever," which ends with the unsuccessful suicide attempt of a young prostitute, and "Hollow," where the protagonist Buddy violates all codes and values, there is a moral negation, yet these characters still find some degree of release even in this world of nothing.

Possessing an even more limited range of moral possibility are stories like "The Honored Dead," which ends with a young man unable to shake the ghosts of the past; "First Day of Winter," in which Hollis sullenly resigns to a suffocating life on a barren farm, and "The Salvation of Me," in which a young man, gas-pump in hand, ceases to dream and accepts his fate without a struggle. Yet, these more limited, emotionally seething stories are no less moving or powerful.

In addition to the intense emotional pressure, what makes Pancake's fiction fully developed and explored is the often overlooked mythic quality of Pancake's imagination, a quality that aligns him with an earlier tradition in southern writing and a quality that is obscured by his meticulous attention to realistic detail and texture. Mircea Eliade describes how myths of cosmogony, of how the world was created and what the world was like before each individual was born into it, are vital in healing those who are sick in mind or body or those who are merely "frightened by a dream." He describes how in primitive societies "a patient is projected out of profane time into the fullness of primordial Time; he is carried back to the origin of the 'World' and is thus present at the cosmogony." This process, according to Eliade, remedies the sickness and revitalizes the patient, offering a "return to origins," to first things, which are "significant and valid."[20]

Here, Colly's obsession with finding a trilobite, a prehistoric fossil, is essential to his return to origins, the remedy for his soul sickness. That he can't find one is yet another layer of frustration and denial; he is stuck in the profane world of realistic failures and human inabilities, of crude sex and violence, a world he very much wants to transcend or at the very least escape. Instead of seeing a pterodactyl, the sign of his return, he is angered by discovering that the mythic "shadow" that passed over him was nothing but further evidence of the profane world; "It was a damned airplane," he tells Ginny. It is a tribute to the mettle of his character (Pancake's characters' kind of "grace under pressure") that Colly remains tough-minded and resolved to at least search for the more immediate past by retracing the steps of the father in hopes of finding peace and safe haven from fear. "The Honored Dead," "Hollow," "Fox Hunters," "The Mark" and "In the Dry" also have this mythic quality.

"In the Dry" reminds us of the mythic wasteland, the drought-stricken land lacking fertility—a condition unbelievable in a mimetic representation of West Virginia—yet here in this story where both love and sexuality cannot grow, Ottie sees "their droughty valley, but cannot understand—the hills on either side can call down rain." Perhaps, as Ruel Foster has suggested, Pancake is using the dry bones of Ezekiel as the central motif in this story,[21] but it is the wound that is so deeply felt and experienced by Ottie that tells us how similar this is to the mythic journey of the Fisher King, returning with the hope of renewal and restoration. The "pink-lipped wound in one dimple of Beagle's chest" hints at Ottie's deeper wound of rejection and lovelessness, and, since his return to the Gerlock farm, he becomes aware that the wound has not healed and the drought of love and life will continue since "what turned them all will spin them forever." But of course the story is more complicated than that, borrowing from myth, and from the Bible—"If they do these things in a green tree, what will they do in the dry?"—and from natural history—that wasps will always return to the place of their nest—and from stories of the Kanawha Valley—"sin crops" growing in the valley—and from biography—Breece raised prize beagle pups with his father—and from other writers. For instance, the well-timed refrain "I'll show you something" and the death of Ottie's beagle is a variation of Steinbeck's telling of the death of Candy's dog in *Of Mice and Men*.

However, it is myth and biblical allusion that deepen Pancake's stories below mere surface and sociological intimations of reality. Hemingway, too, worked with the mythic idea of the wound in his stories and novels and thereby acknowledged, as Edmund Wilson has pointed out, that "the condition of life is pain; and the joys of the most innocent surface are somehow tied to its stifled pangs."[22] It was something of which Pancake was instinctively aware, being a hunter, an outdoorsman.[23] So in Pancake's "In the Dry"—and in many of his stories—the most innocent of encounters are reminders of the wound.

When Ottie returns to the Gerlock farm, Sheila Gerlock, the woman he wanted to love, is on the porch burning nesting wasps with a paper-cone torch. "'Please don't, honey,' says her mother. 'A thing alive can feel.' But Sheila held her paper-cone torch to another nest, careful to keep flames and falling wasps from her hand. She balanced on the banister, held the brace, and he sees the curve of a beginning breast crease her shirt." For Ottie, love cannot bloom through these ironies. He only becomes painfully aware of his separation and love's inabilities. The cruelty inherent in human encounters with nature appear again and again in his stories—Big T in "The Mark" smashing a ground mole with the heel of his boot, or Colly gaffing a "turkle" in "Trilobites," or Buddy shooting the ragged spitz through the crack of the trailer window. These incidents signal a recurring wound, which for Pancake's characters is impossible to heal.

These little deaths in nature, these little reminders of separation, signify the unavailability of love or redemption which is spiritually mortal. Pancake was looking for the rule, the boundaries of morality and behavior, and that is why his characters spend so much time preparing, making amends, sacrificing, revisiting circumstances that might play some part in the healing process. For instance, the elaborate, drawn-out prelude to the brutal boxing match in "The Scrapper" is also a psychic preparation to heal the wound.

In *The Golden Bough*, Sir James Frazer argues that there is "a curious application of the doctrine of contagious magic," a "relation commonly believed to exist between a wounded man and the agent of the wound, so that whatever is subsequently done by or to the agent must correspondingly affect the patient either for good or evil."[24] This appears to be nothing more than a variation of the Golden Rule or the eye-for-an-eye rule of the Bible; yet, these biblical rules do not allow for any accidental or unconscious wounding; rather, they imply conscious, purposeful choices which in some way must be atoned for; whereas Frazer's study suggests a more primal understanding; that is, "a sympathetic connexion . . . between a man and the weapon which has wounded him, probably founded on the notion that the blood on the weapon continues to feel with the blood in his body."[25]

From this, it may be assumed it is not love and compassion but rather blood and injury that are the ties that bind in "The Scrapper." If that is true, then the slack-jawed, brain-rattled Bund "sitting on a Coke case in front of the Gulf station begging change" is forever tied to Skeevy, who is, after all, the agent of Bund's wound. Clearly, from the beginning of this story the imperative to atone for and to heal Bund is on Skeevy's mind, and the incredible "sympathetic connexion" between Bund and Skeevy at the end of the story, perhaps, is based on Frazer's observation about primitive man. During the climactic boxing brawl, Gibson floors Skeevy. "As he went down he could hear Trudy screaming his name above the cheers." And now at this moment in the story, present and past time merge and the place of the wounding, the Sunflower Inn, and Bund re-enter Skeevy's consciousness again. "He lay for a time on the cold floor of the Sunflower Inn: the jukebox played and he heard Bund coughing. He rolled to his side. Cephus threw water on Skeevy, and he spat the bitten-off tip of his tongue. Gibson waited as Skeevy raised himself up to squat. His head cleared, and he knew he could get up." For good or evil, Skeevy can continue, risking himself in the healing quest, but at what price? And is it something that can ever be paid?

The elusive price, the ineffable mystery of atonement, is at the heart of all Pancake's stories. His passionate conversion to Catholicism, with its rituals of confession and absolution, prove his personal quest for atonement. The biblical images and phrases that appear throughout his work and even some of his titles, "The Salvation of Me" and "The Mark," help define his work as a search for a moral and spiritual sanctuary in an undefined, nebulous world of banality and evil—something that can also be found in Flannery O'Connor's work.

In Pancake's "Fox Hunters," for instance, young Bo Holly walks down the road to work and notices the early morning highway steam "give birth to little ghosts beneath his feet" through oncoming headlights. We come to know he is haunted by the age of sixteen, haunted by the death of his father, haunted by the uncertainty of where he stands in life. During the course of the story, evil will intrude. Wanting to fit in with the older men, his father's friends Virg, Bill, Enoch, Cuffy, Bo will have to choose between the evil and what else is left. As the men talk of the crimes they have committed, the murders of Dawn and Anne, Bo dozes in and out, half-awake, half asleep. "He caught bits of conversation, then his mind drifted into hollow sleep, and the voices jerked him awake again. 'He's sittin' in the Holy Seat,' said Bill's voice in Bo's darkness. Bo kept his eyes closed."

The "Holy Seat," the middle seat, the mystical in-between world, is where things are decided, where evil intrudes, where all can be lost. What saves Bo, what helps him decide, is the portent of Enoch's old tricks, an inkling of his nature, that occurs early in the story. "Enoch was up to his old tricks again, but only the men were supposed to know." At this point in the story, there is a warning that presumably floats into Bo's consciousness, for it is a sentence in the middle of the paragraph, not connected to a voice or a place, not grammatically connected to a listener; nor do we know the effect it has on the listener. It just appears: "Not even the angels in heaven shall know the hour of his coming." The phrase is from Matthew 24:36 and refers to the prelude of the Second Coming when "heaven and earth shall pass away, but my words shall not pass away," when the Judgment Day is at hand, and the Son of Man will return. It is an apocalyptic warning, but one with the hope of grace and paradise. In "Fox Hunters," and in many of his stories, Pancake, unlike Peter Taylor, peels away time and tradition, negates them, and then examines the moral weaknesses and strengths of human lives, human families, to see what will remain, or should remain, and endure.

The deep and subtle power of these stories lies submerged beneath the mimetic surface rendering of the world Pancake created. Remarkably skillful, the realistic texture of his fiction has often distracted readers and critics from understanding what his stories mean. "Breece Pancake's eye and ear for detail are superb," noted Joyce Carol Oates,[26] and John Casey said of him, "the one thing he did so well—he could use familiar particular details and conjure them into the universal. There's a physical reality to the stories that picks up a whole spiritual dimension."[27] The physical reality of a story like "Hollow" describes methods of mining and hunting that parallel the spiritual condition of its characters. However, in addition to this concrete sense of things, Pancake also had the eye and ear of a poet, as can be seen in the opening paragraphs of "Hollow"; rhythm, repetition, sound, and image elevate detailed mimesis to poetic fiction:

> Hunched on his knees in the three foot seam, Buddy was lost in the rhythm of the truck mine's relay; the glitter of coal and sandstone in his cap light, the setting and lifting and pouring. This was nothing like the real mine, no deep tunnels or mantrips, only the setting, lifting, pouring, only the light-flash from caps in the relay. In the pace he daydreamed his father lowering him into the cistern: many summers ago he touched the cool tile walls, felt the moist air from the water below, heard the pulley squeak in the circle of blue above. The bucket tin buckled under his tiny feet, and he began to cry. His father hauled him up. "That's the way we do it," he laughed, carrying Buddy to the house.
>
> But that came before everything: before they moved from the ridge, before the mine closed, before welfare. . . .[28]

Also adding to this convincing realistic texture is Pancake's studious use of regional idiom and dialogue. The two miners, Estep and Buddy, argue over calling a strike and use "doghole" for deep mining and "dump the water" for a labor walk-out.

> "Whadya know, Mad Man?" Estep said as Buddy climbed in, coughing.
> "Answer me this—Why'd ya reckon Curt wants props for?"
> "To shore the damn face, dumbshit."
> "An' doghole that goddamn seam, too. He's a ol'time miner. He loves doin' all that ol'time shit."
> "Whadya drivin' at?"
> "How many ya reckon'd walk out if I's to dump the water Monday?"
> "Buddy, don't go callin' strike. I got family."[29]

Pancake's realistic technique, of course, is peripheral to his real purpose; it is a sleight of hand. He was, after all, a moralist, concerned with the rules of living. Pancake tested these rules by setting out to destroy our illusions of reality and placing his characters in an environment where failure seems almost predetermined. In "Hollow" the protagonist, Buddy, cannot get beyond the physical and immediate obstacles in his life: he doesn't have enough money, enough love, enough sense of the past. He responds to his predicament without illusion and without vision, which inevitably leads him to commit a list of transgressions that elucidate the meaning of the title of the story. He chastises a young boy for collecting old fossils (emblematic of the mythic past), shoots a ragged spitz dog from the window of his trailer to keep the others away from his "bitch in heat" (a metaphor for his relationship with Sally), decides to go against kin by calling a strike, and then, finally, without a second thought or feeling, shoots and kills a pregnant doe because he is hungry, guts her, and kicks the still squirming unborn fawn into the snow. Without vision, a sense of the past, or a sense of moral direction, Buddy can only respond to his environment in terms of physical survival, which, according to Pancake's moral sense, makes him subhuman, without spiritual substance. The story's purpose has little to do with exposing living conditions in West Virginia hollows as symptomatic of an overall social malaise. A character like Buddy can be found in any town in America or the world.

The naturalism seemingly evident in Pancake's work has convinced many readers that his characters are at the mercy of deterministic forces. To complicate matters even further, many readers have often misread Pancake's fiction as a biographical and sociological portrait of a region, another instance where an author's work has been the natural outcome of the circumstances of his life: the predictable result of social and economic forces common to Appalachia, the obvious expression of a region's cumulative history, and the necessary conclusion of an individual biography. Of course, it is any writer's hope to create works of art that will endure through time and space, to transcend those influences and details of a particular life, and to reach into the hearts and consciences of men and women who may never even have heard of an author's birthplace in West Virginia.

Pancake attempted things far more challenging than merely cataloging the social ills of a region and suggesting ways of improvement, as he humorously suggests in the opening paragraph of "The Salvation of Me": "Chester was smarter than any shithouse mouse because Chester got out before the shit began to fall. But Chester had two problems: number one, he became a success, and number two, he came back. These are not your average American problems like drinking, doping, fucking or being fucked, because Rock Camp, West Virginia is not your average American problem maker, nor is it your average hillbilly town."[30]

Though he was consciously fastidious in his manipulation and use of detail, Pancake, like Taylor and many other "moral" writers of the South, was more concerned with the interior than the exterior, more concerned with his characters' moral condition than with the fact that they may be living in a rundown trailer in a hollow or seeking shelter in a cheap hotel room. It is a tribute to his ability as a descriptive artist, however, and to his power of empathy that readers cannot escape the dominating effect of his mimetic rendering of place and character and often confuse "the localized raw material of life and its outcome as art."[31]

7

The Prisoning Hills of Home

I want to haul my ass out of here—I have been inside too long.

—Breece Pancake, "A Room Forever"

Knowledge of place, of a region, gives writing power, a power that is further enhanced if the reader, too, knows the region in which the writer has rooted his fiction. C. Michael Curtis introduced the 1992 edition of *Contemporary New England Stories* by giving the reader some rudimentary knowledge of the region the collected stories grew out of. "What is a New England Story?" he asks. "What, for that matter, is a New England attitude or stance towards the world?"[1] Curtis attempts an easy and jocular understanding of certain commonly held characteristics that loosely link stories and writers together under a regional banner, for purposes of an anthology, but also for purposes that may yield a better appreciation of the collected stories. Curtis goes on to name those regional characteristics: a connection to a regional past through history or family, religious practices, geography (and how people interact with that geography), climate, population density, and language—the same cultural criteria can be identified for any region. What, then, is an Appalachian or West Virginia story? What, for that matter, is an Appalachian stance or attitude toward the world?

For Appalachian fiction, there still too often exists a sociological expectation that the writing should conform to social science research, which confuses the art of storytelling with reporting, and fiction writers who don't reinforce that sociology, or who are not fashionably politically correct, run the risk of censure. Furthermore, whereas the social scientist may be bent on reconstruction and social change, the editor and literary critic are intent on tracing the imaginative links between author and story, on finding the sources that have informed the writer where to go and what to do.

This sorry state of affairs is perhaps mainly due to the sheer amount of sociological writing that has, so far, dominated discourse about the region. In the early part of this century, few fiction writers born in the Appalachian mountains chose to write about the place of their birth. Then the work of a handful began to appear—Harriette Arnow, Jesse Stuart, Thomas Wolfe, James Still, Davis Grubb. Not until the post–World War II generation, which was encouraged to attend college to escape the economic circumstances of the past, has there been a significant increase in the number of writers born in the mountains who have also used their individual experiences of place in fiction.

Lee Smith of Virginia, Fred Chappell and John Yount of North Carolina, Cormac McCarthy of Tennessee, Gurney Norman of Kentucky, and numerous native sons and daughters of West Virginia at times have bound their fiction to the memory and recreation of their native homes. West Virginia writers born before the Depression—Mary Lee Settle, Davis Grubb, and Tom Kromer—have been joined by a large number of postwar writers— Denise Giardina, Meredith Sue Willis, Chuck Kinder, Jayne Anne Phillips, Breece Pancake, Lee Maynard, Vic Depta, Pinckney Benedict, Lisa Koger, and Richard Currey.

These contemporaries of Pancake have also noted the same sociological misunderstanding of their work. Like Pancake, these writers have intentionally selected a "realistic" representation of place to create an effect in their fiction, not to develop a positive regional image. "There's no responsibility to put the best face on everything," as Denise Giardina has said, "and there's no responsibility to have characters represent a certain group of people. That's not the writer's job. The only responsibility I have is to tell a story the best way I can."[2]

Yet, these distinctions between sociological portraits and imaginative literature do not prevent misunderstandings from occurring. For example, after the football squad of Marshall University died in a plane crash in 1971 while Pancake was in his freshman year there, the university recovered from its loss; in 1993, a new "Thundering Herd" competed in the NCAA Division II National Championship. Vying for the national title, Marshall faced Troy State University in the semifinals. In the pre-game publicity hype, Tom Ensey, the sports director of Troy State, named "Dead Genius" Breece Pancake as guest celebrity captain. (Ensey often named famous alumni from the opposing school as a way to provoke interest.) For the pre-game press release Ensey wrote: "Pancake . . . published one collection containing 12 bleak short stories of sad, desperate people that evoked his home state as a land rich in beauty, sorrow, and grim hope of life itself. Sadly, on the night of

April 8, 1979, Breece reached the depth of a valley we hope grace will spare us, stuck a shotgun in his mouth and pulled the trigger. He was 26. Breece D'J Pancake, it is our loss that you will write no more beautiful stories, but we hope you are at peace. Rest well, and CALL THAT TOSS!!!"[3]

Almost immediately, the phone lines buzzed with Marshall alumni and angry West Virginians demanding an apology. An apology for what, Ensey wanted to know. "I'm surprised anybody took me seriously. Whoever read it, misunderstood what I was trying to do. Breece Pancake is one of my favorite authors. I certainly wasn't trying to make fun of him."[4]

The perception remained that again someone from outside West Virginia was poking fun, making light of unfortunate people inappropriately. An editorial by Dave Peyton in the Huntington *Herald-Dispatch* was typical of the angry response: "It is said that outsiders have tried, and succeeded in taking about every treasure West Virginia ever had—our coal, our timber, even hefty portions of our rich heritage. Now, in an apparent attempt to be humorous—an attempt that fell flat on its face—the sports information director at Troy State University has attempted [to] take Breece Pancake from us."

According to Peyton, himself a classmate of Pancake's at Marshall, the press release was an insult wrought by a colonial mindset (however unconscious it may have been): "The suggestion here," Peyton wrote, "at least to many who read it, is that Pancake was a native of this place, which Ensey calls 'rich in beauty, sorrow and grim hope of life itself,' and it led to his demise. It only proves that, while Ensey may be a fan of Pancake's writing, he totally misunderstood what Pancake had to say."[5]

Not everyone took Ensey's gesture so badly. Rick Blenko, Pancake's best friend from Milton, submitted a letter to the editor explaining that "Pancake wouldn't have minded at all." Blenko wrote:

> I would like to respond to the controversy created when Troy State sports information director referred to Breece Pancake, the talented writer who died in 1979. Breece was my best friend for years, and I spoke to him two weeks before he died. Breece wouldn't have been offended by the mention of his name at the Marshall University vs. Troy State game. He would have found it amusing and he would have been pleased by all the accolades that have been given him these past years. The Troy State sports information director mentioned his name out of admiration. It's sad when someone so young takes his own life or dies, but at least his talent has been vindicated. He had a real insight into the world around him. It's too bad he isn't here to see his impact on American prose narration.[6]

In one way, this incident shows the strength of the Breece Pancake phenomenon: the people of the region have fiercely claimed him as their own. In another way, the Marshall incident is just one more example of the heightened sensitivity of people in the mountains to outside perceptions, evidence of a sore nerve rubbed the wrong way too many times. A firm and vivid sense of place is usually judged a plus in American fiction written anywhere else, but in rural Appalachia too much sense of place turns out to be a handicap, and further misconstrues the object of fiction.

Pancake's fictional West Virginia confuses some who are uncomfortable or frightened by the realistic texture of his writing. "Although [Pancake's] setting and culture is American," noted *Boston Globe* writer David Bosworth, "they will seem strange to most readers, as exotic as the author's name."[7] Daphne Merkin could not penetrate the "impassive" landscape or the subject matter of Pancake's stories, which, "like Pancake himself, don't invite lavish involvement. They are spare, undoubtedly, but they are also pitiless; try to get close to them and they rebutt [sic] you."[8] The Appalachian landscape may be indifferent, but it is not "impassive," and in Pancake's fiction the West Virginia setting serves at times "as a metaphorical equivalent to the lives of his characters,"[9] as Towers noted and, at others, as a formidable physical and moral proving ground on which his characters must struggle to endure.

By equating vision with sociological reality, critics have also inadvertently perpetuated the idea of Appalachia, and especially West Virginia, as the "cultural other," that is, as a region lacking any artistic possibility in the contemporary American literary marketplace. In a 1984 review for the *Plain Dealer*, James Frakes wrote, "West Virginia was the place where the bartenders usually don't ask for proof of age, where Nighttown pleasures were available to the more daring teenagers, and where for (I think) 25 cents you could destroy your innards with a poisonous foot-long hot dog. None of us sophisticates ever thought of it as providing material for fiction. And yet, by gum, here are a dozen crackling stories about the bleak landscape by a young man who obviously knew the territory. . . . This posthumous collection contains no mistakes, no ugly ducklings. . . ."[10] Frakes, in a self-consciously self-deprecating way, labels himself the outsider-sophisticate looking into the "bleak landscape" of another, more exotic world.

Michael Harrington, in his 1962 classic sociological study, *The Other America*, taught a generation how to think of Appalachia as this "other" world where people are victims of their own history and geography, isolated from any real culture. Harrington wrote: "It seems likely that Appalachia will continue going down, that its lovely mountains and hills will house a culture of poverty and despair and that it will become a reservation for the old, the apathetic, and the misfits."[11] With ideas like these leading the way, it is understandable how onlookers might sometimes fail to distinguish Appalachian fiction from Appalachian reality, especially in the case of Pancake, a writer with a fine eye and ear for convincing detail.

Realistic details can obfuscate and mislead; instead of fiction, stories are too often understood as journalistic snapshots. "The problem with fiction," agrees Richard Currey, "is that people assume that fiction is literally true— well obviously the test of fiction is how true it is, but not in the autobiographical sense. . . . The point of storytelling is exaltation, evocation, and the transfer, hopefully, of an emotional knowledge as opposed to factual knowledge or even just point of view. . . . It seems to be a general problem of Americans . . . in order to accept something and value it, it has to be factual, and Americans, for the most part, believe that the work of the imagination is not going to teach them anything."[12] Hence Americans' attraction to works of nonfiction rather than fiction. The imaginative is not to be trusted as a storehouse of wisdom or practical knowledge. It is an American habit of mind that, in this case, confuses the understanding of Pancake's life and work.

For Pancake and for Currey after him, place has been something that brings an "authentic sense" to a story. "You know how it is," Currey has said, "[t]here's nothing wrong with the words on the page. They look fine, they work well, but the thing that happens between the words that really does lend the work its particular strength, truth, and energy might be lacking." The detailed imaginative remembrance of place, in Currey's words "may, in fact, bear little connection to the real place. And it's that kind of imaginative drive that brings a sense of authenticity to a piece of work."[13]

This "authentic sense" in fiction, however, can also be misunderstood. "I think that somebody described Pancake's work to me as full of despair," recalls Lee Maynard, the author of the Appalachian coming-of-age novel *Crum*.

> I know Milton where Breece grew up and compared to Crum or Dunlow or Turkey Creek, Milton is uptown. So when I read Pancake, I don't see it necessarily as "despair," I see it as "accurate." . . . In Pancake's "The Scrapper" there's Skeevy driving along in a pick-up truck and there's a single sentence in there—that he reaches down under the seat and pulls out his pistol and starts looking for groundhogs to shoot. Well, I go right on by that. That's nothing new to me. Every guy in the Appalachian Mountains has driven down the road looking for groundhogs to shoot. But if you are from mainstreet Philadelphia, and you read this, you want to shoot Skeevy. Why would you kill an innocent groundhog from a moving vehicle out an open window firing randomly with a pistol? So it stops the Philadelphia guy right in his tracks, while I read it, and say, "Hey, sounds like home."[14]

Maynard's perception is influenced by an intimate knowledge of the region; he more readily understands these details as part of the "realistic texture" of the story, while his hypothetical reader from "mainstreet Philadelphia" may see this behavior as a social problem that needs fixing. "Does it need to be fixed?" asks Maynard. "I'm not at all sure it's something that's broken. Maybe it is something that is unattractive to outsiders, something that makes them feel uncomfortable. But I think the people to answer whether or not it needs to be fixed or changed are the people in the hollers. If they want it to be fixed, let them do it."[15]

While people from within the region have been very sensitive to the mainstream preference for regional stereotype, they, too, have had their own difficulties distinguishing stereotype from factual reality and understanding the purpose of fiction. Robert DeFrancis, writing for the *Parkersburg* (W.Va.) *News*, responded testily to Joyce Carol Oates's review of Pancake's stories even before he himself had read the book, taking issue with Oates's reckoning of Pancake's life as synonymous with a "slowly dying" geography, which, Oates had written, "Breece Pancake identified so intensely with. . . ." De Francis wrote in reply:

> It was with initial mixed feelings . . . that I read a front page review in last Sunday's edition of *The New York Times Book Review*. . . . My mixed feelings were these: it should be a cause for celebration, even under tragic terms, that a young West Virginian's works have been given such national attention and approval—yet the works deal with an "impoverished" West Virginia, a "doomed" West Virginia, a "slow-dying" West Virginia. I was just about to feel betrayed by what seems to be West Virginia's fate when I realized I was ignoring my own view of what constitutes good fiction—does it help us to better understand man's condition? Does it offer us, no matter how much pain is imparted in arriving at the end, an appreciation of why the characters acted and reacted in the way they did? I realized that my objection to the West Virginia hillbilly image in reality is an objection to a cartoon image that nobody, really, can obliterate. Breece Pancake's stories, it appears, offer a look at the dark side of the cartoon, the image that should concern us, a fact of West Virginia life for some of our residents that we all should be made to understand more completely.[16]

The "dark side of the cartoon" alarmed DeFrancis as yet another reinforcing image of the stereotype, but he also accepted the notion that this may be representative of a point of view "that we should be made to understand more completely," a kind of unflattering *Let Us Now Praise Famous Men* portrait that might be good, if unwelcome, medicine.

Of course, Pancake selected a "realistic" representation of a place to create an effect in his fiction, not to develop a regional image. Yet, in the truest sense, Pancake was a regional writer, one who rooted his personal vision of the world in his own experience of place, both uniquely individual and widely shared. "Each part of the country has a separate and special experience of its own," as Meredith Sue Willis has pointed out. "Maybe I say that too easily," she said, "because my part of West Virginia is not the *Night*

Comes to the Cumberlands part of West Virginia. It was an industrial area. It was mixed culturally; my own particular family came from different parts of the Appalachians. And my experience is very precise, and I think that the precision of one's own experience is essential. Without that there's nothing." Without the precision of individual experience or personal vision, there wouldn't be any fiction at all because the measure of good art, good fiction, she reminds us, "comes out of whatever your life is."[17]

However, labeling Breece Pancake as a regional writer does not mean his imaginative region is bounded by lines on the map or enclosed by James Still's "prisoning hills" of geography,[18] nor does it mean that regional facts overshadow emotional truth. For these regional writers like Pancake—or for that matter any writer—there is a place that drives their writing, engages their creative powers, to form unique distinctions between the raw material of what is seen and the meaningful expression of what is felt. Out of the individual memory of place comes literary art intended to transcend the limits of physical reality, and without that transcendence there remains only documentary, a journalistic montage of perception.

Richard Currey acknowledges this debt to place in his own art.

> West Virginia becomes a much more mythic ground. It's a fertile place that sends my imagination into motion. . . . The mythic ground for me is like what Scott Momaday refers to as the "remembered earth"; it is the imaginative point of departure, a place I can fix in my head, knowing it well, having long, deep roots there, and a great sense of history, of at least my family, more than a true history of the state itself. That in turn sends things into motion and allows me to start making connections that tend to move into, hopefully, good stories. . . . History is what connects us. Within Appalachia, there are certain broad historical currents that inform all of us. You can see certain connections from Pancake to Phillips to Settle to me in shared subject matter. But the perspectives and approaches are very different, influenced by the psychology of each writer.[19]

Knowledge of place and its history, of course, helps shape the individual artist's vision of the world, of how it works, and how the people in it live. Jayne Anne Phillips explains how sense of place also translates into a sense of family and how both can affect memory and the imagination:

> Home place becomes a memory. . . . Even for people who stay in the same place all their lives, that place is going to change. Hopefully, there's enough that remains familiar so that the nature of their place stays intimate. But I think we all lose our homes and our families. We grow up, most of us anyway, in a nuclear family, and we leave that family at age 18 or 19, and that's when we lose our parents. And the place where we came from changes whether we're there to watch it change or not. It becomes a kind of memory. But I think we carry home around with us in the way we perceive things, in the

way we look at things. Your view of the world, the kinds of things you notice, the things you select to remember, are what home really is. And that's something you carry with you anywhere.[20]

Pancake's view of the world, rooted in his experience of the Kanawha Valley, was shaded by the loss of his father and grandfather, the illness of his beloved Aunt Julia, a longing for the place he remembered in his youth, and the sad knowledge that "the place changes whether you were to watch it change or not." For Pancake and for many of his contemporaries, this longing was complicated by what Phillips has observed about her hometown of Buckhannon, West Virginia, since the years of her youth:

> I think of the West Virginia I grew up in as being lost, as being gone, because it really has changed so much. I remember it as being very beautiful, no chain restaurants of any kind, no McDonald's, no Long John Silver's, none of that. And Main Street was a thriving concern, always so crowded on Saturdays, when everyone went to town. There were two movie houses and all the various rituals of small town life were very visible and alive. Now there are malls and chain restaurants and the highways have gone through, big highways that bypass town. My grandmother's house, the house where my mother grew up, was actually torn down to build a McDonald's. . . . I would have preferred West Virginia to stay the same: a green island in the United States. . . .[21]

The physical changes that occur to a place over time prevent any kind of real return home; the only true return is through memory to the kind of place it was before. For these writers from West Virginia, the impulse to return was confused by real economic and psychological realities. Fortunately, for writers like Phillips and Pancake, their fiction afforded them a spiritual return home where none other was possible.

Pinckney Benedict has paid homage to Pancake, who had, as Benedict remembers, helped navigate his own spiritual passage home:

> I had discovered Pancake's work when I was freshman at Princeton University. His work to me was like a homecoming. His stories were a return to some places I knew about. You know the guy in "Time and Again" who drives the snowplow? I mean—Big Sewell Mountain—well, geez, that's just west of here. And there's Chimney Corners he goes through, down Route 60 from Ansted to Gauley Bridge. So my stories, similarly, were a way for me to return imaginatively to these places. They became for me a way to combat my homesickness when I really wanted to come home. So I owe him a great deal spiritually, and his stories were literally an inspiration to me when I was writing in college, where most of the stories in Town Smokes come from.[22]

Pancake's stories reflect this spiritual need. Yet the characters in these stories are often trapped by economic or psychological circumstances, unable to leave their home in the first place. His characters routinely search (sometimes symbolically) for parts to broken-down Impalas and Pontiacs, look for work, dream of a "stake" that will take them far from home. However, the cost of physical escape is often too great an expense of the soul. Pancake was fond of quoting Steinbeck: "Anything that just costs money is cheap."[23]

In Pancake's "Fox Hunters," Enoch tells young Bo, "I'll sell ya parts real cheap," but Bo feels his stomach contract, his hands grow cold at the offer, and says, "No thanks." The cost of buying parts from a car that carried classmates Anne Davis and Dawn Reed to their deaths is too high. In "First Day of Winter" Hollis's escape can only be bought by abandoning his feeble parents on a farm that cannot sustain them, and in "Trilobites" Colly measures the price of escape against the moral cost of leaving his homeplace, the land, and his connections to the past.

It seems that returning to the past and home in Pancake's fiction has more to do with redemption than with any practical outcome or possibility, perhaps in the same way that Jayne Anne Phillips has described the nature of fiction writing: "I think the function of fiction is basically religious. It has to do with redemption really. That if you are dealing with elements of the past, your past, someone else's past, the past of a country, county, town, you are basically trying to redeem that past, trying to make it live again and save something of it. . . . Keep something from fading away. . . . Keep something from being forgotten . . . writing is very similar to prayer."[24]

The many biblical allusions that appear throughout Pancake's work and the facts of his own biography evident in his correspondence attest to this view. In "First Day of Winter," though Hollis aches to escape while his parents weep, Pancake closes his struggle and the story with an image of prayer: "He heard the cattle lowing to be fed, heard the soft rasp of his father's crying breath, heard his mother's broken humming of a hymn. He lay that way in the graying light and slept.

The sun was blackened with snow, and the valley closed in quietly humming, quietly as an hour of prayer."[25]

The kind of redemption sought by his characters is not often found. In only one of his stories does Pancake allow his protagonist to escape and return. The foster prodigal son Ottie, of "In the Dry," lives in exile as an independent trucker and one day returns to the Gerlock farm, the place and past of his youth. Instead of extending welcome, Old Gerlock curses him: "God forgive my wore out soul, but I hope you burn in hell." The biblical passage "For if they do these things in a green tree, what shall be done in the dry?" spins through "their droughty valley" and reverberates in the surrounding hills rusting "with dying trees." Ottie confirms what he sometimes knows, "no breaks are his, no breaks for foster kids" and that the Gerlocks are "people of name, not past," people incapable of love, forgiveness, and all that matters. His redemption is an "awful" kind like the gears of his departing semi that "strain to whine into another night."

Similarly, the redemption sought by the man who drives the snowplow along Route 60 in "Time and Again" turns out to be only a temporary stay of anguish and psychosis. "I hear my hogs come grunting from their shed, thinking I have come to feed them. I ought to feed them better than that awful slop, but I can't until my boy is safe," that is, he cannot give them the human kind of feed that he did before his boy "ran off." His gruesome compulsion of collecting hitchhikers for hog feed is, of course, why his boy fled. "I told him not to go look . . . but he went and looked." Though the man is mad, his murderous habits are temporarily held in check by the memory of his son. This memory is brought to life by a young hitchhiker who is on his way home to Charleston for Christmas and his recalling of his World War II past, which is brought to mind by the December snowfall. "All the way up the mountain, I count the men in France, and I have to stop and count again. I never get any farther than the night it snowed." It is a kind of redemption, a payment of dues, that he refrains from killing the young hitchhiker (although he would dearly love to) for the sake of his son and for a memory of the past.

In "The Mark" Reva's search for redemption for past and present sins— her sexual love for her brother Clinton and the burning of the lockhouse along the river—brings about a series of bitter revelations. Reva's ambiguous exclamation, "I done it. . . . I done an awful thing, T," suggests many admissions of the soul. She acknowledges setting fire to the lockhouse and, tacitly, her sexual love for her brother.

The meanings of that "awful thing" could also point to her witness of the monkeys in the cage who "bucked in their breeding," marking her, or "her secret" for "the child that never was." "She felt the spot where the baby should be, closed her eyes, and tried to imagine her blood in the rabbit's veins. It would pump into the ovaries, making them swell, the doctor had said, if she was pregnant. They were going to kill the rabbit and look for her secret in its organs, but the sinkings in her belly came on too hard and frightening, too much like her worst month. She told herself that they would find no confessions in the rabbit ovaries."[26]

"Her secret" makes Reva wish "the deed undone, even forgotten," but what she wishes undone is still a secret by the end of the story. The redemption she seeks eludes her because of the pain revealed in her past. The jumble of anger and grief from being left behind by her parents, who had died eight years earlier, and her brother, who left her for his "Cincinnati whore," makes it impossible for her to redeem the past. Furthermore, she knows "the rabbit had died for nothing" and that somehow she is responsible. These conflicting emotions, along with her husband's unsympathetic and cruel nature, may also explain her inability to love anyone other than those in her family.

Nevertheless, Reva's truncated redemption is a secret and terrible kind, one that is hidden by Jackie's idiot head, which obscures the "two moons" of her past, Clinton's "hanging quietly above Ohio" and the moon of her lost parents reflected in the river where they had drowned. This is as far as her admission will probably take her, as Jackie, the retarded tenant farmer, responds "C'mon, git up'ar" as if he were handling livestock, which are incapable of redemption. Metaphorically, Reva is incapable of redemption as well.

The pain of return to the past and a place and the fervent prayer for redemption in Pancake's stories can also be found in the work of his contemporaries, who also have looked "homeward" for a place to anchor their art and have lived in either a self-imposed or circumstantial exile. In addition to the regional spirit that sometimes drives their writing, they also share certain regional economic realities common to their generation, and these realities at times have informed them where to go and what to do in their writing.

The collective West Virginia experience suggests some basic assumptions about history and social structure; stories about the mine wars, or the geographical and social ravages of strip mining, or the struggle of families coping with scarcity continue to be the métier of many West Virginia writers. Pancake's story "Hollow" makes the assumption that the "do or die" dependency on coal is a condition in extremis, and he uses it to dramatize the stark lives and moral predicament of the story's characters. West Virginia writer Denise Giardina shares that view:

> I do make an assumption that the coal industry has devastated and blighted the land and people's lives. I think it's a legitimate assumption to make because I think you do have to make value judgments. In writing a book about the Holocaust, I would begin with the basic assumption that what happened was pretty evil. I think there are some things you can assume, and I think growing up here and seeing that, it's just something I assume. I'm sure that troubles some people, especially people outside the coal fields who maybe think I'm exaggerating or something like that, but I feel like I'm saying what I'm seeing.[27]

Historically, West Virginia and most of Appalachia have been predominantly rural; farms and small towns dot this land of "make do or do without," where a poor economy has been the uniform rule. In his letters home Pancake echoed this common complaint, here made by Jayne Anne Phillips: "Jobs have never been the strong point of the economy in Appalachia. Work is not easy to come by. If the country is doing badly economically, Appalachia is doing worse. And if your whole identity depends on what you do, and you can't earn a living, everything falls apart."[28]

Hence, in Pancake's story "Trilobites" Colly's fractured identity is due, in part, to his inability to keep the farm, and, having no economic flexibility that would allow him to stay, he will be forced out of the region to a city in another state. Economic realities leave little room for choice; the option to stay or leave, in many instances, has nothing to do with individual preference or desire.

According to writer Lee Maynard, who now lives in New Mexico, these economic realities have psychologically affected a large segment of the population:

> After living in various places in the country you meet people who have had it so damned hard by any measure you want to make. But mostly those people I have met out here in the West have been individuals—a couple of guys in Prescott, Arizona, for example fall into that category, but not the whole population of Prescott. On the other hand, in West Virginia, it's the whole place, it's not just individual, it's everybody. Everybody's life has been hard. I think a certain mindset has to come of it. People in southern West Virginia don't rub shoulders with anybody else. The guy in Prescott who has had it hard is still rubbing shoulders with somebody who hasn't. He's got some measure, but people down there in Wayne County—I'm not sure who they rub shoulders with.[29]

This phenomenon has created a more classless society in West Virginia—where the population is less concentrated and poverty has been so widespread—sensitive to the boundary between have and have-not.

In Pancake's fiction, characters instinctively know this boundary to be something they can never cross. In "The Scrapper," for instance, the beautiful, clog-shod Calley has been to college "looking for rich boys," and she consequently now belongs to another world that is unreachable for the protagonist Skeevy, who realizes "even if she stood beside him, he couldn't have her." In "The Mark" Bill, Carlene, Tyler, and Reva are on their way to the county fair. The discussion turns on the virtues of livestock with an eye always on the chance for breeding good if not superior stock, and hints at Reva's barrenness.

> "New Angus in the County," she heard Bill say, and felt Tyler's fingers flex. "Whose?"
> "Feller name of Jordan or Jergan—I forget, but the bull's called 'Imperial Sun'—S-u-n. All the way from Virginia."
> "Good stock?"
> "You couldn't afford the fee."
> Carlene leaned up again. "What you gonna call the baby?"
> "Imperial Sun," Reva's voice was hollow.[30]

Reva's sarcastic reply underscores a contempt for the very material status that Bill and Tyler admire.

In "Trilobites" Colly sprays "turkle" blood on the pants of the loansman/land developer, Mr. Trent, who, in Pancake's fiction, is the epitome of material contempt. "Sorry," Colly says, but he hopes the stain doesn't come out, and Ginny, who now wears "too much jewelry," who dreamed of "peacocks," and whose skin "is almost too white in the faded evening," is also a bitter reminder of the social class to which Colly can never climb.[31]

Even more disdainful, however, is a character like Chester in "The Salvation of Me," who temporarily crosses the boundary and returns home the image of success in a brand new Camaro, sporting capped teeth and a new girlfriend who licks "her teeth in toothpaste ads on TV." He has come home to flaunt his new status and "to kill everybody's magic." Chester now believes that "his shit doesn't stink," that he has become better than those he left behind.

Pancake describes the desire for success in this story as a "germ," the kind that causes the "disease" of unfulfilled longing:

> When Chester left town, he left a germ. Not the kind of germ you think makes a plant grow, but disease, a virus, a contagion. Chester sowed them in the cafe when Deputy recognized him, asked what he'd been doing with himself. Chester told Deputy he was on Broadway, and gave away free tickets to the show he was in, and a whole slough of people went up to New York. They all came back humming show songs. And the germ spread all over Rock Camp, made any kid on the high-school stage think he could be Chester. A couple of the first ones killed themselves, then the real hell was watching the ones who came back, when Pop told them there was no work at the station for faggots.[32]

The need to establish a validity of the self in the context of a larger world, apart from the identity of family and small town, and the need to find an identity through vocation are contradicted by the unspoken understanding that the escape to the larger outside world may bring about an ambivalent result, like that produced by Chester's return.

Chuck Kinder, the author of *Snakehunter*, describes this as a unique condition of small town life that can make a person feel "frozen in place":

> Setting is almost enough to make a book a West Virginia book. The people there, the uniqueness of growing up in adversity, everyone in West Virginia is a legend in their own mind. I've knocked around the country and every place you go, of course, you meet eccentric people, but there's something about West Virginia and especially the Kanawha Valley. It's not class, that idea doesn't have much meaning for me. It's the people in the towns, in the valley, the people there are in their own position, in that strata. You have a certain position in that strata of society, of who you are. Everybody knows your family, your history. You're there. You're frozen in place in a sense.
>
> The only thing you can do is to sort of invent yourself in your own personal way, and it often ends in being eccentric, in being weird. You have to

invent yourself because in a sense you are frozen in people's perceptions of you. They know your dad and they know who your granddad was. They know all that you are. Within that you have to define yourself. You have to invent yourself.[33]

Pancake's penchant for role playing and adopting personae may perhaps have been his way of reinventing himself and may also help explain his ability to empathize with his characters.

The stultifying effect of community perceptions and family expectations places a "lid in terms of what's possible," as Lisa Koger has pointed out. "I want to know who put the lid there?" Koger has said. "Who says if you are a kid growing up here, that right out of high school you've got to get married, you've got to settle down? Who says you can't go to other places? And who says you can't experience everything and bring that experience back? . . . If I want to do anything as a writer, I want to blow the lid off. . . . I want it off in terms of behavior, possibility, and ways of thinking."[34]

The need for self-determination and identity during adolescence is difficult enough, but in a small town, the security of family and the familiarity of a friendly but narrow community can squeeze the individual. This is the paradox of small-town life and the West Virginia experience. The inevitable tension created by these circumstances provides impetus for escape. "I had to leave West Virginia. That's all there was to it," admits Jayne Anne Phillips. It is a common refrain among writers from the region. "Even when I was very young," she recalls. "I remember sitting on the back porch of my parent's house, looking out at the fields and wondering how far I would travel from this exact point. I wanted to leave. . . . I think I was struggling to define myself outside the family, yet family was all that mattered: they were the whole story. . . . I felt that the pull home was so strong that if I didn't leave, I'd sort of freeze in place."[35]

Pancake's protagonists, like those of Anderson's *Winesburg, Ohio* and Joyce's *Dubliners*, face the same struggle, but Pancake's stories show a marked intensity reminiscent of the battle of the preacher's hands in Davis Grubb's *Night of the Hunter*, fingers tattooed with "love" and "hate," clenched in conflict. In Pancake's story "Fox Hunters," sixteen-year-old Bo Holly wants to "break out like gangbusters" from the rigidly defined town of straw bosses and miners and his ineffectual, failing mother, yet "insecurity crawfished through his blood, leaving him powerless again." In "The Salvation of Me" the young protagonist dreams of leaving the hills of home to become a disc jockey in Chicago, like Dex Card, but is "frozen" in place by the betrayal of his best friend and the passage of time, and the dream "never hummed to [him] again." In "Trilobites" Colly begs Ginny to take him with her to Florida but knows that the land and the ghost of his father will forever hold him back, and in "First Day of Winter" middle-aged Hollis is "looking for some way out of the tomb Jake had built for him," longing to escape the responsibility of caring for his aging parents and the failing farm left to him by his brother, even contemplating murder; but a cracked engine block, his parents' bitter recrimination, and the snow-darkened sun shut him in.

Pancake's characters are also held in place by the boundaries of their sex; men and women live in segregated worlds kept apart by notions of sexuality and propriety and by a narrow definition of the roles of men and women. "In Appalachia men are favored over women in terms of what you are allowed to do,"[36] Lisa Koger has observed, and Phillips suggests why this is so:

> West Virginia is a place in which men are men and women are women. All the old ideas about what makes a man a man still held in the '50s, '60s, and even the '70s. . . . I also had a very strong sense of rebellion against my parents and their values, all of society. I embraced the whole '60s and '70s mentality.[37] These were uncompromised political beliefs, about not wanting to live the lives I saw women living around me. I was extremely angry at the waste of their capabilities, at their entrapment, and I was saddened.[38]

Even though Pancake has been criticized for "an annoyingly narrow-minded attitude toward women"[39] in his fiction, John Casey remembers him as being "extremely sympathetic to women" in life, although "inept with pretty women at a bar."[40] His fiction, however, does show a sadness and empathy for his women characters, which in a few stories adds to the male protagonist's sense of futility.

For example, in "Fox Hunters" fatherless Bo Holly, coming of age in the close-knit society of Parsons, cannot "claim kin" with the men of the town "by tolerating their music, their cards, their fox hunting," which are not only practical habits but also habits of mind. Fox hunting, Bo discovers, parallels their idea of women as prey, something Bo rejects. In an attempt to fit in with his father's friends, Bo tells a tall tale of sexual prowess, but when he learns the secret about the deaths of Dawn Reed and Anne Davis during a night fox hunt, he drunkenly shoots his father's .45 automatic not at the frightened fox trying to escape but at the pursuing hounds. "Try'n save foxie," Bo slurs, but really he is trying to save Dawn Reed, Anne Davis, and all women from the narrow and brutalizing attitude of men. Bo's drunkenness illustrates the futility of his effort. In his society, he is resigned to the fact that Dawn would "never stare down a husband . . . so maybe it's best." The same brutal revelation appears in "The Mark" when brother Clinton warns his sister Reva that if she gets married she will "get slapped down like a 'ol catfish," and in "The Way It Has to Be," the murderously possessive ex-con Harvey subdues young Alena on the very brink of escape and freedom.

Furthermore, the rough treatment of Sally in "Hollow" typifies a sympathetic but nonetheless destructive virgin-whore conception of women that appears throughout Pancake's work. Sally stays, or rather survives, with Buddy only on the promise of money. When Sally soberly recognizes the kind of relationship it has turned into, Buddy slaps her because it is the kind of relationship, one without virtue or the illusion of love, that he cannot consciously accept or abide.

> "Never had a pot to piss in, neither. Stick 'round Sal."
> With her fork, Sally drew lazy curves in her beansoup, and shook her head. "Naw, I'm tired of livin' on talk."
> "This ain't talk. What made ya stay with me this long?"
> "Talk."
> "Love? Love ain't talk."
> "Whore's talk."
> His hand flashed across the table, knocking her head askance, and she flushed. She got up slowly, put her plate in the sink, and walked down the hall to the bedroom.[41]

It is Pancake's judgment on this attitude that the fourteen-year-old prostitute in "A Room Forever" keeps looking at the young male protagonist "like she is the Wrath of God." In Pancake's "prisoning" environment, this defeating and often violent sexual attitude victimizes both women and men. The young tugboat operator can't help but hurt the young girl he wants to protect, and, although he hasn't "sunk that low"—hasn't attempted suicide as she has—he knows it is a fate not everyone, woman or man, may escape: "I stop in front of the bus station, look in on the waiting people, and think about all the places they are going. But I know they can't run away from it or drink their way out of it or die to get rid of it. It's always there, you just look at somebody and they give you a look like the Wrath of God. . . ."[42]

While also showing the palpable signs of his generation, Pancake's stories capture the irony between his life and work. His stories are filled with themes of escape and impossible flight; yet, in life he longed to return to his home in West Virginia. His characters yearn for love and connection to past and place, which were there for him in life, though he felt he could not hold on to them. His settings emphasize the closed-in darkness of suffocating hollows and the open desolation of drought-stricken landscapes that mirror the emotional lives of his characters; yet, in life he loved to feel the peace and solace of the mountain woods. In both fiction and life, it appears that Pancake could not imagine or realize the physical or psychological freedom that many other West Virginia writers have achieved.

Writer Meredith Sue Willis, who escaped to New York, theorizes about what might have happened had she stayed:

One story I wrote about the same time I wrote "The Little Harlots" was "The Adventures of a Vulture," which is about a funeral lady, a lady who tries to run away from her home which is a little middle-class northern West Virginia town like Shinnston or Buckhannon. She tries to run away and she can't do it, but what she does is she goes back and goes to a town just like her town, almost as close as it could be, just a few miles over the mountain and down the river. And she goes to this town which is totally familiar to her with all of its social structures, and she goes in and instead of being herself with all of her ties to everybody, she becomes a funeral lady. She rents a room, and goes to funerals, and buys the kind of food she likes, and eats it in her room, and eats in her pajamas and nightgown and never takes them off, and she becomes a town crackpot, an eccentric. But she does it right over the mountain from her own town. This, of course, is one of my fantasies—of what might have happened if I had stayed. She's not crazy. She's not a disaster as a human being, but she is the funeral lady.[43]

"I could be dramatic and say I probably would have died if I had stayed," Lee Maynard has said, "but I did have very severe ulcers when I lived there and I felt very trapped. Like my protagonist in *Crum*, I felt very claustrophobic, emotionally so. I do not know what would have happened to me. What I would have done Lord knows. Once I decided I had to go, I never looked back, and I never thought about what I would have done had I stayed. . . . Let's say I might have dated the funeral lady Meredith Sue Willis talks about."[44]

Pancake once told his parents, "I'm going to come back to West Virginia when this is over. There's something ancient and deeply rooted in my soul. I like to think that I've left my ghost up one of those hollows, and I'll never be able to leave for good until I find it—and I don't want to look for it because I might find it and have to leave."[45] Apparently he had been haunted not only by the ghosts of the past but also by the "ghost" of himself, an image or identity, like the trilobite he could not find or hold. Hoping to return but frightened by the possibility of being unable to stay, Pancake's sense of place proved to be a prison. In a way, as Meredith Sue Willis has observed, "[H]e never got of there, and he's still there."[46]

Notes to Part I

1. Emily Miller to Helen Pancake, May 10, 1979, Breece D'J Pancake Papers, West Virginia Univ. Library, Morgantown, and the Pancake Family Estate. All letters are contained in this collection unless otherwise noted.

2. O'Connor in Emily Miller to Helen Pancake, May 10, 1979.

3. Cynthia Kadohata, "Breece D'J Pancake," *Mississippi Review* 18 (1) (1990): 57.

4. Rick Blenko, interview by Marty Buchsbaum, videotape recording, July 28, 1988, Milton, W.Va.

5. Miller to Helen Pancake, May 10, 1979.

6. Helen Pancake, interview by Russ Barbour, videotape recording, Nov. 4, 1986, Milton, W.Va.

7. Breece's cousin.

8. Breece Pancake to Helen Pancake, Mar. 21(?). The letter, found in a notebook, was never mailed.

9. John Casey, interview by Russ Barbour, videotape recording, Nov. 5–6, 1986, Huntington, W.Va.

10. Sam Harshbarger, interview by Marty Buchsbaum, videotape recording, Nov. 4, 1986, Milton, W.Va.

11. Julia Morgan, interview by Russ Barbour, videotape recording, Aug. 1988(?), Milton, W.Va.

12. Fred Glazer, "West Virginia Literary Award," paper presented at the annual awards meeting of the West Virginia Library Commission, Science and Cultural Center, Charleston, Feb. 7, 1984.

13. Lewis Simpson, *The Dispossessed Garden: Pastoral and History in Southern Society of the Old South* (Athens: Univ. of Georgia Press, 1975), 79.

14. Ibid., 91.

15. James Alan McPherson, foreword to *The Stories of Breece D'J Pancake* (Boston: Little Brown/Atlantic Monthly Press, 1983), 9.

16. Pinckney Benedict, interview by Marty Buchsbaum, videotape recording, July 26, 1988, Lewisburg, W.Va.

17. Richard Jones to Helen Pancake, Oct. 22, 1989.

18. Casey, interview.

19. Cited in Ruth Burney Pennebaker, "Remembrances of a Young Writer," (Charlottesville, Va.) *Daily Progress*, Feb. 20, 1983, E4.

20. Ibid., E1.

21. Casey, interview.

22. Grace Toney Edwards, "Memories of Breece," *Appalachian Heritage* 13 (1985): 112.

23. Morgan, interview.

24. Robert Jackson, interview by Marty Buchsbaum, videotape recording, July 28, 1988, Milton, W.Va.

25. Helen Pancake, interview.

26. Morgan, interview.

27. John Teel, interview by Russ Barbour, videotape recording, Aug. 1988, Huntington, W.Va.(?).

28. Morgan, interview.

29. Jackson, interview.

30. Kadohata, "Breece D'J Pancake," 52.

31. Jackson, interview.

32. Charlotte Pancake to Helen Pancake, Jan. 27, 1988.

33. John Casey, afterword to *The Stories of Breece D'J Pancake*, 175.

34. Donnetta Pancake to Helen Pancake, Apr. 1, 1980.

35. Ruel Foster to Helen Pancake, May 5, 1995.

36. G. C. Hendricks, interview by the author, tape recording, June 30, 1995, Wake Forest, N.C.

37. Casey, afterword, 172.

38. Robert J. Higgs, letter to author, July 20, 1994.

39. Cited in Jack Welch, "Davis Grubb: a Vision of Appalachia" (Ph.D. diss., Carnegie Mellon Univ., Pittsburgh 1980), iv.

40. Richard Jones, interview by Russ Barbour, videotape recording, Nov. 6, 1986, Huntington, W.Va.

41. Breece Pancake to Emily Miller, July 1, 1978.

42. Helen Pancake in *Breece Pancake*, video broadcast, by Russ Barbour, WPBY, Huntington, W.Va. Jan. 7, 1987.

· Nowhere on Earth

1. Milton is also known as "Milton-on-the-Mud" for being situated along the Mud River. The town was named for Milton Rece, a prominent landowner in the area during the late nineteenth century.

2. After the glaciers receded, the Teays divided into the present-day Kanawha and New Rivers. The glaciers also changed the east-west course of the Ohio to where it runs today. Because of this geological history, the Teays River bed is rich in ancient fossils. When Interstate 64 was being cut in the mid-1960s, bulldozers unearthed many fossils that were hidden in the ancient riverbed.

3. Sherwood Anderson, *Tar: a Midwest Childhood*, ed. Ray Lewis White (1926;

Cleveland: Press of Case Western Univ., 1969), 15. It is White who observes that Anderson's depiction of Camden resembles Clyde, Ohio, and Marion, Virginia.

4. Ibid., 16.

5. Johanna Maurice, "Station Once Hub of Commerce," *Charleston* (West Virginia) *Daily Mail*, Apr. 18, 1981.

6. Helen Pancake, interview.

7. Rick Blenko, grandson of William Blenko, now owns and manages Blenko Glass. Rick Blenko was a close friend of Breece during high school.

8. See Eason Eige and Rick Wilson, *Blenko Glass 1930–1953* (Marietta, Ohio: Antique Pubs., 1987), and Nick Salvatore, *Eugene V. Debs: Citizen and Socialist* (Urbana: Univ. of Illinois Press), 308–9. "When Blenko died in 1933, his wife, Sarah Blenko, wrote Theodore Debs (Eugene Debs's brother) that 'I'd like to have dad's ashes scattered on [Debs's] grave.' In reply Theodore Debs said that he would 'be happy to meet your wishes,' but that 'the complete estrangement between our family and Gene's wife' made it impossible" (*Letters of Eugene V. Debs*, vol. 2, 1913–1919, ed. J. Robert Constantine [Urbana: Univ. of Illinois Press, 1990], 531n.)

9. C. R. Pancake to Breece Pancake, Sept. 9 1970.

10. "Gerlach" is a name that appears in Pancake's notes as a character in a planned novel. Another spelling of the name, "Gerlock," appears in "In the Dry."

11. On April 5, 1863, a few months before West Virginia gained its statehood, the bridge was attacked by a small troop of Confederates under the command of Capt. P. M. Carpenter. The Confederates were repulsed after a one-day encounter. The Union force, commanded by Captain Dove, preserved the bridge, but when the unit abandoned its garrison near the end of the war, the soldiers left the church in a wreck, having torn up the floorboards, gallery, and pews for firewood. This history is transformed into a minor detail in Pancake's story, "The Honored Dead."

12. The Teays River Turnpike is mentioned in "Trilobites."

13. Pancake, *The Stories*, 22.

14. Ibid., 44.

15. "The most distinctive Adena legacy in West Virginia and the Ohio Valley consists of hundreds of earthen mounds. The Adena people . . . built mounds over the remains of chiefs, shamans, priests, and other honored dead or as temples and houses for chiefs. They exposed the bodies of common folk after death and, once they were denuded of flesh, burned the bones. They then buried the remains in small log tombs on the surface of the ground. The forces of nature and the cultivation of the soil by European settlers later removed nearly every trace of these burials" (Otis K. Rice, *West Virginia: a History* [Lexington: Univ. Press of Kentucky, 1985], 5).

16. Pancake, *The Stories*, 116.

17. For a more detailed explanation of the Mothman, see John A. Keel, *The Mothman Prophecies* (New York: E. P. Dutton, 1975).

18. "A Breece Pancake Report," (Huntington, W.Va.) *Herald-Dispatch* Dec. 5, 1966.

19. Helen Pancake, letter to the author, May 26, 1993.

20. "Sue," C. R. and Breece's prize beagle pup, often competed in time trials. A beagle puppy plays a significant role in Pancake's story "In the Dry." "I'm going to show you something, Ottie" (*The Stories*, 156).

21. C. R. Pancake to Breece Pancake, Sept. 30, 1970.

22. Sam Harsbarger, interview by Marty Buchsbaum, videotape recording, Nov. 5, 1986, Milton, W.Va.

23. Breece Pancake to C.R. and Helen Pancake, May 5, 1975.

24. Breece once gave his father a copy of Hemingway's *The Old Man and the Sea* for a birthday present and wrote this inscription: "Life is a struggle that knows no age—Breece Pancake. With love to Pop."

25. C. R. Pancake to Breece Pancake, Oct. 31, 1970.

26. Ibid.

27. C. R. Pancake to Breece Pancake, Sept. 30, 1970.

28. C. R. Pancake to Breece Pancake, Oct. 1, 1970.

29. Pancake's beagle dog. A small beagle plays a significant role in Pancake's "In the Dry."

30. C. R. Pancake to Breece Pancake, Sept. 9, 1970.

31. Breece Pancake to C. R. and Helen Pancake, Jan. 15, 1972.

32. Breece Pancake to Helen Pancake, Sept. 24, 1975.

33. Breece Pancake to Helen Pancake, Sept. 17, 1975.

34. Breece Pancake to Helen Pancake, Aug. 14, 1978.

35. Harshbarger, interview.

36. Breece Pancake to Helen Pancake, Jan. 11 1976.

37. Breece Pancake to Helen Pancake, Oct. 15 1975.

38. Breece Pancake to C. R. and Helen Pancake, Oct. 21, 1974.

39. Supervising officer at Staunton Military Academy.

40. Breece Pancake to Helen Pancake, Mar. 28, 1976. Breece added the following P.S.: "Save mail from Educational Testing Service in Princeton, N.J. It contains a ticket I'll need at M.U. [Marshall University]."

41. Breece Pancake to C. R. and Helen Pancake, June 10, 1973.

42. Breece Pancake to C. R. and Helen Pancake, Jan. 22, 1972.

43. Breece Pancake to C. R. and Helen Pancake, Oct. 12, 1974.

44. Helen Pancake, interview.

45. Ibid.

46. Ibid.

47. Sarah Nutt related: "He had a somewhat unhappy event with another Pancake relative in Staunton—I think a cousin, but for some unknown reason that family did not accept him. Maybe they had broken away from the log cabin Pancakes in West Va.—and possibly felt superior. Who knows? The result was no contact after that and I feel the negative contact added to Breece's withdrawing from people or making contacts at the school" (Sarah Nutt, letter to the author, Oct. 10, 1992).

48. Janet (Nutt) Lembke, letter to the author, Feb. 22 1993.

49. Breece Pancake to Helen Pancake, Oct. 22, 1975.

50. Breece Pancake to Helen Pancake, Oct. 12, 1975.

51. Breece Pancake to Helen Pancake, Aug. 14, 1978.

52. Breece Pancake to Helen Pancake, Oct. 22, 1975.

· Cadillac Cowboy

1. Pop Amick, one of Breece's "walking encyclopedias," owned and operated the American Oil service station in Milton for twenty-seven years. Breece wrote an article about him for the *Cabell Record* in 1975 and transformed him imaginatively in his story "The Salvation of Me."

2. Jackson, interview. Robert Jackson became the banker in Milton and served as the real-life model for the fictional character of Chester in "The Salvation of Me."

3. "Rat Boy," written in high school, was Breece's first serious attempt at reworking a story and having it published. He sent the story to Jesse Stuart for comment in 1974 and then to the *Atlantic* for consideration. It was published for the first time in the *Appalachian Journal* (Fall 1991).

4. Breece Pancake to Marshall University students [1974?].

5. Blenko, interview.

6. Jackson in *Breece Pancake,* video broadcast.

7. Blenko, interview.

8. The young protagonist in "The Honored Dead" draws on some of Pancake's experience in high school athletics.

9. Jackson, interview.

10. Breece Pancake to C. R. and Helen Pancake, Sept. 7, 1974. Pancake MSS.

11. Ball in Cynthia Reuschel, "Milton Friends Remember Talented Author," (Milton, W.Va.) *Cabell Record,* Aug. 24, 1983, A2.

12. Breece Pancake to C. R. and Helen Pancake, Mar. 6, 1972.

13. Breece Pancake to C. R. and Helen Pancake, June (?) 1971.

14. Ibid.

15. Breece Pancake to C. R. and Helen Pancake, Jan. 22, 1972.

16. Helen Pancake, letter to author, Aug. 16 1990.

17. Morgan, interview.

18. Helen Pancake, interview.

19. Breece Pancake to C. R. and Helen Pancake, Feb. 8, 1972.

20. Breece Pancake to C. R. and Helen Pancake, Mar. 21, 1972.

21. Breece Pancake to C. R. and Helen Pancake, Jan. 21, 1972.

22. Breece Pancake to Helen Pancake, Apr. 14, 1977.

23. Breece Pancake to C. R. and Helen Pancake, Jan. 22, 1972.

24. Breece Pancake to C. R. and Helen Pancake, Mar. 16, 1972.

25. The title, according to Breece's notes, comes from Confederate general Jeb Stuart of Civil War fame.

26. "Wobblie," a member of the IWW, Industrial Workers of the World, an organization that figured prominently in the socialist and union movements of the early twentieth century. Breece carried an IWW membership card around in his wallet.

27. Breece made several lengthy trips to Arizona, one in 1972 and another in the following year. He also visited the West in the summer of 1978.

28. Breece Pancake to Donnetta Pancake, June 6, 1977.

29. Pancake cited Matthew 24:36 of the *New American Standard Bible*—"Not even the angels of heaven shall know the hour of his coming"—to focus the young protagonist's revelation at the end of "Fox Hunters," and "In the Dry" he used Luke 23:31—"For if they do these things in a green tree, what shall be done in the dry?"

30. Howard Burton Lee, Marshall University graduate, former West Virginia state attorney general, and author of *Bloodletting in Appalachia,* a recounting of the coal mine wars, *Burning Springs and Other Tales of the Little Kanawha,* and other books about West Virginia history and folklore.

31. Breece Pancake, Marshall University notebook, 1972, Pancake MSS.

32. Breece Pancake to Helen Pancake, Oct. 29, 1976.

33. The famous "Hatrack" scandal of 1926:

Tom Kromer graduated from high school in the spring of 1925 and the following fall enrolled at Marshall College, a small, conservative institution in Huntington. . . . The professors with whom Kromer was most friendly were Watson Selvage,
head of philosophy and psychology, Arthur S. White, a member of the economics
and political science department, and W. Page Pitt, who established a department
of journalism at Marshall during Kromer's second year there.

In the spring semester of that year, Marshall became involved in the backwash
of a controversy that had made headlines elsewhere in the country a year before—
the famous "Hatrack" case involving H. L. Mencken, the *American Mercury*, and
the Boston Watch and Ward Society. The April 1926 issue of the *Mercury* had carried a reminiscence by Herbert Asbury entitled "Hatrack"—a humorous piece
about a small-town prostitute. When the issue was banned from public sale in
Boston, Mencken decided to test the ban in court. On April 4, he traveled to Boston and at 2:00 P.M. that day sold a copy of the *Mercury* issue containing "Hatrack"
to J. Frank Chase, secretary of the city's Watch and Ward Society. The sale had been
prearranged, and Chase had brought along officers of the law. Mencken allowed
himself to be arrested, booked, and arraigned in court for selling obscene literature. The case went to court, and on April 6 Mencken was exonerated. It was a
signal victory for the Baltimore Sage and for liberal-thinking Americans but in
towns and cities throughout the country, files of the *Mercury* were removed from
library shelves and destroyed. In the spring of 1927, a year after Mencken's victory in Boston, files of both the *American Mercury* and the *New Republic* were
taken out of the library at Marshall College, an act which polarized fundamentalists and free-thinkers on campus. Watson Selvage and Arthur White both protested the removal of the magazines, and as a result both men were fired from
the faculty. (from "In Search of Tom Kromer," in *Waiting for Nothing and Other
Writings,* ed. Arthur D. Casciato and James L. West III [Athens: Univ. of Georgia
Press, 1986], 264–65)

34. Breece Pancake to Helen Pancake, Sept. 9, 1977.

35. Tom Kromer, *Waiting for Nothing and Other Stories*, ed. Arthur D. Casciato and
James L. West III (Athens: Univ. of Georgia Press, 1986), 257.

36. Ibid., 259.

37. Ibid., 42. "He had the guts and now everything is all right with him . . . ," etc.

38. Breece Pancake to Helen Pancake, Jan. 4, 1977.

39. Pancake in Carlos Santos, "We Teach Them to Rewrite at U.Va.," *Richmond
Times-Dispatch*, Jan. 7, 1979, E1. The image of a millstone about the neck is taken from
the Bible. Jesus taught many parables in Jerusalem and among his teachings—the
necessity to avoid offense: Luke 17:2: "It were better for him that a millstone were
hanged about his neck, and he cast into the sea, than that he should offend one of
these little ones."

40. Pancake in Chuck Hyman, "The Big Break," *The* (U.Va.) *Declaration*, Dec. 1, 1977.

41. Ibid.

42. Ibid.

43. Ibid.

44. Casey, afterword, 172.

45. Breece Pancake, Univ. of Virginia manuscript note, 1977(?), Pancake MSS.

46. In 1924, Sherwood Anderson had described the evolution of an artist in *A
Storyteller's Story*. "Those who are to follow the arts," he wrote, "should have train-

ing in what is called poverty. Given a comfortable middle-class start in life, the artist is almost sure to end up becoming bellyacher, constantly complaining because the public does not rush forward at once to proclaim him." It is an interesting comparison to note that Pancake acknowledged his debt to Anderson: "[I]t is my first memory of a really big Ohio farm, the kind that made Sherwood Anderson's stories so vivid in my mind. Without Anderson, I'd never have written a word" (Breece Pancake to Helen Pancake, Oct. 30(?), 1977).

47. "Toy Soldier" (unpublished) was written in 1976 and is based on Pancake's experience at Fork Union and Staunton Military Academies. The only remaining copy is incomplete. Pancake MSS.

48. According to U.S. Census Bureau estimates, West Virginia lost 14 percent of its population between 1960 and 1970 due to outward migration. The population recovered slightly in 1974, growing by 2.5 percent to 1,791,000. Current estimates predict the population will decline to 1,722,000 in the year 2000 and further decline to 1,617,000 by 2010.

49. Breece Pancake to C. R. and Helen Pancake, Sept. 19, 1974.

50. Breece Pancake to C. R. and Helen Pancake, Sept. 7, 1974.

51. Ibid.

52. Breece Pancake to C. R. and Helen Pancake, Feb. 16, 1975.

53. Breece Pancake to C. R. and Helen Pancake, Oct. 21, 1974.

54. Breece Pancake to C. R. and Helen Pancake, Sept. 19, 1974. Pancake is referring to a song by Phil Ochs.

55. Breece Pancake to C. R. and Helen Pancake, Sept. 15(?), 1974.

56. Breece Pancake, Fork Union demerit report, Nov. 8, 1974.

57. Southern Teachers Agency of Richmond placed Breece at Fork Union Military Academy for a fee.

58. One of Breece's girlfriends from his college days at Marshall.

59. Shorty Hollandsworth, family friend and car salesman in Huntington.

60. Breece Pancake to C. R. and Helen Pancake, Sept. 15(?), 1974.

61. Breece Pancake to C. R. and Helen Pancake, Apr. 8, 1975.

62. Breece Pancake to C. R. and Helen Pancake, Oct. 21, 1974.

63. Ibid.

64. Breece Pancake to C. R. and Helen Pancake, Sept. 7, 1974.

65. Breece Pancake to C. R. and Helen Pancake, Oct. 4, 1974.

66. Many of Pancake's professors at the University of Virginia have commented on Breece's fiery temper and volatile disposition. John Casey's phrase in the afterword to *The Stories,* "He struggled hotly to be a gentle person" (175), seems to be an apt description.

67. Breece Pancake to C. R. and Helen Pancake, Nov. 1, 1974.

68. Breece Pancake to C.R. and Helen Pancake, Oct. 21 1974.

69. Breece Pancake to C. R. and Helen Pancake, Jan. 6(?), 1975.

70. Breece Pancake to C. R. and Helen Pancake, Mar. 21, 1975.

71. For an interesting discussion of the idea of space in Pancake's fiction, see Grace Toney Edwards, "Place and Space in Breece Pancake's 'A Room Forever,'" in *The Poetics of Appalachian Space,* ed. Parks Lanier, Jr. (Knoxville: Univ. of Tennessee Press, 1991).

72. Breece Pancake to C. R. and Helen Pancake, Sept. 19, 1974.

73. Casey, afterword, 171.

74. Breece Pancake to John Casey, Aug.(?) 1975.

75. Breece Pancake to C. R. and Helen Pancake, Sept. 4, 1975.

76. Breece Pancake to Helen Pancake, Sept. 20, 1975.

77. Breece Pancake to C. R. and Helen Pancake, Sept. 5(?), 1975.

78. Breece Pancake to C. R. and Helen Pancake, Sept. 4, 1975. Pancake MSS.

79. Grandpa Fred Frazier.

80. Breece Pancake to C. R. and Helen Pancake, Sept. 17, 1975.

81. Helen Pancake, interview.

82. Ibid.

83. Ibid.

84. Breece Pancake to Helen Pancake, Sept. 20, 1975.

85. Breece Pancake to Helen Pancake, Oct. 12, 1975.

86. Breece Pancake to Helen Pancake, Mar. 21(?), 1976.

87. Breece Pancake to Helen Pancake, Oct. 12, 1975.

88. Sarah Nutt, letter to author, Oct. 10, 1992.

89. Breece Pancake to Helen Pancake, Oct. 5, 1975.

90. Breece Pancake to Helen Pancake, Oct. 28(?), 1975.

91. Breece Pancake to John Casey, Mar. 25, 1979, Pancake MSS, Univ. of Virginia.

92. Breece Pancake to Helen Pancake, Sept. 24, 1975.

93. Breece Pancake to Helen Pancake, Mar. 3(?), 1976.

94. Ibid.

95. Breece Pancake to Helen Pancake, Apr. 16, 1976.

96. Breece Pancake, "Toy Soldier" [unpublished manuscript], 1975, 1. Pancake MSS.

· Aristocrat in Blue Jeans

1. Breece Pancake to Helen Pancake, Sept. 22, 1976.

2. Breece Pancake to Helen Pancake, Mar. 3, 1976.

3. Breece Pancake to Helen Pancake, Nov. 2, 1976.

4. Breece Pancake to Helen Pancake, Sept. 4, 1976.

5. Breece Pancake to Helen Pancake, Sept. 2, 1976.

6. John Casey's novel *An American Romance* (1977).

7. Breece was doing research for "Hollow."

8. Breece Pancake to Helen Pancake, Mar. 21, 1976.

9. John Casey, interview.

10. McPherson in Kadohata, "Breece D'J Pancake," 46. McPherson also remembered his friendship with Pancake this way in a letter to the author, Apr. 13, 1994: "There was, indeed, a secret country that we shared over the short time that I knew him; . . . I had not realized he was truly the friend he had said he was until the day of his death. . . . My daughter . . . was born almost at the same time that Breece was dying. I still have not been able to figure out the true meaning of this."

11. Breece Pancake to Donnetta Pancake, June 6, 1977.

12. James Alan McPherson, letter to author, Apr. 13, 1994. Pancake MSS.

13. Eleanor Ross Taylor, letter to author, Dec. 21, 1995.

14. Breece Pancake to Helen Pancake, May 22, 1976.

15. Ibid.

16. Breece Pancake to Helen Pancake, Nov. 8, 1976.

17. Breece Pancake to Helen Pancake, Oct. 16, 1976.

18. Breece Pancake to Helen Pancake, Oct. 24, 1976.

19. Jones in Edward Fox, "Pancake's Imagination Rooted in West Virginia Soil," *Charleston Gazette*, Apr. 23, 1984, B6.

20. Breece Pancake to Helen Pancake, Sept. 9, 1977. Pancake MSS.

21. McPherson, foreword, 7.

22. T. B. Shutt, "Bright Hosannas and Eyes in the Night: Breece D'J Pancake, Writer," *Virginia Country* (June 1983): 38.

23. Ramsey in Kadohata, "Breece D'J Pancake," 43.

24. Charles Perdue, letter to author, Sept. 21, 1994. Pancake MSS.

25. Nelson in Kadohata, "Breece D'J Pancake," 44.

26. Mary Lee Settle, *The Clamshell* (New York: Lawrence/Delacorte, 1971), 27.

27. Lee Maynard, interview by author, tape recording, Jan. 20 1993.

28. Settle in Kadohata, "Breece D'J Pancake," 37.

29. Breece Pancake to Helen Pancake, Oct. 20, 1976.

30. Breece Pancake to Helen Pancake, Apr. 6, 1977.

31. Breece Pancake to Helen Pancake, Aug.(?) 1976. Pancake MSS.

32. McPherson, foreword, 6.

33. Jones in Fox, "Pancake's Imagination," 6B.

34. Breece Pancake to Helen Pancake, Nov. 2, 1976.

35. Breece Pancake to Helen Pancake, Nov. 8, 1976.

36. Breece Pancake to Helen Pancake, Feb. 28–Mar. 1, 1977.

37. Breece Pancake to Helen Pancake, Oct. 10, 1976.

38. Breece Pancake to Helen Pancake, Sept. 16, 1976.

39. Breece Pancake to Helen Pancake, Sept. 2, 1976.

40. Breece Pancake to Helen Pancake, Oct. 20, 1976.

41. Breece Pancake to Helen Pancake, Sept. 16, 1976.

42. Breece Pancake to Helen Pancake, Sept. 25, 1976.

43. The *Declaration* published two of Pancake's stories, "Hollow" and "Cowboys and Girls."

44. "Will o' the Wisp" was the working title for "Trilobites." The first versions of this story included sections that were to become "Trilobites" and "The Honored Dead."

45. *Tattoo* (1974) and *A Garden of Sand* (1970) are novels by Earl Thompson.

46. Breece Pancake to Helen Pancake, Oct. 20, 1976.

47. "Quits ain't the answer" is a phrase from "A Room Forever." Variants of this phrase and idea, the ability or inability to "stick," appear in "The Honored Dead," "In the Dry," "Fox Hunters," "Trilobites," and "The Scrapper."

48. Breece had submitted these stories to Robie Macauley at *Playboy* magazine in the early spring of 1976. Macauley responded: "I like your writing style. The style—especially in the narrative and descriptive parts—is fresh and clean. There are a lot of good graphic touches, especially, I think, in "the Mark." That's a fine, reflective story and the exploration of Reva's guilt and longing is excellent—but, of course, it's a very feminine story and that, I'm afraid, makes it unlikely for this magazine. . . . Even though none of these stories is just right for *Playboy*, I think all are publishable stories. And as you can see, I'm interested in your work" (Robie Macauley to Breece D. Pancake, May 25, 1976).

49. Carlos Santos, "'We Teach Them to Rewrite' at U.Va.," *Richmond Times-Dispatch*, Jan. 7, 1979, E1.

50. Breece Pancake, "The Honored Dead" (manuscript), 1977, Pancake MSS.

51. Breece Pancake, Course Syllabus, U.Va. Dept. of English., ENWR 250 Writing Short Fiction, Spring 1977, Pancake MSS.

52. Breece Pancake to Helen Pancake, Sept. 9, 1977.

53. Pancake, Course Syllabus.

54. Shutt, "Bright Hosannas and Eyes in the Night," 43.

55. Helen Pancake, interview by author, tape recording, Spring Hill, Fla., Nov. 9, 1992.

56. The 1920 Underwood no. 5 typewriter Aunt Julia gave to Breece.

57. *Paint Creek Miner* is a songbook about the Coal Mine Wars in southern West Virginia. Mary Lee Settle was working on her novel *The Scapegoat*.

58. Camden Park is a well-known amusement park in Huntington, W.Va.

59. Breece Pancake to Helen Pancake, Feb. 28–Mar. 1, 1977.

60. Breece Pancake to Helen Pancake, Feb. 25, 1977.

61. Pancake in McPherson, foreword, 12.

62. Ibid.

63. Breece Pancake to Helen Pancake, Mar. 28, 1976.

64. Weston La Barre, *They Shall Take Up Serpents* (Minneapolis: Univ. of Minnesota Press, 1962). The sketch, entitled "Shouting Victory," is in this second part of this volume.

65. Perdue, letter to author, Sept. 21, 1994.

66. Letter from around 1973, Pancake Papers, West Virginia Univ. Library, Morgantown.

67. Breece Pancake to Donnetta Pancake, June 6, 1977.

68. Breece Pancake to Helen Pancake, Mar. 25, 1977.

69. Helen Pancake to Breece Pancake, Mar. 31, 1977.

70. Ward Just (b. 1935), journalist, short story writer, novelist. His books include *A Soldier of the Revolution* (1970), *The Congressman Who Loved Flaubert and Other Washington Stories* (1973), *Nicholson at Large* (1975), *A Family Trust* (1978), *Honor, Power, Riches, Fame and the Love of Women* (1979), *In the City of Fear* (1982), *The American Blues* (1984), *The American Ambassador* (1987), and *Jack Gance* (1989).

71. Breece Pancake to Helen Pancake, Apr. 2, 1977.

72. Breece Pancake to Helen Pancake, Apr. 3, 1978.

73. Breece Pancake to Helen Pancake, June 11, 1977.

74. Breece Pancake to Helen Pancake, Aug. 12, 1977.

75. Casey, afterword, 172.

76. Breece Pancake to Helen Pancake, Nov. 11, 1977.

77. Wendy Jacobson to Breece D'J. Pancake, Nov. 3, 1978.

78. Colly's hunt for turtles in the story "Trilobites" is described this way: "I wade in. He goes for the roots of a log. I shove around, and feel my gaff twitch. This is a smart turkle, but still a sucker. I bet he could pull liver off a hook for the rest of his days, but he is *a sucker for the roots that hold him* while I work my gaff. I pull him up, and see he is a snapper" (*The Stories,* 26).

79. Breece Pancake to Helen Pancake, Feb. 29, 1976.

80. Breece Pancake to Helen Pancake, May 24, 1977.

81. Breece Pancake to Helen Pancake, Sept. 9, 1977.

82. Breece Pancake to Helen Pancake, Jan. 21, 1977.

83. Breece Pancake to Helen Pancake, Sept. 25, 1976.

84. Laura Owen Keene to Helen Pancake, Dec. 10, 1984.

85. Breece Pancake to Helen Pancake, Oct. 22, 1975.

86. Breece Pancake to Helen Pancake, Oct. 29, 1976.

87. Breece Pancake to Donnetta Pancake, June 6, 1977. A similar lyric can be heard on the 1973 Tom Waits album, *The Heart of a Saturday Night*.

88. Breece Pancake to Helen Pancake, Apr. 16, 1977.

89. Breece Pancake to Helen Pancake, Jan. 11, 1977.

90. In his last letter to John Casey, Mar. 25, 1979, Pancake admits he had been thinking of becoming a priest: "[W]hen it became clear I would have no work, I wanted to become a padre. Me a padre?"

91. Breece Pancake to Helen Pancake, Feb. 25, 1977.

92. Jones, interview.

93. Breece Pancake to Helen Pancake, Sept. 9, 1977.

94. Possibly "In the Dry" or "The Honored Dead."

95. Breece Pancake to Helen Pancake, Oct. 18, 1977.

96. Breece Pancake to Helen Pancake, Mar. 3, 1978.

97. Breece Pancake to Mary Roberts Rinehart Foundation, Mar. 21, 1978.

98. Breece Pancake to Helen Pancake, Nov. 11, 1977.

99. Breece Pancake to Helen Pancake, Sept. 3, 1978.

100. Breece Pancake to Helen Pancake, Oct. 25, 1978.

101. Breece Pancake to Emily Miller, July 1, 1978.

102. Breece Pancake to Helen Pancake, Sept. 22, 1978.

103. Breece Pancake to Helen Pancake, June 22, 1978.

104. Breece Pancake to Helen Pancake, Nov. 11, 1978. Breece mistakenly writes that Thomas Wolfe died in a cab in New York. It was James Agee who died in a cab in New York City on May 16, 1955. Thomas Wolfe died in Johns Hopkins hospital on September 15, 1938, in Baltimore due to a tubercular infection of the brain.

105. Breece Pancake to Helen Pancake, Jan. 20, 1979.

106. Breece Pancake to Helen Pancake, Sept. 9, 1976.

107. Breece Pancake to Helen Pancake, Apr. 3, 1978.

108. Breece Pancake to Helen Pancake, June 24, 1977.

109. Breece Pancake to Helen Pancake, Aug. 14, 1978.

110. A cat playing a guitar and singing is pictured on the front of the greeting card.

111. Breece Pancake to Helen Pancake, Dec.(?) 1978.

112. Breece Pancake, diary, 1979.

113. John Casey, interview.

114. Breece Pancake, introduction to "The Honored Dead" reading at the Methodist Student Center, Charlottesville, Spring 1979, Pancake MSS.

115. Breece Pancake to Helen Pancake, Feb. 28, 1979.

116. Breece Pancake to Helen Pancake, Jan. 20, 1979.

117. Breece's cousin.

118. Breece Pancake to Helen Pancake, Mar. 21, 1979.

119. Breece Pancake, memorandum, Apr. 7, 1979.

120. Kathleen Devereux to Breece Pancake, Mar. 28, 1979.

121. Sheriff's report in Thomas Taylor, "Breece D'J Pancake and His Literature of Last Words," (Marshall Univ.) *Parthenon*, Mar. 22, 1990, 6.

122. Kadohata, "Breece D'J Pancake," 56.

123. Fox, "Pancake's Imagination."

124. Mead in Kadohata, "Breece D'J Pancake," 57.

125. Helen Pancake in Paul Hendrickson, "The Legend of Breece D'J Pancake," *Washington Post*, Dec. 10, 1984, C6.

126. James Alan McPherson to Mrs. C. R. Pancake, Apr. 11, 1979 (Western Union).

127. Breece Pancake to Helen Pancake, Aug. 5, 1978.

128. Ibid.

129. Laura Owen Keene to Helen Pancake, Dec. 10, 1984.

130. Helen Pancake in Hendrickson, "The Legend of Breece D'J Pancake."

131. Raymond Nelson in Kadohata, "Breece D'J Pancake," 58.

132. Breece Pancake to John Casey, Mar. 25, 1979.

133. Breece Pancake to Helen Pancake, Apr. 14, 1977.

134. Breece Pancake to John Casey, Mar. 25, 1979.

135. Casey, interview.

136. Casey in Kadohata, "Breece D'J Pancake," 56.

137. Settle, ibid.

138. Helen Pancake, interview.

139. Virginia Meade to Helen Pancake, May 16, 1979.

· **A Room Forever**

1. Robert Merritt, "Writer Leaves an Earthy Legacy," *Richmond Times-Dispatch,* Feb. 20, 1983.

2. Robert Manning to Breece Pancake, May 3, 1977.

3. Edward Weeks to Breece Pancake, Mar. 23, 1977.

4. Peter Davison to Barbara Bannon, Oct. 22, 1982.

5. Phoebe-Lou Adams to Breece Pancake, Apr. 27, 1977.

6. Helen Pancake to Phoebe-Lou Adams, Aug. 18, 1979.

7. Ibid.

8. Jayne Anne Phillips to John Casey, May 5, 1982, Pancake MSS, Univ. of Virginia.

9. See, for example, Geoffrey Harpham, "Short Stack: the Stories of Breece D'J Pancake," *Studies in Short Fiction* 23 (1986): 265–73.

10. Casey in Thom Cole, "Young Writer Was Haunted by the Troubles of the Less Fortunate," *Stuart Florida News* (UPI), Jan. 2, 1983, D11.

11. Randy Hogan, "Review of *The Stories of Breece D'J Pancake,*" *Village Voice,* May 3, 1983, 40.

12. Peter Davison to Barbara Bannon, Oct. 22, 1982.

13. Ronald Sharp to John Casey, June 1, 1982. Pancake MSS, Univ. of Virginia

14. Andre Dubus to Richard Todd, Oct. 10, 1982, Pancake MSS, Univ. of Virginia.

15. Several titles and themes of Pancake's stories suggest those in Hemingway's collection *Winner Take Nothing:* "A Way You'll Never Be," "The Natural History of the Dead," and "Fathers and Sons."

16. Joyce Carol Oates, "The Stories of Breece D'J Pancake," *New York Times Book Review,* Feb. 13, 1983, 1.

17. Ibid., 24.

18. Robert Towers, "Violent Places," *New York Review of Books,* Mar. 31, 1983, 11.

19. Albert Wilhelm, "Breece D'J Pancake," *Dictionary of Literary Biography: American Short Story Writers Since World War II* (Oneonta, N.Y.: SUNY, 1993), 254.

20. See reviews by Tony Tanner, David Montrose, Eileen Battersby, Colin Walters, John Domini, Joyce Carol Oates, Bud Foote, and others.

21. John Domini, "Crying the Beloved Country," *Boston Phoenix,* Mar. 15, 1983.

22. M. K. Dieckman, "The Stories of Breece D'J Pancake," (Ithaca, N.Y.) *Grapevine,* Aug. 25–31, 1983, 34.

23. Bolton Davis, "The Stories of Breece D'J Pancake," *San Francisco Review of Books*, May–June 1983: n.p.

24. Eileen Battersby, "South Forks," *Irish Times*, Feb. 6, 1993.

25. Pancake knew what an automobile could symbolize. About his experience in Mexico he wrote, "Like much of W.Va., there are old cars sitting dead in front yards as a testimony to those inside the adobe hut that they had tried and failed to achieve that wispy, illusive [*sic*] dream of being rich." (Breece Pancake to C.R. and Helen Pancake, 21 March 1972. Pancake MSS.)

26. Leslie A. Fiedler, *Love and Death in the American Novel* (New York: Criterion Books, 1960), xxiii.

27. Ibid., xxii.

28. Ibid., xxiv.

29. David Bosworth, "A Writer's Death Haunts His Stories of Pain and Beauty," *Boston Globe*, Mar. 13, 1983, B12.

30. Robert Monroe, "A Single Flame," (Cambridge, Mass.) *Harvard Crimson*, Feb. 28, 1983.

31. Samuel Hazo, "A Dozen Good Stories," *Pittsburgh Press*, Mar. 13, 1983.

32. Michael Bakunin in A. Alvarez, *The Savage God* (New York: Random House, 1972), 26.

33. Adams in Peter Davison to Barbara Bannon, Oct. 22, 1982.

34. Oates, "The Stories of Breece D'J Pancake," 24.

35. Monroe, "A Single Flame."

36. Daphne Merkin, "The Aura of Suicide," *New Republic*, May 9, 1983, 36.

37. "Three West Virginia Writers: He's Gone, He's There, and She'll get There—Breece D'J Pancake, the Writer Who Was," (Summersville) *West Virginia Hillbilly*, May 21, 1983, 1.

38. Randall Short, "Pancake's Vivid Stories a Fit Legacy," *Virginia Pilot-Ledger Star*, Feb. 27, 1983.

39. Merkin, "The Aura of Suicide," 37.

40. Bud Foote, "The Pain of Creation, Pancake's Legacy: Simple, Direct, Honest Prose," *Detroit News*, Mar. 13, 1983, H2.

41. Dieckman, "The Stories of Breece D'J Pancake," 1.

42. Ibid.

43. Davis, "The Stories of Breece D'J Pancake."

44. Raymond Nelson, "The Hills of Home," *Virginia Quarterly Review* (Winter 1984): 169. Raymond Nelson shared an office in Wilson Hall with Pancake during their graduate school days at the University of Virginia. Nelson dedicated his book on Kenneth Patchen "to the memory of Breece D'J Pancake."

45. Bosworth, "A Writer's Death," B10.

46. Martin Kirby, "Stories of Life's Grim Side by a Gifted, Tragic Artist," *Philadelphia Inquirer*, Feb. 13, 1983, E5.

47. Foote, "The Pain of Creation," H2.

48. Jim Dent, "Presence of Death Lurks in Pancake's Stories," *Charleston Gazette*, Feb. 20, 1983, 16.

49. Kirby, "Stories of Life's Grim Side," E5.

50. Mike Ritchey, "Stories That Give Clues to Their Young Author's Despair," *Ft. Worth Telegram-Star*, Feb. 20, 1983, E8.

51. Alan Cheuse, "A Greatly Gifted Storyteller and Tales Not Quite Ripe," *Los Angeles Herald Examiner*, Feb. 27 1983, F5.

52. Carolyn Wilkerson Bell, "The Stories of Breece D'J Pancake," *Magill's Literary Annual* (1984), 824.

53. Sharon Barrett, "A Posthumous Voice from Somewhere Deep in the Hills," *Chicago Sun-Times*, Feb. 6, 1983.

54. Patricia Vigderman, "K-Marts and Failing Farms," *The Nation*, Mar. 19, 1983, 345.

55. McPherson in Kadohata, "Breece D'J Pancake," 46.

56. Gregory Morris, "Bare Gaping Wounds," *Prairie Schooner* (Fall 1983): 89.

57. Foote, "The Pain of Creation," H2.

58. Barrett, "A Posthumous Voice."

59. Towers, "Violent Places," 11.

60. Bell, "The Stories of Breece D'J Pancake," 824.

61. Domini, "Crying the Beloved Country."

62. Tony Tanner, "Review of Trilobites and Other Stories," *Guardian*, Nov. 3, 1992.

63. David Montrose, "In a Melancholy State," *Times Literary Supplement*, Oct. 23, 1992.

64. Battersby, "South Forks."

65. "Review of Trilobites and Other Stories," *Glasgow Herald*, Dec. 5, 1992.

66. Tom Butterworth, "Review of Trilobites and Other Stories," (London) *City Limits*, Oct. 29, 1992.

67. Erica Wagner, "A Dead Poet's Fossils," *London Times*, Oct. 20, 1992.

68. Several film scripts are in the Breece Pancake manuscript collection at Alderman Library, Univ. of Virginia.

69. Hendrickson, "The Legend of Breece D'J Pancake," C6.

70. Pancake in Hyman, "The Big Break," 12.

71. Casey in Kadohata, "Breece D'J Pancake," 61.

72. Wilhelm, "Breece D'J Pancake," 253.

73. Bob Snyder to Helen Pancake, Feb. 15, 1992.

74. Jane Tompkins, *Sensational Designs: the Cultural Work of American Fiction, 1790–1860* (New York: Oxford Univ. Press, 1985), xi.

75. See Jim Wayne Miller, "A People Waking Up, Appalachian Literature Since 1960," *Appalachian Symposium: Essays in Honor of Cratis Williams* (Boone, N.C.: Appalachian Consortium Press, 1989), 47–76.

· The Only Value

1. Leonard Lutwack, *The Role of Place in Literature* (Syracuse: Syracuse Univ. Press, 1984), 142.

2. Jones in *Breece Pancake*, video broadcast.

3. John Casey, interview.

4. Robert Wilson, "Tales from West Virginia Hills and Hollows," *Washington Post Book World*, Mar. 6, 1983, 3.

5. Shelby Foote, interview by Noah Adams, National Public Radio broadcast, Nov. 3, 1994.

6. Peter Taylor, *A Woman of Means* (New York: Frederic C. Bell, 1950), 27.

7. *The Stories*, 116.

8. John Casey, afterword, 173.

9. Peter Taylor, *A Summons to Memphis* (New York: Knopf, 1986), 24.

10. Fox, "Pancake's Imagination," B1.

11. Michiko Kakutani, "Books of the Times," *New York Times*, May 15, 1984, 23.

12. Taylor, *A Summons*, 20.

13. Foote: "In Peter's later writings, in the Memphis book about the old forest there's a good deal of talk about why that old forest is there, what it represents historically. He writes about a times that's been *forgotten almost,* but he doesn't romanticize it; he just describes it the way it is. A young girl disappears in the thirties, and not only is her family wondering where she is but the chief of police and the city judge and everybody else is terribly concerned about this young woman. Sort of *loco parentis* back in those days. Now nobody cares what happens to anybody" (Shelby Foote, interview by Noah Adams).

14. Breece Pancake to Helen Pancake, Sept. 25, 1976, June 11, 1977, Aug. 14, 1978, and others.

15. *The Stories,* 21.

16. Harpham, "Short Stack," 267.

17. *The Stories,* 35.

18. Ibid.

19. *The Stories,* 36–37.

20. Mircea Eliade, *Myth and Reality* (New York: Harper and Row, 1963), 24–34.

21. Ruel Foster, interview by Marty Buchsbaum, videotape recording, Morgantown, W.Va. Aug.(?) 1988.

22. Edmund Wilson, *The Wound and the Bow* (Cambridge, Mass.: Houghton Mifflin, 1941), 216.

23. "Well, Pop, the forestry you taught me when I was kid paid off. I have to escape to the woods in my free time to get away from the noise and the kids. I've seen more snakes than you could shake a stick at—mostly because I look for them. There are entire herds of deer, and watching them graze is a beautiful sight. I set a rabbit snare and bated [*sic*] it with apple. Caught a coon by the paw, and when I found him, he was trying to chew the line in two. He was so mad, I couldn't get close enough to cut him free, so I stayed with him until he had frayed the nylon cord down (to keep the dogs off), freed himself then went off dragging this green string of nylon behind him" (Breece Pancake to C. R. and Helen Pancake, Sept. 19, 1974).

24. James George Frazer, *The Golden Bough* (New York: Macmillan, 1951), 47.

25. Ibid., 49.

26. Oates, "The Stories of Breece D'J Pancake," 24.

27. Casey in *Breece Pancake.*

28. *The Stories,* 23.

29. Ibid., 47.

30. Ibid., 133.

31. "When I speak of writing from where you have put down roots, it may be said that what I urge is 'regional' writing. 'Regional,' I think, is a careless term, as well as a condescending one, because what it does is fail to differentiate between the localized raw material of life and its outcome as art" (Eudora Welty, "Place in Literature," *The Eye of the Story: Selected Essays and Reviews* [New York: Vintage, 1979], 132).

· · · · · · · · · · · · · · · · · **The Prisoning Hills of Home**

1. Michael Curtis, foreword, *Contemporary New England Stories* (Old Saybrook, Conn.: Globe Pequot Press, 1992), viii–xii.

2. Denise Giardina, interview by author, tape recording, July 10, 1992, Whitesburg, Ky., *Appalachian Journal* (Summer 1993): 384–93.

3. Ensey in Tim Stephens, "Director's Attempt at Humor Falls Short," *Herald-Dispatch*, Dec. 7, 1993, 1A.

4. Ibid.

5. Dave Peyton, "Troy State Can't Have Pancake—He's Ours," *Herald-Dispatch*, Dec. 8, 1993, 8A.

6. Rick Blenko, "Pancake Wouldn't Have Minded at All," *Herald-Dispatch*, Dec. 13, 1993, 6A.

7. Bosworth, "A Writer's Death," B10.

8. Merkin, "The Aura of Suicide," 37.

9. Robert Towers, "Violent Places," *New York Review of Books*, Mar. 31, 1983, 11.

10. James Frakes, "Your Choice: Stories Hard or Soft," *Plain Dealer*, Mar. 20, 1983, C19.

11. Michael Harrington, *The Other America: Poverty in the United States* (New York: Macmillan, 1962), 43.

12. Richard Currey, interview by author, tape recording, Albuquerque, N.M., June 6, 1992, *Appalachian Journal* (Summer 1993): 374–82.

13. Ibid.

14. Lee Maynard, interview by author, tape recording, Jan. 20, 1993.

15. Ibid.

16. Robert DeFrancis, "West Virginia Writer Celebrated," *Parkersburg* (W.Va.) *News*, Feb. 20, 1983, 16.

17. Meredith Sue Willis, interview by author, tape recording, South Orange, N.J., June 30, 1992.

18. James Still, "Heritage," *Hounds on the Mountain* (New York: Viking, 1939), 55.

19. Currey, interview.

20. Jayne Anne Phillips, interview by author, tape recording, Dec. 7, 1992, Boston, Mass., *Appalachian Journal* (Winter 1994): 182–87.

21. Ibid.

22. Pinckney Benedict, interview by author, tape recording, Aug. 19, 1991, Lewisburg, W.Va., *Appalachian Journal* (Fall 1992): 68–74.

23. Breece Pancake to C. R. and Helen Pancake, Feb. 22 1975. Pancake MSS.

24. Phillips, interview.

25. *The Stories*, 169.

26. Ibid., 90.

27. Giardina, interview.

28. Phillips, interview.

29. Maynard, interview.

30. *The Stories*, 94.

31. "Ginny is no more to me than the bitter smell in the blackberry briers up on the ridge" (*The Stories*, 25).

32. *The Stories*, 144.

33. Chuck Kinder, interview by author, tape recording, Sept. 29, 1992, Pittsburgh, Pa.

34. Lisa Koger, interview by author, tape recording, Glenville, W.Va., July 28, 1992.

35. Phillips, interview.

36. Koger, interview.

37. It is worth noting that Pancake, unlike Phillips, did not embrace the mentality of the sixties and seventies.

38. Phillips, interview.

39. Michiko Kakutani, "Books of the Times," *New York Times*, May 15, 1984, 23.

40. Casey, interview.
41. *The Stories*, 45.
42. Ibid., 60.
43. Willis, interview.
44. Maynard, interview.
45. Breece Pancake to C. R. and Helen Pancake, Sept. 7, 1974.
46. Willis, interview.

Part II

*Selected Letters
and Fragments*

8

1970–1975

Milton, W.Va.
Sept. 9, 1970

West Virginia Wesleyan College
Buckhannon, W.Va.

Hi Pal,

Not much to write about, but I know you must look for mail, so I'll try to update you on any news.

I haven't as yet got back on the regular job. Brown is still working my job. In fact I ain't doing much. Jerry hasn't been getting much FRT from UCC[1] but I'll change that soon. I understand Charley's wife is sick but is improving. We haven't got any mail from the girls latley [*sic*], but I guess no news is good news, you see it's about the same at home. Hope it's more interisting [*sic*] with you. I am sure it is, and most thankful you can be exposed to better living.

On the care packages, let me know when you need one. Call when you need to anytime.

Sue[2] is entering a trial Saturday 9/12, the first this season. May or may not place, I'll let you know.

Best wishes,
[signed] Pop

1. Union Carbide Chemical.
2. C. R. and Breece's beagle hunting dog. A beagle dog plays a minor but significant role in Pancake's "In the Dry," "I'll show you something."

Huntington, W. Va.
Jan. 11, 1973

John and Barbara Shaffer
Buckhannon, W.Va.

Dear John & Barb,

Since last you heard from me (Arizona) I've been the rounds. I came home in time to resume my "education"—12 hrs. last summer and 18 hrs. this past semester—a lot of hard work and long nights but I've earned the right to call myself a "dean's list man"—for what it's worth.

I'm taking 18 hrs. again this semester and it looks as if things get worse instead of better—I honestly have no regrets about leaving WVWC but if I am going to work this hard down here I can find no justification for former actions.

My father is better but has been diagnosed as an unsalvageable case of M.S., so much of my free time is involved with him. M.S. is a drawn out process producing the antithesis of life but he adjusts like a champ and is always enjoying life to its fullest.

I was in Buckhannon in October and meant to drop by but Gilligan and the bottle got in my way and before I knew it I had to get back to M.U.—hungover and blown out. Thank God for pressure valves!

Belcher is here, well so much for that topic. Cebe was around this summer but I didn't see much of him since we both stay pretty busy with class. He did, however, relate the tale of Jay's reaching "manhood"—still nothing to do in Buckhannon—huh?

Well, enough of me, what of you two? I devine [sic] that you'll graduate, John,[1] around May. Correct? Then what? Ah, the golden question! The answer from your guru says: "Get your wife a job." John, with a blessed beauty like your bride you should beg for a job in the salt mines; I mean, nobody should be lucky twice in the same year. It's Un-American!

Well, write if you can, give my regards to all and keep in touch if you move. I'll do the same in hope of one day seeing my old friends again.

Love you both,
[signed] The Pancake

P.S. Any great expectations? I mean children?

1. David Belcher, Cebe Marpe, Jay Boyd, John Shaffer, and Breece were all members of the West Virginia Wesleyan Theater Company. James Calligan was Breece's roommate while he attended college there.

La Vista Grande
Phoenix, Ariz.
June 10? 1973

Mr. & Mrs. C. R. Pancake
Milton, W.Va.

Dear Folks,

It's been so long since I've written to you I thought I'd better get one off before you give me up for dead. . . .[1]

Anyway, I went up to Sedona and then Flag [Flagstaff] to escape the heat. I camped two nights and came home—getting more like Pop daily. Those mountain beds don't agree with my bones like they used to. Getting old and soft, I guess, but the next trip I take probably won't be camping trip. Maybe I rough it too much—a sleeping bag just isn't good padding for rock. But the lakes were beautiful with the Sacred Peaks rising above them and making the entire area a warm Montana. There weren't too many people either— it's a good piece off the main highway. Saw some deer, ducks, and rabbit but no snakes—still too cold for them, I guess. It isn't too cold in Phoenix—107 degrees—110 at day with an average of 95–98 at night. Night is when the snakes[2] come out and La Vista has it's [sic] share because the new owners don't cut the weeds or trim the flowers back. Donnetta killed a baby snake night before last. Personally, I don't bother them unless they bother me the way that monster snake did two weeks ago. He scared hell out of me so I killed him. It was very unfair—he couldn't help it because he was ugly and big and besides two people helped me so Ole snake didn't have a chance.

The stories are coming along and I'll send Beasley[3] the first rough drafts for possible suggestions as soon as they're finished. I'm really proud of "Rat Boy"[4] and I hope Atlantic takes it. They pay $100 a page (mine or theirs I don't know) which could mean $1,000 or $200 depending on how you mean it. Doni did the typing and it was perfect. She's a darn good secretary and she works cheap too. I might send off some poems[5]—I'll have to revise them first. That doesn't pay much but it's print any way and right now that's all I'm after. I have plenty of time to get rich—baloney. It takes Atlantic a while to decide on a story but if they get swift, forward anything from Arlington St., Boston, Mass. If they reject it? Big deal. Atlantic is the best but not the only literary magazine. . . .

I don't want any "help." If I can't make it on my own I don't want it.

Glad to hear you're getting around so well Pop—don't get too close to that river bank, Pal, the fish have enough to eat as it is. I hope you're enjoying yourself—have a happy father's day. Doni and I went together on something for your sitting room. I hope you like it. Well, I'll get back to work now, my regards to all esp. Aunt Julia. I'll write her soon.

Love,
[signed] B.D.P.

1. Here and in subsequent letters, a series of four ellipsis points indicates deleted portions that are judged to be redundant or too mundane. A series of three ellipses indicated ellipses that were in the original letters.
2. Pancake's preoccupation with snakes surfaces in his fiction, most notably, "Trilobites."
3. Mike Beasley, Breece's friend and teacher at Marshall University.
4. See letter from Jesse Stuart to Breece Pancake July 19, 1974. "Rat Boy" was first published in *Appalachian Journal* (Fall 1991).
5. Many of these poems are included in this volume.

· **Poem, 1973**

[Untitled]

He scratched and stirred as the
Rain washed the wine from his nerves.
Electric stars reflected from
The wet brick mosaic. "The
Alley Moves" he thought, and
Belched as he reached to touch
A blue reflection turned
Black by his finger shadow.
Bell ringings chilled him
He knew what they wanted
He knew where they would
Take him. He was wise to them.
Move out, he thought, by God,
Follow that dream. And slept.

· **To the** *Atlantic Monthly*

To whom it may concern,[1]

The following letter from Jesse Stuart (a fellow Appalachian) speaks strongly for the quality of my short story. Of course, I am working under the premise that anything turning Jesse's switch off must have something going for it.

Thanks,
[signed] Breece D. Pancake

P.S. Pancake is really my name.

1. This note typed on the letter from Stuart served as a cover for "Rat Boy," which Breece sent to the *Atlantic Monthly* for consideration.

W-Hollow
Greenup, Ky.
July 19th 1974

Breece D. Pancake
1054 R & 60 East
Milton, W.Va. 25541

Dear Breece Pancake:

Usually, when someone sends me material,[1] I return it unread. It's got to the point, I get so much, it would take all my time to read and comment on it if I would. The way I look at it is, I am another writer, not an editor and stories, poems, essays and articles should be sent to editors. I never in my life would let anyone read my material but editors and later after I married, my wife.

Really on your story, which I tried to read, I couldn't get through the first page which is very important to an editor. Even a first sentence is. I have no particular love for a rat, except the old packrat. He's a pretty good fellow. But when it comes to cannibalism among rats I have to turn the switch off. Wish I had a better comment. Some one might like it.

One thing about you, you know how to write a letter (most people don't). Another thing about you is, you sent return postage. So many don't. I post their material back to them. You are well trained and I do hope luck with your writing.

Sincerely,
[signed] Jesse Stuart

1. Breece had sent "Rat Boy" to Jesse Stuart (1907–1984) for comment

· · · · To C. R. and Helen Pancake, September 7, 1974

Fork Union, Va.   Sept. 7, 1974

Mr. & Mrs. C. R. Pancake
Milton, W.Va.

Dear Folks,

I guess now that Char[1] has gone back to Seattle, the house is settling back into the usual routine. I hope this finds you well.

My students range from creative to brilliant to leaden slugs, but I'll get by, I'm sure. I sort of like working with the little ones, especially the homesick cases—I know just how they feel. I must be getting old; today I decided my hobo days were gone forever—I have no desire to live in Europe any-more, I don't even want to go back out west for a while. I'm going to come back to W.Va. when this is over. There's something ancient and deeply rooted in my soul. I like to think that I've left my ghost up one of those hol-lows, and I'll never be able to leave for good until I find it—and I don't want to look for it because I might find it and have to leave.

I like my work and tolerate most of my co-workers, but there's no animosity—we just don't share the same interests. I've discovered that not everybody likes to read a book a week. It was quite a shock at first, but I'll get by. . . .

Anyway, Mom, get this straight; I want to pay my bills. I appreciate your help, but you and Dad have given me my life up to this point and it's time I earned my own and started acting like a man. If'd I'd been more re-sponsible, none of this mess would have happened.

For recreation, I walk, write and read. Today, I hiked about five miles saw a passle of snakes—copperheads mostly—a few garters (which have a darker coloring over here) and one timber rattler that I swear must of have been four feet long. I've set up a hiking-forest survival intermural [sic] pro-gram for the boys who don't want to play ball (I know I never liked to), but I'm going to take them on tamer trails until cold weather sets in.

Paula's[2] getting a new place in November or before: Terrace Park East. I've seen it and it's the kind of place I'd planned on retiring to. But she's happy with it so I guess she'll enjoy it.

This place is o.k. if you just keep cool and when the day's over quit playing soldier. There's good noise about me in the commandant's office. "Pancake's Company," or so I've heard. I don't do anything but keep good relations with cadet officers and men—they run this showboat, I just give them pointers now and then, make recommendations and reward good work. And they said war was hell—ha ha.

My temper? It's almost gone. I've also discovered that life without beer is not necessarily unbearable. But tell the preacher I still smoke cigarettes and have no intentions of becoming a Baptist.

It's not all peaches and cream—the dinner tonight had dogmeat and rotten eggs disguised as—I've forgotten what Sarge called it. I hope I never see it again. Otherwise, the grub is decent.

I was glad to hear about Grandpa and tell him I said to take good care.

Pop, I guess you're taking a bone out of Mom? Don't work her too hard, now. If she'd up and drop dead on you, it might be Sunday before Jimmy Johnson found you. Then who'd take care of you? Sure, you'd go to some V.A. hospital, but they don't give love, just medicine.

Well, better get to what they pay me for. remember, I love you and I'll fly in T-giving. Paula said she'd pick me up at the airport so don't sweat it.

Love you
[signed] Breece

P.S. Regards to any who ask.

1. Charlotte Pancake, Breece's sister.
2. Breece's girlfriend.

· · · To C. R. and Helen Pancake, September 19, 1974

Fork Union, Va.   Sept. 19, 1974

Mr. & Mrs. C. R. Pancake
Milton, W.Va.

Dear Folks,

My students are taking one of my surprisingly easy tests, so I'm writing this now in the classroom. Since classes began we have worked seven days out of eight, not counting the two days of helping incoming students. To top it off, I pulled duty Monday night (6:00 pm–10:30) on top of my regular work. Then some idiot gave me the high right arm salute of the Nazi Army, and I had to put him on report (two typed pages) and supervise his punishment—the cleaning of our common restrooms in "A" company.

The work is hard, but the long periods of free time on the weekends don't help me much, so I'd rather work. I found a cave, of a sort, in the end of a hollow about four miles from here. That was my first act of colonization. It is a foxden at the present time, but this winter I plan to camp in it on weekends. It's an off grade of granite, so there's no danger of a cave-in.

As far as textbooks are concerned, the days of the McGuffy Readers are over, although what I'm using is just a modernized version of them. To my opinion McGuffy was as bad as Allen Ginsberg's "Howl" except to the other extreme. Ginsberg thought he had something new when he incorporated perversion into poetry, but Sophocles wrote about a son who killed his father and married his mother. This was written nearly four thousand years ago, and it's much finer poetry than "Howl."

I guess I find fundamentalists—hard-shells, foot-washers—even Methodists a bit hard to take at times. Super-dedicated people bore me. They have no sense of humor, no reception to different ideas, nothing—only their cause, and that makes them singly hard-headed, and generally sickening.

No, private schools aren't the answer either. The answer, Dear Folks, is that there is none.

Well, anyway I'm glad to hear the supersleuth is on the trail of the crook that knabed [*sic*] my wallet. I honestly hope he doesn't find the guy. I know that sounds crazy, but all I lost was some money and a fivebuck piece of plastic. The crook stands to lose his job, or even the chance of ever getting another job. I'd rather not see that, because he'll just become a bigger crook without a job.

Tell Shorty I saw a T-V ad for a Granada, and it looked pretty good. I'd like to get some information on it if I could—tell him that no matter what, I'm buying my next car from him.

Well Pop, the forestry you taught me when I was a kid paid off. I have to escape to the woods in my free time to get away from the noise and the kids. I've seen more snakes than you could shake a stick at—mostly because I look for them. There are entire herds of deer, and watching them graze is a beautiful sight. I set a rabbit snare and bated [*sic*] it with apple. Caught a coon by the paw, and when I found him, he was trying to chew the line in two. He was so mad, I couldn't get close enough to cut him free, so I stayed with him until he had frayed the nylon cord down (to keep the dogs off), freed himself then went off dragging this green string of nylon behind him.

I try to get letters off to Mammaw and Grandpa and Aunt Julia, too. That's tough to do, but it means a lot to get mail. Sort of means that despite age and loneliness, somebody cares about you.

I hope you don't mind if I pass on Janet and Carolyn—we have nothing in common. Instead I'm going to look up some Pancakes just for the hell of it—to find out if they're nicer than the Huntington Branch. Aunt Julia will fill you in on what I've heard to date.

During my wood-treks, I've picked up several arrow-head ferns, some teaberry, some red-green lichens and some moss. I built a box for the window and I've got them in it—now we'll see if they live.

Pop, I hope you're doing o.k. Want you to know that I think about you and Mom a lot. These kids are in one hell of a shape and if it hadn't been for you two, I'd have been that way too. A long time ago we heard a folk song: "There but for fortune, go you and I."[1]

I was very fortunate to have you two.

Love,
[signed] Breece

1. A song by Phil Ochs.

· · · · · · To C. R. and Helen Pancake, October 4, 1974

Fork Union, Va.   Oct. 4, 1974

Mr. & Mrs. C. R. Pancake
Milton, W.Va.

Dear Folks,

I am pleased to announce I've saved a whopping $322.00 for the month of September. I know it doesn't sound like much, but when it's all you have, it's a pretty big sum. I intend to dump about $20.00 in C'ville with Matt,[1] but I've earned it. Got to get these creatures out of my hair at least once a month.

I am also happy to announce my adjustment was successful. I was tested today when my hiking team and I strayed through a farmer's field (which wasn't posted) and he gave me hell for trespassing. Said he was going to report me—oh, just generally made an ass of himself—and I didn't explode back. I hope to God my temper remains in check. I apologized, but he said, "Well, sorry's not enough," and I nearly laughed at him. What did he want me to do? Disappear into thin air? So I very politely informed him of my name and rank, told him exactly who to call to report me, and politely apologized again, took my troop, and left. I hope he does report me. If his land is so important, why doesn't he post it thus: "Shit-Faced-Son-of-a-Bitch—Beware of Bastard."

Mom, thanks for the cookies—there was not too much flour! They were delishous [sic]. I made the mistake of getting them during my free period, so I had to share, but they were very good. Damn Matt. He hopes I get more! Glutton. Thanks again.

Jezzuz! I've got duty again tomorrow night. Oh, Leave Weekend, where is thy sting?

It will be nearly a month and a half before I come home, and I miss you, but don't worry, I'll get there if the plane doesn't crash. I'm beginning to think I'm jinxed about traveling for a while. Wonder if I broke a mirror? You know, if the plane crashed, it would be my luck to walk away—wouldn't even get a good week's rest in the hospital. I've thought a lot about my car wreck.[2] I should have got out that minute and checked the tire pressure. Like that guy on the bridge[3]—"Be a good time to grease it."

You may tell the Rev. Mr. Pyles that they make you go to church here, but it's so watered down that it's easy to ignore it. The Chaplin's a pretty nice fellow, but that's as far as I care to go. I don't like being made to do things in the way of religion, but this is a private institution and I've signed my rights away—or so it seems. So I sit there mentally reciting logic rules and the few fiery words I remember from the Constitution and Transcendental philosophers.

Well, I hope this finds you well and happy—my regards to all.

Love,
[signed] Breece

P.S. Ask Bob Reese if he has any Tax-Shelter plan or special investment plan I could enter. The stock market is horrid, and I'd rather have security at 7% than desperation in a depression.

1. Matthew Heard.
2. Breece had two serious auto accidents while he lived in Huntington. He totaled the family car, a Chevy Impala, in one of them.
3. An incident that becomes fictionalized in "In the Dry."

· · · · To C. R. and Helen Pancake, November 1, 1974

Fork Union, Va.   Nov. 1, 1974

Mr. & Mrs. C. R. Pancake
Milton, W.Va.

Dear Folks,

Halloween is over, and all the spooks have gone back into the earth till next year. Hope this finds you well, and unhaunted.

Perhaps I should explain my comments of my last letter. I am leaving F.U.M.A. this spring, and heading for Morgantown.[1] That decision was the direct result of the nervous breakdown I almost had last week. No joke. I thought about the "Ripoffsky" plan, but I'm just not cut out for it. There are a number of things I am qualified to do besides teach at F.U.M.A. and I have figured it up, I can pay off my loan by May, and have a little left over. I've started that wheel already, and I'm going to try for law school. With the first loan paid, I'll have no trouble getting the second one. It will mean work and school at the same time, but that can't be the pressure I've been under the last two weeks.

A lot has happened to me, and I've decided the only dependable thing in my life is my own ambitions. Everything else is here and gone, but a dream is something to make you get up in the mornings. When one has sold one's soul the roof falls in, and one must build the soul again. So I will start now. I will eat the food because I earned it, will teach because they hired me to, and will do the best job I know how because it isn't the kids' fault I have to lie to them.

Nov. 2, 1974

Parents day is over. Boy was that a winner. Most of them were pretty civil about their kids grades, but one father insinuated I was not doing my job because his son made a B, and last year his son made straight A's in all subjects. Hell, I couldn't help it if the kid blew a test. Then there was a very pretty lady who told me she would appreciate it if I or the commandant told her son that his father (her ex-husband) was in jail in Richmond for murder . . . said she didn't have the heart. As it turned out, neither did I, and W.C. had to tell him.

Excuse the mistakes in the last paragraph; the machine[2] is going hay-wire on me. I'm still not sure I've got everything together.

My figures on paying my debts would astound you. I get $440.00 after taxes, pay the agency 120.00, the school 25.00, the bank 200.00. The little left over goes into the Breece Pancake Survival Fund, a non-profit organization which contributes to the delinquency of myself. If I can really claim a loss on my car, I'll get 300.00 bucks back from the government, but I'm not counting on that. Yet dispite [sic] my poverty, the thought of being a free man again is enough riches. I dislike the restriction here . . . both in thought and action.

I know you both are saying I'm dumb to leave with the cost of living going up all the time, but I want the right to be me, even if I have to fight to get it. Thing is I can't see why we aren't allowed to be ourselves. Everybody here has an education, and should be able to handle his or herself, and still do the job . . . guess not, huh?

Well, I'll quit boring you with my prattle.

I'm glad the yard is in shape again, and that you got a boy to do it. Can't believe the people out back raked leaves as celebration. Takes all kinds I guess.

Hope this finds you well, Pop. Don't work Mom too hard, she isn't that much younger than you. I tried to call you all last week, but there was no answer, so I assumed you were out driving around. That's good, and it really helps to get out now and then.

Just three more weeks till I'm home. So get your arguments against my leaving ready. I've looked them all over, and I can say there are no good reasons to stay.

Love,
[signed] Breece

1. West Virginia University is located in Morgantown. Breece was thinking of applying to graduate school and / or law school there.
2. The 1920 Underwood no. 5 typewriter Aunt Julia had given him.

Fork Union, Va.   Nov. 10, 1974

Mr. & Mrs. C. R. Pancake
Milton, W.Va.

Dear Folks,

Many thanks for your last letter. We all want to be understood, and I think that's why humans began to speak, but if you don't understand my dilemma, don't worry about it. You are removed from the real essence of the problem, and I haven't written the WHOLE truth about FUMA because I'm afraid to put things like that in print, and sign my name after it. That's called paranoia.

Rita went to Paris? I'd love to go there, and just sit in a bistro on the Champs Elysees with a glass of calvados. As it is, I am drinking Bosco, and trying to convince myself that my students are not as dumb as I thought. If I stayed here another year, I would have to take courses in Special Education just to teach them how to read. By the way, the boy who threw the fit is gone.

Good old Gloria,[1] sounds as if she had her hands full. Did she say she hates blacks? It's true. At least it was when I knew her. You couldn't pay me enough to teach in one of those places. My advice to her would be to get the hell out of the city, and marry a rabbi.

I saw Lucas Tanner[2] too. Matt and I jointly wrote the producer a nasty letter. Told him that his show assumed too much; like one can reach a student, that students are all human, that students care, that parents care, that anybody cares. Personally, I could never deliver a baby if I had to. Education has nothing to do with the real world, and shows like that one only fill a kid's head with a bunch of illusions, and the kid wonders why his teacher can't be a Lucas Tanner. Maybe if they put cameras in my room and paid me $40,000 a year, I'd be able to do what he does for one hour a week.

When and if I ever get into politics, I'd like to work on the quality of public education and public health. West Va. needs a total social medicine program, and a revamped education program. Why should someone like you, Pop, who worked all his life, and payed state taxes have to rely on your workman's insurance alone without any state aid? What about Aunt Julia? Uncle Mont left her well off . . . unless she gets sick. Then she can't go home, because the bills took everything, and she has to rely on her social security, and the nursing home takes that.

There has been so much sickness in our family, and I've often thought of how bad it could be if we weren't prepared for it, and how easier it could be made through a good medical program. I'm glad to hear Grandpa and Mammaw are at least doing better. Sounds as if you've had your hands full, Mom, but it also sounds as if you had a pretty good time.

Donna Poe invited me to her apartment for dinner this coming week-end, and I'm going to take her up on it. "I ain't had a home-cooked meal/ and Lord, I need one now." Besides I get pretty bored sitting around here. She's working as a dental technician in C'ville, and I ran into her at a ball-game last week. She didn't know me without my beard, and was pretty mad because I hadn't tried to contact her. But her anger was mostly bark, and she invited me to dinner and offered to come down and get me in the same breath. That, my friends, is a hustle. Don't worry, I can take care of myself.

To top that off, her father came down yesterday for the hell of it (I don't think he believed I shaved). He has shoulder length hair and a mustash, and dresses like I used to. The man's forty-five, but you couldn't tell it. He's sell-ing the West Va. area, and doesn't get home much, but says he's making money. I guess that's what it's all about.

So it is that I have actually worked three months shy two weeks and I'm tired. I'm looking forward to my stay at home. Mom, could I ask for a diet of seafood and greens? This meat and potatoes is killing me. I feel like I'm 100 years old and one foot in the grave.

Give my regards to all. My plane ticket is on its way, and I'll be in when I get there, so don't look for me until you see me.

Til I knock on the door.

Love,
[signed] Breece

1. Gloria Nicknowitz, one of Breece's former girlfriends.
2. *Lucas Tanner* was a popular TV show.

· · · · To C. R. and Helen Pancake, February 22, 1975

Fork Union, Va.
Feb. 22, 1975

Mr. & Mrs. C. R. Pancake
Milton, W.Va.

Dear Folks,

Finally I get a chance to answer your letters. This week hasn't been at all hectic, just the routine insanity. I'm getting ready for the next grading period, and trying not to worry about how I'm going to pass the silent ma-jority this time. I was glad to hear that you complied with my wishes on the insurance. Dishonesty is too rampant in our land to be excused on an individual basis, rather, like charity, honesty should begin at home. The price doesn't matter. As Steinbeck once said, "Anything that just costs money is cheap."

Weather was so good today, I took a friend's bike out for a five mile trip. I'll feel that tomorrow morning. Walked the last mile as one of the gear guides got mucked in with the chain, and the whole damn thing fell apart. That little venture should cost me about $10.00. I hate those English bikes . . . too much junk to break.

I'm taking a bunch of the boys out to the farm for their Survival Merit Badge some time in the future. They can't take anything with them except a knife, and have to build camp, make fire, all the neat tricks. Boy, that will be a laugh. Can't get Matt to go. Said he wasn't going to let any damn snake eat him. Said I was crazy. Well, I don't consider getting concussions in the rugby field very sane. . . .

I have not seen the Doc about my ear, as I found out that both of them are rather incompetent. Told one of the faculty members to take two aspirin, etc. . . . he nearly died from acute and ruptured appendicitis. Happy note. . . .

The impossible happened. Beas[1] wrote me a letter. He sends his love as he is too broke to send himself. He's in Mississippi, not Texas. Time to go now. Send my love to all as I am in much the same state as Beas.

Love,
[signed] Breece

P.S. Mom, cash that damned check. You're fouling up my bank book. bdp.
P.P.S. Paul Newman has no beard. My first duty upon leaving FUMA is to dispose of my razor. Sorry, girls, Paul will have to do.

1. Mike Beasley, Breece's former teacher and friend at Marshall University.

· · · · To C. R. and Helen Pancake, February 28, 1975

Fork Union, Va.
Feb. 28, 1975

Mr. & Mrs. C. R. Pancake
Milton, W.Va.

Dear Folks,

No news. Just a note to say hello. I have to work this weekend, plus I have duty, so I probably won't have much of a chance to notice any news should it happen.

Mom, I hope the world is still intact. I haven't gotten a clipping in ages. Don't tell me Huntington has no new scandals. Somebody might knock up

————'s daughter . . . that would be real news. Tell them to get busy down there. I don't want just another sleepy town.

Pop, you going to take that ride with me? What if I let Mom drive? Would you trust her? Maybe I'd better, I couldn't find a plastic Jesus, or even one of those scented skunks Pop Amick[1] used to sell. I tell you, America has gone to seed.

Enclosed is the monthly. I've got the monthlies now, oh brother, what next?

I'll be in. Don't look for me till I get there. It'll be after Mar. 8, but I refuse to say when.

Love,
[signed] Breece

1. Pop Amick owned and operated the Milton Amoco station when Breece was a boy. He is fictionalized in Pancake's "The Salvation of Me" and "Fox Hunters."

· · · · · · · To C. R. and Helen Pancake, April 13, 1975

Fork Union, Va.   April 13, 1975

Mr. & Mrs. C. R. Pancake
Milton, W.Va.

Dear Folks,

There isn't a whole lot of news in big Fork Union this week. The usual amount of family shootings . . . etc. For the most part, the biggest thing was my fight and win of a fried egg. I'll explain when I get home. And, by the way, I was accepted into W.V.U. Graduate School of Writing, but still hear nothing from Law School. Will you please get Mike Sunderlands address for me, as I want to ask him about cost of livings, jobs, etc.

The most exciting thing I did this weekend was to watch Matt play rugby, and discuss the problems of the world with a C'ville lawyer who probably wishes I'd let her watch the rugby game. I'll say this, if she was any example of a female lawyer, I want into that Law School as of now. I've just been away too long.

Something I'd like to know: if Jr.[1] is plowing so much, why isn't my garden plowed? Now, I don't want to be rash, but If I can't garden this summer, I'll get a job and apartment in Huntington., and you can get that Smith laddie to mow the yard. W.Va. just has too many reminders of something I lost to let me sit around. I'd go nuts in Milton if I didn't have something to work the piss out of me. Hope you understand. . . .

You may tell Aunt Julia that there is a typewriter[2] just like this one in the Smithsonian. She'd get a kick of that.

Glad to know Grandpa got somebody to do the yard. Glad (mostly) that he's feeling better.

Well you all take care, and I'll talk to you next week.

Love,
[signed]
Breece

1. Jr. Blake was a factory worker and a part-time farmer. A line in "The Honored Dead"—"Somebody's got to dig in the damn ground" (*The Stories*, 123)—has been attributed to him.
2. A 1920 Underwood no. 5.

· · · · · · · · · To C. R. and Helen Pancake, May 5, 1975

Fork Union, Va.
May 5, 1975

Mr & Mrs. C. R. Pancake
Milton, W.Va.

Dear Folks,

You can always tell when I am running out of typing paper. I type on the backs of things. Please keep this one as it is my only record of a request to the dean at M.U.[1]

Well, I was right. They offered me a contract, and avoided offering one to the poor bastards who needed their jobs—and sadly, they are all dedicated to their work. $5522.40 isn't enough to make me endure another year of social isolation, educational sins, and institutional food. I dreamt of one of Mom's pineapple cakes the other night, and nearly cried. But despite that, Matt is hacking his way, and it looks as if he'll be back. His father was really upset with the raise they offered—said the cost of living had gone up 12%, and these people have the male organs to offer us 4%, which isn't even maintenance. By refusing mess I & III, Matt got thirty a month out of the deal, and another ten for living in the barracks, and despite that, he didn't make it close to $6,000. Yeah, it's the old Russian game of Ripoffsky. As Lightfoot said, "If you make a mistake, don't make it twice."[2]

Give us your tired, your poor, your huddled masses . . . It says that at the base of the statue of liberty, yet we're raising hell over those poor people trying to get to our country. I'm never amazed by Americans. I hit a possum the other night and didn't stop to pick him up for stew, so I'm sure this party can hold a few more people.

Harry [Truman] might have loved me, but I found Harry no better than Ford. At least he was better than Nixon—Harry was honest. As for clothes,

I could use a half sole on my boots, but if I walk in the grass they should last another season. I still wear stuff I bought three years ago. It's just getting to the point where it's comfortable. Nice to think I made it through this year on $1200 spending money—I didn't go hungry, and I won't have anything to show for it either, but . . .

Did you ever get a bill from the doctor? Slow fellow. That's about it for this week—I guess the cockroaches will sure miss me when I'm gone—there won't be any Raid to eat. Sure will be good to see home.

Love,
[signed] Breece

P.S. Keep the money! For godsake take it while I've got it to give!

1. Marshall University.
2. A line from Gordon Lightfoot's "Cold on the Shoulder."

· · · · · · · · To C. R. and Helen Pancake, May 11, 1975

Fork Union, Va.
May 11, 1975

Mr. & Mrs. C. R. Pancake
Milton, W.Va.

Where will you be at 65?
"On food stamps, you turkey."

LIFE-TIME PROGRAMS
Life Insurance—Estate Planning
Chase Manhattan Bank Bldg.

Dear Folks,

Mother's Day was started someplace in W.Va.[1] back in the 1800's. That's all I know about it. You see, when I must celebrate a holiday, I must know all about it, and quite frankly, I hope not to become a Mother. But all that aside, HAPPY MOTHER'S DAY, MOM!

About that camping trip . . . Matt went, but I kidded him about sleeping in the car. At three a.m. that ground got the hardest it had been all night, so I spent the next four hours in the front seat of my Whale. Then I rented a row boat, and all they had were canoe paddles—no oar-locks, no oars, just two canoe paddles. Of course, Matt was still at camp, so I had to paddle the jon back to our campsite (we were right on the lake). After making enough circles and figure-eights to qualify for a ticket for drunken boating, I made it back to camp only to be welcomed with, "Oh, I see you got a boat." We explored the vast reaches of Bear Creek Lake, but never found Bear Creek Lake, let alone the Bear, and still can't figure out where all that damn water came from. Maybe they piped it in.

Pop, the ranger at the park was Mr. J. C. Woody. He said he used to work at South Chas.[2] in the gas-separation, and in plastics. He retired around 1960, although he didn't recall your face, he remembered the name. Do you remember him? He was really a nice old guy. Let me use the boat all day for three bucks, then offered to lend me a pole, but I didn't have a license, so I refused.

Besides, I'm sure that with Matt and I splashing around out there all the fish were more concerned with when we were going to leave than with food. Then Mendy came down from D.C. and laughed at us for about four hours. The wind blew my lean-to to pieces, I burned my hand picking up the coffee water, spilled it, and put out the fire. I decided to take a dip, and since the last bit of pride I had left could only be saved by making a good dive from a running start, I did. The dive was one of the most graceful things I've ever done, but the water must have been thirty-three degrees— just one above freezing. The shock sent me swimming back to shore in a speed that must have put Johnny Weissmuller to shame. Matt and Mendy took off for Richmond, and I took a shower (also cold) and broke camp. Next week is the survival thing, and I hope it goes better.

In the meantime, take care.

Love,

[signed] Breece

P.S. The nearest testing center for the LSAT is in Columbus on July 26—so don't make any plans for me that weekend.

1. Mother's day, the second Sunday in May, proposed to honor the mothers of America in 1907 by Anna Jarvis of Grafton, W.Va.
2. Union Carbide is located in South Charleston.

· · · · · · · · To C. R. and Helen Pancake, May 19, 1975

Fork Union, Va.
May 19, 1975

Mr. & Mrs. C. R. Pancake
Milton, W.Va.

Where Will You Be at 65?
"In a hell of a shape."

LIFE-TIME PROGRAMS
Life Insurance-Estate Planning
Chase Manhattan Bank Bldg.

Dear Folks,

The survival campout was a total loss. First, the original group cancelled out due to a class trip they'd rather go on. Then it rained the first day we were supposed to be out, so I called it off for a day, and caught hell. Finally, with the knowledge it was going to rain later that day, I took them out Saturday. I have never seen a more inept group in my life—they couldn't even build a fire. As I was the only one who was dry and had a fire, I said I was staying. Of course, they were all for it. Since they couldn't get much wetter without swimming, I told them to get hiking around to find the plants they needed for their meal (we'd gone over this a hundred [times] before the actual trip). After they were gone over an hour, I got into the car, and took off. They had gone at least two miles up the road to another farm, where they were asking permission to use a tarp the farmer had left out. Thatch roofs (especially the way they made them) didn't seem to be dry enough for them. But because they had knowingly gone off, I took them back [to school].

Been packing like a rat on a sinking ship. Funny how I'm not leaving with much more than I brought. Matt is talking quitting. While on duty, one of the finer young men called him a "stupid son of a bitch", to which, Matt grabbed the kid by the arm, shook him, and told him to watch his mouth. The kid called da-da, who called Matt, and more or less threatened him. It was really bothering him until I told him that if I'd been called an etc., I'd have probably beaten the kid within an inch of his life, and called Whitescarver[1] two minutes before so that I couldn't be held responsible to the Academy (in other words, quit then beat the shit out of the little bastard, and if his old man wanted to get froggy on the phone, tell him to hop on over and get me.)[2] That's what Johnny Cox[3] would have done to me, plus I'd get it from both of you when I got home.

Mom, you knew about my pool-room background. I was one of the best. Haven't played since I left home. Stupid Va. doesn't have a billiards table[4] that's half white or at all safe. I've tried to get a game to bet Matt on, he doesn't believe I'm any good. . . .

This week is finals, so I'll probably not write again unless it's a note.

Take care, and remember, I love you.
[signed] Breece

P.S. Will be in the 30th.

1. Dean of Fork Union Military Academy.
2. Breece was working on "The Scrapper." A line very similar to this appears in the story: "[A]nytime you get to feelin' froggy, just hop on over to your Uncle Skeevy."
3. Milton High track coach.
4. Breece was fond of playing pool.

[Summer 1975]

Mr. & Mrs. C. R. Pancake
Milton, W.Va.

Hi Folks,

"Jarfly" Johnson[1] claimed there was a catfish under the big rock at Zoar Church, and it was so big he had to cut his line for fear of drowning.

Well, Jr. Blake and me, we got this idea as to catch that monster. We took his tractor and winch over there with a logging hook, but we still needed live bait. So we got Dick Bias' wig and put it on Ching Ball along with one of Mom's old Lois Lane dresses (you know—with the shoulder pads like a line backer?), and roped Ching to the logging hook and threw him in.

Ching, he swum under that rock, and directly there was a great commotion. The sky got all dark, virgin timber shook its roots free and ran, and that big old rock, it quivered till the water was foamy as the cup in Glenn Perry's shop.

Pretty soon that big catfish came out of there like a torpedo from hell. He was going so fast they had to close the flood gates at Huntington to keep down the waves, and the explosion sent that big old rock clear up into the yard at Zoar Church—five souls were saved on the spot.

Well, Ching crawled out of that mess all slimy and grinning ear to ear, but his wig was gone.

Jr., he said, "What's you do to that fish?"

"I kissed him," said Ching.

We had to buy Dick another wig, It's been that way all summer.

Love,
[signed] Breece

1. Breece was trying to outdo the storytellers back home with this tall tale about "Jarfly" Johnson.

Milton, W.Va.
[August] 1975

Mr. John Casey
Rugby Rd.
Charlottesville, Va.

Dear Mr. Casey,

The hill-country was grand. The fishing only fair, but I brought a few back, and a piece of the hills (enclosed since I can't mail you the fish.) This is yours, and you don't have to read it, comment or anything. Mostly I'm sending it to show you I'm still writing. It has been my experience that CW teachers don't believe CW students write. I'm sure there's precedent for this, and justification.

Your house-sitter said you were vacationing. Enjoy it. Teachers are in season before turkeys, you know.

My home-town paper just called, and they want me to do some feature writing. It's only a tabloid, but for the Catch-22 of the job market, it's experience, anyway.

Did you get all that junk I sent to Rugby Rd.? I took the LSAT, and have little hope of ever joining that learned profession. Veni, sedi, excessi.[1]

Let me know if any waves break, etc. In the meantime, I remain, etc.

Sincerely,
[signed] Breece Pancake

1. Breece changed Julius Caesar's "Veni, vidi, vici" (I came, I saw, I conquered) to "I came, I saw, I exceeded."

· · · · To C. R. and Helen Pancake, September 4, 1975

Staunton, Va.
Sept. 4, 1975

Mr. & Mrs. C. R. Pancake
Milton, W.Va.

Dear Mom and Pop,

S.M.A.[1] was even better than I anticipated. Outside of the great pay, the headmaster[2] is a genuine educator, an artist, and easy going as hell. He's the opposite of Ronnie Clark.

One of the fringe benefits is Mary Baldwin College—next door—a girls school of great size! Of course the snooker table is in walking distance. The rooms are small, but plentiful. I can use as many as I like . . . all unconnected, except by a hallway.

I feel as if I shouldn't have left you at this time, but I want you to know I'll be home as soon as I can. Promise you'll call if you need me. If anything happens, call.[3]

Everything considered, this year promises to be much better than last. I'm going into C'ville to see Casey about "sitting in" on his writing classes. You may inform all concerned that I'm happy (beardless, but happy) and give them my love.

Mostly, my thanks for summer, and my love to both of you. You put up with me, and that says a lot.

More as it develops,

Love
[signed] Breece

P.S. Save my mail until I can send a decent address.

1. Staunton Military Academy.
2. Preston Doyle.
3. C. R. was gravely ill at the time. He died four days later on Sept. 8, 1975.

· · · · · · · · · · To Helen Pancake, September 14, 1975

Staunton, Va.
Sept. 14, 1975

Mrs. C. R. Pancake
Milton, W.Va.

Dear Mom,

Just a note to tell you I've made it back to Staunton. Everything's O.K. I guess Doni will be leaving tomorrow, and by the time you read this, you'll be wrapped up in red-tape and paper. If you need me for anything, please call, but I trust your common sense will get you through most decisions. Legal matters, however, should be given to Sam[1] since the law is not based on common sense.

Soon, the leaves will be turning on Afton Mountain, and I hope you'll will be here to see them. You could bring Helen S. and make a dual trip, or you could come alone.

A truck wreck on 60 made me re-route via turnpike—460–N81. A much better but longer route. Maybe you'll want to come that way rather than battle the mountains. See you soon.

Love,
[signed]
Breece

1. Sam Harshbarger (1928–1992) former West Virginia Supreme Court chief justice, family friend, and attorney. He helped settle the estate after C. R. Pancake's death on Sept. 8, 1975.

· · · · · · · · · · To Helen Pancake, September 24, 1975

Staunton, Va.   Sept. 24, 1975

Mrs. C. R. Pancake
Milton, W.Va.

Dear Mom,

Just got off Barracks Duty and will jot this note as I relax before bed. Thanks for the letter and clippings. Despite the slantedness of the articles, etc. it was sad that he had to die. I've been tempted to buy a pistol before they legislate them off the market, but I don't know. Guns are good for one thing. Poor Jerry[1] had better stay clear of California—third time is charmed.

Casey finally got "The Scrapper," and used it in his class last night. It went over well, and most of the complaints were things I'd already noticed—minor stuff, like things Cally says, or the snake-eater image. Casey's offered to write a facing letter for the story to "Atlantic" after I've been baptized by fire from "Playboy." He seems to think it's worth the postage, but I don't—at any rate I've got to send it to "Playboy" before he will write the letter to "Atlantic"—I know that sounds silly but it's the difference between 1000 and 2000 dollars "Playboy" paying the latter.

Going to see the Frazier-Ali fight with Casey next Tuesday.[2] Keep your fingers crossed for Joe he's waited a long long time to beat Ali. The fight-game is almost gone but I remember Pop watching the big names on T.V. It was the only sport he ever enjoyed and in that respect I'm his son. I find myself becoming more like him. I've been doing it for years and I guess it was what I've always wanted. At least I'm comfortable at it. He was a good old boy and to imitate him wouldn't be a mistake.

Please tell Aunt Julia I don't want to put her through the desk thing. That desk is very much a part of her life and while she is living it should be with her as a reminder of the well-organized man[3] she loved. "There is a time for every purpose" and now is not the time. I'd much rather have her come here for T-giving if she could make it (and if you're willing to bring her). Perhaps I could come in the following weekend.

Whale[4] is sick. She's took to screaming at me when I want heat or air of any kind. I can't get her fixed before payday but will drive as little as possible until then.

For the first time in over a year I'm really teaching. Things are working out quite well. If only I weren't playing "Big Army" as Danny used to say it would be quite satisfactory. Better stop now. Remember to save some coleus this winter.

All my love,
[signed] Breece

1. Breece is referring to the two assassination attempts on President Gerald Ford that occurred on Sept. 5, 1975, in Sacramento, Calif., when Lynette "Squeaky" Fromm pointed but did not fire a .45 caliber pistol, and on Sept. 22, 1975, in San Francisco when Sara Jane Moore fired a .38 caliber pistol in the direction of the president.

2. Heavyweight championship fight between Muhammad Ali and Joe Frazier in Manila, Philippines, Oct. 1, 1975. Ali barely defeated Frazier in this brutal bout. See Pancake's letter to John Casey, Mar. 25, 1979.

3. Mont Ward (1881–1964), Aunt Julia's husband and Breece's great-uncle, the former mayor of Milton.

4. Breece's nickname for his blue 1964 Cadillac was "The Great Blue Whale."

· · · · · · · · · · · · To Helen Pancake, October 5, 1975

Staunton, Va.
Oct. 5, 1975

Mrs. C. R. Pancake
Milton, W.Va.

Dear Mom,

Received your note upon return Sunday. O.K.—around 2 pm the 25th, and plans O.K. all around. As it were, I didn't get to Uncle Ray's or the Heards'. The Heards were leaving when I called from Union Station—going to Harrisonburg, Va. I then called Melinda,[1] whose parents were in from Fla., and she asked me to join their party, etc., and by departure 26 hours later, I'd had a grand total of three hours to talk to Melinda. She's doing well, and I implored the Heard's to continue plans as it is only twelve bucks RT and a very nice ride on the train. Nonetheless, I'll get to Rockville before T-giving—I hope to God.

Cellar is quite warm, home, etc. I'm sure you'll love it. Will probably have the money for instant oats when you arrive, so M & G as well as yourself will eat here. What is their diet? I can't cook it if I don't know it. This is important to me. My sanity was ready for this apt. Too long I've been subject to dictates. Both Preston[2] (Head master) and Chuck[3] (Commandant) were here to congratulate me on the place, and drank a stout to celebrate.

Rumor has it that the Alumni Assoc. is planning to buy SMA from Leoffler.[4] This could be the best thing going, but if Leoffler continues to run the place, it only has inches to go before ground. He's a fish (a Born Again

Christian), and tries to force Jesus down all our throats. The families are against it, the faculty, the administration, the cadets are all against it. Last mandatory Chapel, I marched my young ass to Mass, and later to the First Presbyterian, then that night to the Baptists. I spent most of that day in one church or another. This country gave us the freedom of religion, and a right to bear arms, and I'll be a shitass before I let someone rob me of my basic rights. Let it suffice that I'm getting on all right. Yes, I'm looking forward to seeing you, and I hope you feel the same. Let me know how everybody's doing . . .

Love,
[signed] Breece

P.S. Note from ———— (M's wife) with copy of "Scrapper" in which she compared herself to Cally in the story. Cally was described as "the perfect woman"—God, I feel sorry for Mitch.[5]

1. Matthew Heard's girlfriend. Matt Heard died on Sept. 29, 1975.
2. Preston Doyle.
3. Chuck Kegley.
4. Layne Leoffler purchased Staunton Military Academy in 1973 and declared bankruptcy in 1976. He was a former graduate of the school.
5. One of Breece's cousins.

· · · · · · · · · · · · To Helen Pancake, October 15, 1975

Staunton, Va.
Oct. 15, 1975

Mrs. C. R. Pancake
Milton, W.Va.

Dear Mom,
Many thanks for the cookies, they were great. Unfortunately, I got them in the presence of the entire office, so about half of them were gone before I could get to the coffee machine. The entire staff and faculty as SMA now knows what a good cook my mother is. They send their compliments. Everyone remarked about the black walnuts. That's a clincher.

Grades, writing, and the typing of "Scrapper" has been keeping me out of trouble. I've yet to find the time to change my lesson plans to the point where I don't get ten comps. a day. I've created a monster.

Speaking of creations, the latest (are you ready?) story[1] I'm doing is the one about that girl who stared at the monkey cage too long, etc. Because the simple truth (that the monkies marked her baby) is too hard to believe, I'm working in incest as a possible reason for the deformity, but dwelling on the normality of the child's mind. I know you don't like my over-abundance of strange themes, but you must remember people read that kind of stuff because their minds are so normal it bores them.

Mindi isn't coming down, which is a big load off. I was really not in the frame of mind to see her again. She said Mr. & Mrs. Heard are doing O.K. I mailed them Matt's watch. I don't think I told you why I had his watch—we got pretty polluted after the first week here, and I woke up with his watch. Never saw him again.

I have duty all next weekend, plus the fact that it's Parent's Weekend. If you don't hear from me, you'll know I'm going crazy. Planning on going to Ray's the first weekend in Nov. Going either by bus or Amtrak. Whale is bleeding me dry on gas. Won't bring her home Christmas, either.

Speaking of Christmas, I intend to be home if Suzanna (not Suzanne) gets it together. Otherwise, I'd like to split up the holiday, and go to Nag's Head for a week and work on a story.[2] But that's all so far away. I'll tell Beas to drop by. By the way, Suzanna was one of my students at HHS[3] and is now at MU. Dr. Carr gave her my address, and she's been writing ever since. Figure that one out.

I'm sorry but I can't get it together to answer Gloria. It's not that I'm bitter or anything. I can honestly say I have nothing to say to her or Paula. In truth, that isn't all that bad.

It just dawned on me that Mitch never did send that ms. he made such a big deal about not taking stamps for. Could you send me his address? I don't appreciate copies floating all over hell and creation for long periods of time. One guy at Iowa just sent back "Fox"[4] after four months. . . .

Please give my love to everybody especially Mammaw, Grandpaw and Aunt Julia. Glad to know you'll be working. It'll be the best thing. God knows Milton isn't enough to excite people through that stretch in Jan. and Feb.

No. Don't haul a bunch of junk over here for the winter. I'll need the tires, but that's about all. Again, this is a one year job. This time I'm working on Civil Service. (civil). I've got a rating, etc. All I want is a job in West Virginia. Also, something might come up with Iowa or P-Exeter, I'll sign a contract, and if I have to, break it; if I don't, I still have a job.

Hope this finds you well and getting out. I enjoy your accounts of the various trips you've taken. That must be where I get my writing. I meet my share of people, too, and getting along.

All my love, and take good care. Again, thanks for the cookies. They'll make me fatter than gallons of beer.

Love,
[signed] Breece

1. "The Mark."
2. Breece began this story, "The Conqueror," but only a fragment exists and is included in this volume.
3. Huntington High School, where Breece did his student teaching.
4. "Fox Hunters."

· The Conqueror

Of Pancake's many short story fragments, "Conqueror," like "Trilobites" and "The Honored Dead," is a direct attempt to mine the memory of his father. Pancake used his father's war letters as a resource for this story, letters that were subsequently destroyed in the late spring of 1979. The story has to do with an alcoholic war veteran who stops to pick up a young "tramp" who is on his way to work as a "carney" in Kitty Hawk along the outer banks of North Carolina. The Pancake family vacationed there during the 1960s.

CONQUEROR also titled THE SAMARITANS

Characters

Sgt. "Beetle" Bailey (Ret.)—WWII veteran on way to old training camp in North Carolina outerbanks to visit C.O. (Ret.).
Max—A rubbertire tramp whose car has broken down on his way to work a carnival at Kitty Hawk.

[Sketch]

Bailey picks Max up at ——— and a few towns later; stops to buy a fifth, lets Max drive. Bailey talks about his son—a failure, about his wife—a teetotaler old bat, about his war days. He is mild, friendly and thirsty.

Halfway or so, Max stops for lunch and coaxes Bailey to leave the bottle in the car because there's beer inside. In the restaurant, Bailey almost starts a fight, but Max steps in, "He's just a drunk old man. I ain't drunk or old." The challengers back off and Max shuffles Bailey out to the car. He passes out and we get Max's reflections on the situation: Lost Colony [located on Roanoke Island, N.C.] Max tosses the bottle out.

Bailey awakens, claims to be getting sick; Max pulls off on a fire road. Bailey gets the dry heaves and Max feeds him water until it all comes up. Bailey whimpers something about when he was a kid, his mother told him, "Now you gone and put a little pison in your stomach and you'll never get it out." A car load of high school kids pull up, football player types, and razz Bailey's tags: Disabled veteran. Bailey straightens, stops leaning on the hood: "Reach under the seat and hand me my .45. I'm gonna' ventilate their engine." Max reaches, but there is no gun. The bluff works and the car backs out.

Bailey looks for the bottle as Max drives. Max won't own up, but Bailey knows he's tossed it. He orders Max out of his car, cursing: "Goddamn the man that'd pour out another man's drink." Bailey pulls out, weaving and Max looks out across the bay bridge until Bailey's car disappears on the other side. He sees the giant ferris wheel glistening in the sun, its colors barely discernible in the white sky. He is too late to set up, too late even to work. Behind him are the stagnant swamps. He looks in his wallet, picks up his suitcase and tools. He could lay up in motel for a few days: it was still spring, and the college kids wouldn't have the good jobs yet. He started walking across the bridge.

[Fragment of first draft]

Now he lay awake on the shack's floor, huddled in his jacket, and listened to the field mice scratching at the walls. The rain drizzled, turned into mist, and tree frogs clicked, groaned; it was almost morning, and he knew Boss Pruitt would fire him if he didn't set up the ferris wheel in Kitty Hawk today. He watched a blue glow of early light outside the door until he saw Carolina pines against a foggy sky. He stood, squeezing water from his shoes, and brushed dirt from his clothes. He switched on his flashlight, found a last slosh of wine in the bottle, finished it; then he threw the bottle on the floor littered with rags, all dry, but no wood among them for fire. He wanted coffee. He thought of his home in West Virginia, then smiled; years with the carnies, years with the ferris wheel, years gave him no word like home.

He walked through the doorway into the yard. At his feet, packed in mud and ringed by the rain, lay a shiny yellow cat's eye marble. He picked it up, rolled it between his fingers, and it showed yellow lights high in the air, turning. He switched off his flashlight, dropped the marble in his pocket, and looked back at the tar-paper shack. Walking through the white clay fields with broken rows of long-dead cotton, he came to the highway's berm where his convertible was parked. Patche[s] of tape had peeled away in the rain, soaking the seats and leaving puddles in the floor. He raised the hood, looked again at the hairline crack along one side of the engine block, then slammed it shut. From the trunk he took a suitcase and a large wooden tool box, left the keys dangling from the lock. Behind the road's eastern rise, the sunlight pines and a breeze shook drops from them in yellow sparks. He leaned against the fender and watched light glinting from chrome as the first few cars whistled past his thumb.

He had seen Boss fire slackers and no-shows: Boss called them crotch-licking punks and first-of-Mays, and his eyes bugged as he yelled. He tried to think of a sharp answer, but Boss never left room for sharp answers.

He smoked a cigarette and watched a higher sun seep through the fog.

Along the edge of the field a quail piped and led her chicks into the woods; when he looked westward again, a new station wagon was pulling up. An old man rolled down the window, his face straining as he leaned, and he spoke through the half-opened window, a voice without breath: "Can you drive?"

He nodded, but when the old man slid across the seat, he saw the pinchers of an artificial hand unclamp the wheel. He put his suitcase and tools in the back, and climbed in to drive.

The old man laughed, held up his plastic arm "Long drive wears me out. Leg's the same way. He tapped his left leg with the pinchers, then jerked his head toward the convertible as they pulled away. "Your car?"

"Nobody's now." He watched the car disappear in the wing mirror; when they topped the eastern hill, the sun started overhead, out of his eyes. He stared at the road, tried not to look at the old man's arm. "How far you going?"

"To the last stop sign before you hit the ocean. Going for a reunion at the airbase at the outer banks."

"I'll drive as far as Kitty Hawk." He took a ticket book from his shirt pocket, handed it to the old man. "I work for Pruitt's Amusements. You and your buddies have fun on me. Say Max sent you."

"Appreciate it. Got any show girls?" The old man leafed through the tickets and his claw clicked as he turned each one.

"None worth seeing."

He handed Max the book. "Thanks, but I ain't been to a carnival since my boy was little. He didn't take to it much either."

"Kids are funny that way."

The old man reached under the seat, dragged out a fifth of whiskey, poured a cup full and offered Max the bottle. "Kids are a pain in the ass."

He waved the bottle away, pointed to a thermos, and the old man poured Max a cup of coffee then sloshed down his liquor.

"Kids done this to me." He held up his arm, shuffled his leg. "One of them dedicated German youths. Yessir, kids and wives both. You married, Max?"

He shook his head, watched the pines blur by and the bright yellow lines slip past his window.

"Good for you. I been married thirty-five years and this is the first time I been away her since the war."

Max looked at the bottle and grinned: a half-pint was already gone. "Careful you don't founder yourself on that stuff."

"Goddamn it, can't a man take a drink without a tee-totaling wise crack?"

"Didn't mean nothing by it." Max watched the pines fade away to open fields of beans and young cotton. Far back in every field were shacks; some standing, some caved in, some still with families. The field steamed in the sun, and down one side road to a shack he saw ruined toys.

The old man capped the bottle, stuck it under the seat, and leaned his head against the window. He closed his eyes and his jaws went slack, then he opened his eyes, turned to face Max. "Why'd you join a carnival?"

Max shrugged. "Got tired of using a mule's ass for a compass. I wanted to look around."

[end of fragment]

• • • • • • • • • • • • • • To Helen Pancake, October 1975

Staunton, Va.
Oct. 28? 1975

Mrs. C. R. Pancake
Milton, W.Va.

Dear Mom,

After Nov. 1, my address should read 324 East Beverly St., Cellar, Staunton, etc. After pulling duty all weekend, I was awakened at 6 a.m. by the screams of cadets. Pardon my French, but I said, "Screw this shit."

On my constitutional, I stopped off at Mrs. (Pancake) Mandeville's house, and she told me of the apt. It is furnished with antiques, has a fireplace, back yard complete with squirrel, two bedrooms, dining room, sitting room, garage, and is within walking distance to the Academy. Of course, it's in the best side of town, in the basement of a really neat old house, and a widow named Mrs. Nutt lives above me. She wanted somebody in the house because she's away a lot, or so I gather. On top of that, I can afford it and still save money as long as I eat at the Academy twice a day. . . .

Mom, you don't know what a relief it is to get out of these barracks. I must be asocial, but I can't exist under these conditions. I haven't told anybody about it, and plan to keep this room as a sort of stop-over when I pull duty. I'm moving a little at a time so no one will notice. Don't worry about it jeopardizing my job. Preston won't give a good damn whether I'm here or not, as long as I do my job. . . .

You can stay at my place, and if Mammaw and Grandpa can take sleeping in the same bed, they're welcome, too. When you come, I'd like you to meet Mrs. Mandeville—she's really a nice lady. I'm so glad you and Pop taught me to respect and be friendly to elders. It's never been a bad thing.

Work to do—Love,
[signed] Breece

· · · · · · · · · · · To Helen Pancake, November 9, 1975

324 E. Beverly St.   Staunton, Va.
Nov. 9, 1975
Sunday 8:30 a.m.

Mrs. C. R. Pancake
Milton, W.Va.

Dear Mom,

Thanks for the letter updating me on all the goings on. Before I forget, I don't need curtains, but I would like my plates, pans, silver, etc. There is only some (willow) odd pieces and no flatware. That and the tires I need, and if you can't get the rest of the junk in the car—leave it. I realize you have to have a suitcase, etc, and even have doubts about getting those tires in the trunk. (By the way, let some man get those out—they are too heavy.)

Yesterday I picked up the rake Mrs. Nutt had leaned against my stoop and began to rake. I thought it was a hint, so I raked up all the leaves in the back. It hadn't been a hint, and she was rather surprised to find that tools fit my hands (now, I've really got a problem). She then took me to her farm in Middlebrook and let me fish in her trout pond for free. Caught a 3 lb. rainbow and a smaller spotted, which we had for lunch. She's really very nice— somewhat difficult to relate to her D.A.R. Republican party attitude, but a nice lady. She really wanted to meet you all, but she's leaving for her kid's house the 17th. . . .

Granted, I've got it pretty plush here, but I can't count on SMA being here after June. Leoffler is really a sick puppy. Mom, that school has a dedicated faculty and administration—mostly decent kids—it could be so much, yet it's sad to see Leoffler make public statements like, "I hated it when I went there, now I'll see it close." Revenge? Who knows? The turkey's flipped a gobble. . . .

Tuck[1] like Grandpa is too good. The world is very harsh for good people. Harsh and hard to understand. Both men have gone on in smiles and tears while people walk on their hearts. It isn't fair. Mom, there's no place in Staunton worth eating at. All are starchy spoons, etc. Let me cook. Why do you think I rented this place? Because I like privacy and good food. I'm glad you're proud of me. Hope I can do more and better in the future. Once in a while, the gypsy comes back, but her song means less—is harder to hear. Better get ready for the organ prelude at First Pres. Bach today, I think.

All my love,
[signed] Breece

P.S. Would like my blue wool boatman's coat and blue coffee pot.

1. Clifton "Tucker" Frazier, Breece's uncle.

9

1976–1977

To Helen Pancake, January 2, 1976

324 E. Beverly St.
Staunton, Va.
Jan. 2, 1976

Mrs. C. R. Pancake
Milton, W.Va.

Dear Mom,

Many thanks for your letter. I'm eating hot tuna, and trying to get this out before tonight. Story work slow and hard, but that's a sign—nearly had a breakdown writing Scrapper. What I have so far is pretty good—one more draft should do it.

Had New Years with Mrs. Nutt, and sundried Pancakes. She had a dinner party. For me I think. At any rate, I was then invited to a party on Waverley Hill (the home of Mrs. Pancake of UVA, Wilson, board fame—now, of course, dead). That turned out to be cousin Robins [*sic*] P. and Emily and Dorie Smith—also cousins. That is the first time I've ever been served creme de menthe for desert, and I was afraid to ask what it was. Figured it out later. Waverley Hill is a goddamn mansion. Makes Monticello look cheaply built and small. Boxwoods, too. Think I'll introduce Robins to Mindi. He lives in D.C. and has a UVA law degree, isn't bad looking and has a good personality. Our combined efforts on the family shows that I descended from Abe, they from Phillip, and most likely the Huntington clan from Isaac. E.g., we're as close in kin as the pin oak, the white oak and the red oak—if you want to go back to the first tree, they are the same breed.[1]

Amtrak over sold seats, and that was a real bummer of a trip. You know people can really be shits, and they always seem to take it out on the waiters. Spent most of the trip standing up between cars as I did on the way to Mazatlan, Mx.,[2] and talking to the conductors between stops. Just got bored with the people in the cars bitching their heads off. Been thinking about that certificate you have in the bank for me, and appreciate the thought. Nonetheless, you and Dad gave me a lot, good breeding, background and education. I can take it from there. I want you to keep that money and use it as you need to. You may not need it now, but it can serve you far better than I. I'm young and can make my own place—I'm Saturday's child, remember? Just thought you'd sleep better knowing you weren't so short on savings.

Got to get a note off to Char, then back to work. Love you and think of you often. Regards to all.

[signed] Breece

1. Abraham Pancake settled on Storms Creek near Ironton, Ohio, Isaac Pancake (Abraham's brother) settled on Bear Creek near Ironton, and Phillip Pancake (another brother) settled near Romney, West Virginia, ca. 1758.

2. Breece traveled to Mexico in 1972.

· · · · · · · · · · · · To Helen Pancake, January 11, 1976

324 E. Beverly St.
Staunton, Va.
Jan. 11, 1976

Mrs. C. R. Pancake
Milton, W.Va.

Dear Mom,

The story[1] is coming along really well, and may mean something after all—many thanks for telling me that weird story this summer. Without you, I might be writing like John Boy Walton—soft soap. If you pick up anything else weird, let me know.

Moving again, but not so far—Just upstairs. Mrs. Nutt has found a renter for this apt. who promises to stay awhile, so she's offered me a room in the main house, the Library, and kitchen priv's for a lot less rent. Why not?

Preston is leaving soon, and I guess things must get worse from that point on. Nonetheless, I've made my bed for the next few (Maybe very few) months, and I'll lie in it. What the hell, Pop put up with much more than this, and I can wear his clothes.

Mom, Im afraid my being first on the list as Aunt Jul's exec. is pretty worthless. The only thing that matters is the old gal herself—when she dies, we can only say good-bye. I reckon I'll say it as a mourner, and go on my way. Let them take what they want, and as much thereof as they can carry, we knew her, and that's what counts most. By only asking me to do it, she recognized my adulthood, and that means so much to me, I have no words for it. I hope she sees a hundred.[2]

As for yourself, I hope this finds you well. I wanted to call you this afternoon, but I got my bill this week, so I'm being a good boy. Soon the phone will be out, so if you need to call me, just call Mrs. Nutt after five—I'm usually home at that hour. Don't call on a Wednesday. Class at UVA.

Guess I filled you in on the happenings after New Years, so I won't bore you with that. Mostly I've been writing like a SOB, and doing my physical program. The sweats are very handy, and on cold nights, I sleep in them.

First chance, I'll get a letter off to Shorty and Ray Glenn[3]—two fantastic people. We have a fellow here who was once a pilot—pilot?—yeah—and he used to drink a lot. Well, one day his wife called the maintenance office about her furnace being out, and the man said, "Is your pilot lit?" and his wife said, "Oh, is Austin drunk again?"

Wrote to Char and Doni, but no word as yet. Again, hope this finds you well. Many thanks for the clipping on the bridge as it fit (Silver Bridge)[4] into my story very well. Don't work too long a week.

Love, [unsigned]

1. "The Mark."
2. Aunt Julia Pancake Ward died three months before her one-hundredth birthday in 1981.
3. Shorty Hollandsworth and Ray Glenn, two friends from Milton.
4. A bridge collapsed in Point Pleasant, W.Va. This served as a detail in "The Mark."

· · · · · · · · · · · To Helen Pancake, January 14, 1976

324 E. Beverly St.
Staunton, Va.
Jan. 14, 1976

Mrs. C. R. Pancake
Milton, W.Va.

Dear Mom,

I guess you got the letter I mailed Mon., so there isn't that much news with me. Just wanted to let you know I'm not in the hospital—it seems everyone else is. Also, I'd like to send my regrets to Glen.[1] I didn't know his wife very well, and mostly I was afraid to talk to her—she always scared me. I guess I subconsciously recalled asking for Dale, and her reply. But that really doesn't matter, and didn't mean I didn't like her. She was a good woman and a hard worker.

Also, I'm going to have my ear done in soon,[2] and want you to promise to get your foot worked on this summer. I'll be home and more than willing to wait on you and keep the house while you're down. All I'm going to do is get some thing to keep the snakes off my legs, and tramp the rivers with Hinton[3] (if the old buzzard lasts the winter). My next project is the mine wars (and to beat Mary Lee[4] to the punch), so I'll start with him. Also, I'll fish in the mornings, and be back home before nine. Good enough? . . .

We are living one day at a time here at SMA, and as Chairman of English, I can assure you Mr. ———, that your son will leave this school with vertical and horizontal articulation. I don't know what it means either, but I put it on a lot of report cards. Yeah, if the place lasts, I'll be happy for a few more months—I only wish I could deliver a better program, but the Big D won't fork the money we need for materials. I can only get what I make the boys buy, and that's almost always books. We need the aid of posters relating to the themes, things to inspire some imagination, and better prepared lessons.

Just about the time I move in with a permanent chaperone, I get a girl friend in Staunton, Mary Baldwin girl, and quite intelligent, but a little crazy. I always get the weirdo's, don't I? The major thing is that she's from only a mile away from Gloria. Fortunately, she doesn't know Gloria exists. Anyway, she's some kind of companion until May—I never need girls after May anyway. Hope this finds you well, and let me know when you plan to leave for AZ—WA. Give my regards to Mammaw and Grandpa and Aunt Jul.

Love you,
[signed] Breece

1. Glen Crookshank, family friend and hunting partner.
2. Breece suffered severe earaches and headaches probably due to a head injury when he wrecked the Chevy Impala in Huntington.
3. Hinton Richmond. Breece wrote an article about him, "Hinton Richmond: Man of the Woods," in *Cabell Record*, Aug. 13, 1975. He was one of those old-timers whom Breece called a "walking encyclopedia." Hinton Richmond was born in 1897 and lived east of town on Route 60. He worked for International Nickel and spent the rest of his time walking the woods and fishing.
4. Mary Lee Settle. She was beginning work on *The Scapegoat*, a novel about the mine wars in West Virginia. Pancake soon began working on "Hollow."

324 E. Beverly St.   Staunton, Va.
Feb. 8, 1976

Mrs. C. R. Pancake
Milton, W.Va.

Dear Mom,

Hope this finds you well, and into some kind of routine again. The craziness of this place is too much to discuss in a short letter, but somehow, we are staying above the water line. Only four more months, and the last two will go quickly. . . .

Have heard nothing from nobody. If you didn't write, I'd only get mail from the IRS. By the way, I screwed up my taxes like all hell, but have the comfort that 75% of the public made the same mistake.

Next Friday, I have a date at Casey's for dinner, and a Writer's breakfast the following Sunday at UVA's Lawn. The Pancake's had me to dinner last week, and Mrs. Wm. Pancake had me Thursday. You won't believe this—a ——— maid served dinner to the left side, and the whole bit. What a trip these Southerners are. Tonight I dine with Mrs. Nutt, and tomorrow her ——— is coming to be a maid. I don't believe this. Mother, this can't be happening to me.

Church was pleasant today—all musical service, and so much time to think about things. My old building in Huntington burned down,[1] so that was bothering me.

Preston is much happier in N.C., and the office here is going nuts trying to get accreditation—too many teachers who aren't certified to teach. . . .

Let me know if I can help with anything, and plan some things for me to do while I'm not writing. A clean story this time, but I'll find something weird to interject into it.

Must plan tomorrow's lessons.

Love you,
[signed]
Breece

Letter from Rivanna—U.Va.'s Literary magazine—they are interested in "The Mark" for their next issue. Hold your breath, I may be published!

1. Breece's apartment building where he lived during his student days at Marshall University in Huntington burned down.

324 E. Beverly St.
Staunton, Va.
Feb. 29, 1976

Mrs. C. R. Pancake
Milton, W.Va.

Dear Mom,

It has been something of a trying week, and the worst is yet to come with grades and duty. The coast of Mexico has never looked better in my mind, but I'd feel as if I was letting you and Pop down if I flew the coup. [sic]

It looks as if I'll be taking German all summer at MU, so there goes any idea of a vacation. Still, I may get some fishing and roaming in. This is for the grad language requirement, therefore important to get over with. May have to arrange some room with Mamaw and Grandpaw, as I don't want to be shuttling back and forth during the week.

Yesterday I put the top down and drove over to the plant[1] I helped build, visited the Poe's and FUMA, then came home. It took the day, and got some of the gypsy out of my system. The Blue Gill[2] is trucking right along, and giving me 35 mpg. If the weather is this nice at break, I'll drive it over the mountains.

Bob Nutt wants me to help him do some write-ups about the farm, and I'm mulling over an artical [sic] about the Staunton interest in WVa coal to circulate free-lance (and probably for free). To top that, I've promised John[3] a story by the end of March, and I have very little time to write it. May have to put the Staunton artical [sic] on wraps until I finish the other commitments.

Also, Bob hinted at my living in the cabin[4] on the farm this summer (fish for free in the back pond), but all these good things come when I can't take them. So I hinted back at a rain-check.

By now you have the Rivanna, and I hope you enjoyed the story.[5] Getting in print has a strange effect—you feel like writing more because "everybody's read that one." Hope you are enjoying your job and social life. Mrs. Nutt throws about three parties a week, and it really helps her. I'm convinced she'd die without them.

It looks as if the crops will be bad this year unless we have a wet spring. Guess I won't have my garden—again. Give my regards to everyone, and I'll be home the last week in March. Dig some worms.

Love you,
[signed] Breece

1. Located in Louisa, Va.
2. Breece's blue Volkswagen convertible.
3. John Casey. The story is probably "Cowboys and Girls," which was eventually published as "The Way It Has to Be."
4. "Faraway," a hunting cabin on the Nutt farm in Middlebrook, Va.
5. "The Mark" was published in *Rivanna* on Feb. 25, 1976.

· · · · · · · · · · · · · To Helen Pancake, April 12, 1976

324 E. Beverly St.   Staunton, Va.
April 12, 1976

Mrs. C. R. Pancake
Milton, W.Va.

Dear Mom,

Obviously some time has lapsed—I've finished "Hollow," sent it to Casey, gotten a letter (finally!) from U.Va. to confirm my appointment, and sent (again—Mr. Taylor's letter didn't get to Robie McCauley [*sic*] before they sent my stories back—this is getting expensive—$3.00 every trip to Chicago!) my mss.[1] to Playboy's Robie McCauley [*sic*].

Buddy's[2] nuptual [*sic*] came as more of a shock than you might have imagined. The main character of "Hollow" was named Buddy, so whatever chemistry took place launched a space ship—"Hollow" was giving me royal pains until your call. I guess the great respect I've had for Buddy sticking out a hard life made him sort of a demi-God—he had the guts to do something I could never do, at least as long as I knew there was an easier way to get from A to B. But Buddy getting married? That's like saying Hitler found Christ—it just don't mesh. Nonetheless, I'm glad to know he isn't sleeping under a bridge or with a whore. He was always good to me, and I liked him—he'll be a good father—hell, he knows enough tails to wag that boy's ear off. If you get his address, send it. I'd like to congratulate him and wish them well.

When you come over, I'll "get sick"—take a few days off, and we'll buzz around a little—there isn't much to see, but it takes some driving to do it. Plan the middle of May—that's pretty slack and U.Va. is over with on the 1st. Of course, that's always a holiday—May 1st.

Also, I think I'll zoom to the beach the day school is out (June 6) and remain there thru and including the 10th. My test is on the 12th, and registration at M.U. the 14th or something. Anyway, I'd like to get some sun and fun before school starts—this time back on the "other" side of the desk.

Hope this goes well with your plans. No word from my "silent sisters." What gives?

Pulled my left leg playing rugby, and can hardly walk—Mrs. Nutt thinks I should put in for medicare, and I mean it. But I've cut down and lost about five pounds. Gave up meat—not sure for how long, but it seems to be working—and limit myself to six beers—never before nine p.m.—and eat mostly wheat, fruit, cheese, vegetables and fish. No reason for doing this—except to avoid the mess hall, and feel better. There's an interconnection, you know.

Well, I hope you are doing a lot—having some fun along with work. Look forward to seeing you soon.

Love,
[signed] Breece

1. Breece had sent "Fox Hunters," "The Scrapper," and "The Mark" to *Playboy* for consideration.
2. Buddy Everett, Breece's cousin, was a heavy equipment operator and a drifter.

· · · · · · · · · · To Helen Pancake, September 2, 1976

One Blue Ridge Lane   Charlottesville, Va.
Sept. 2, 1976

Mrs. C. R. Pancake
Milton, W.Va.

Dear Mom,

My assumption that the rush of life would cease once settled in Farmington was false. My pins feel like two long-running sores. registration, orientation, et al. was insanity inspired and put to action. I have not been this busy in years.

I talked with Perdeu[1] [sic] yesterday, and my fears were realized. He preferred the "scholarly" paper on narrative style—hard work from here out. Peter Taylor is going to dissolve class after the first few meetings, and that means that most of my work—both for Taylor and Perdeu—will be done on my own. That leaves only Chaucer class twice a week, and happily, only one final exam this term.

I bought health insurance, the car is being inspected, and I still have a million errands to run. My room is ready and moved into—for the most part—I left my guns at David's, and haven't been back since. . . .

The people here are friendly and as exhausted as I am. You know, it's funny to watch new students—they're scared, but they make up for it with dramatic scenes of emotion. I must have seen twenty scenes like Doni[2] makes at registration. . . .

SMA is like a tomb. Nonetheless, Leoffler is still living there—selling bits and pieces of junk—guns, tables, chairs, but as yet, no real estate. Kegley seems to think Leoffler might try to re-open the place, but I doubt that. I can say this much for sure—I wish someone would buy the place and do something with it. It looks so lovely up there.

Looking ahead, I'll be glad to have a job again and not have to study. So many of these turkey-students are staying in for Ph.D.'s, but the whole orientation theme was telling them they couldn't get work with twelve Ph.D.'s from Harvard. I guess there comes a time when you decide the sky isn't the limit and the road doesn't go on forever, and that's where you stop. And I guess I prefer the real world to these ivory towers of learning. . . .

Already the sycamores are turning yellow-green, and I know you must be thinking of Pop. I think that's O.K. to do, but remember, he didn't live very long, but he lived his life very well. That's what counts. Better get to the library.

Love you,
[signed] Breece

1. Chuck Perdue, one of Breece's teachers at the University of Virginia and director of the Virginia Folklore Society.
2. Donnetta Pancake, Breece's sister.

· · · · · · · · · · To Helen Pancake, September 14, 1976

One Blue Ridge Lane   Charlottesville, Va
Sept. 14, 1976

Mrs. C. R. Pancake
Milton, W.Va.

Dear Mom,
   . . . . Went to Staunton this weekend, stayed with Mrs. Nutt, fished, and had a great time. I really felt at home, and really didn't want to leave. She told me I could have "Far-Away" (the cabin on the farm) for Thanksgiving, and any other time. That would be a great place to hunt and write. I really sort of miss being there, at least in any capacity of living other than at SMA—and even seeing it closed hurts a little.

Got to know the Meades a little better, and Mrs. Meade has a piece of needle work reputedly made by Mary Queen of Scots which she invites you to come see. Also, they are going to put us in touch with the guy who can finally tell the truth about the Pancake's beginnings. He's married to, get this, Annastasha [sic], the chick who claimed to be the lost daughter of the Czar of Russia, and rightfully heiress to the Throne.

Of late my Sunday has been spent with Nancy Ramsey at the old swimming hole, and I roughly resemble a sailor lost at sea. Nonetheless, I ran into Lynn, my throb from a year ago, and the big date that flopped. She was repentive, talkative, and asked me to escort her this weekend, at no personal cost, to a party. Why not. Besides Nancy is sane, and it probably wouldn't work out. But I'll keep swimming with her.

Paid my bills. I'm considering substitute teaching this winter.

I want you to write out the stories you told the tape—I'll explain later, but please do it as soon as you can. They were: the monkey story, the token jelly jars, and your dad's token.[1] This is very important. Also, if you can, I'd like the newspaper film prints on the girl and boy who murdered their parents because the parents wouldn't let them marry. As it turned out, they were cousins. I have no idea how to start, but if you start around '67 and move up, you've got it. I realize this is a lot of work, but maybe you can ask around for a better date. Let me know if you can do this, or who I should write to. All this before Nov. Also, this lib. here can't find Oliver Makin. Who should I write to find this stuff? I'm writing John Stuart, but hope for nothing.

Love you,
[signed] Breece

P.S. Tell Aunt Julia hi from me, and tell Grandpa I almost got a deer, but figured the car was worth more. Tell Jr. I let the gas out of his beans, but it didn't do any good. He'll say I didn't do it right.

1. Helen Pancake was in the habit of sending clippings, articles, and anecdotes to Breece for story ideas and details. A similar relationship was enjoyed by Steinbeck and his mother. Apparently, Breece was beginning a folklore project for Chuck Perdue.

· · · · · · · · · · To Helen Pancake, November 19, 1976

One Blue Ridge Lane   Charlottesville, Va.
Nov. 19, 1976

Mrs. C. R. Pancake
Milton, W.Va.

Dear Mom,

. . . . I don't think there's going to be any money in Peter's[1] mag. I sometimes wonder if it isn't just a pipedream.

I've seen so dog-gone many doe it's sickening, and not one buck since the last report. George and some of his friends hunted the farm second day of season, but I had to leave early for class, so I don't know if they got anything, but it sounded like a war, so they saw something. Tell the men back there that I sit on my stump and count shots—three or more, and I know that sucker couldn't hit the side of a barn. Tell grandpaw I go out with my rifle, and before I ready to leave, I potted two or three squirrels. Only I do it with a shotgun. Actually, I found out nobody over here ever heard of hunting small game with a shotgun just a .22 rifle. They must be more concerned with sport than eating.

I've been getting along on three hours sleep since season opened two weeks ago, and now I'm hitting the sack for the entire weekend. Just get up long enough to eat a sandwich and drink a milk. Really, I'm zonked. Running through the wood with two guns has taken a lot out of me, but I'll be better after some sleep. By the way, send me a recipe for cooking game, I'm not too good at it, and it tastes raunchy, but I eat it.[2]

O.K. write me a letter about your trip.

Love you,
[signed] Breece

1. Peter Taylor was planning a regional literary magazine.
2. Breece did eat small game, but also liked to embellish this appetite and shock his listener. He once told of how he cooked a cat and ate it when he was a hungry student at Marshall University.

· · · · · · · · · · · · **To Helen Pancake, January 31, 1977**

One Blue Ridge Lane   Charlottesville, Va.
Jan. 31, 1977

Mrs. C. R. Pancake
Milton, W.Va.

Dear Mom,

Your consideration toward my wardrobe is touching but unmerited. I'm quite warm, although redundant in fashion, i.e. the same four outfits all the time. But it's O.K. since I'm never seen by the same group for more than an hour. If you'd read my mind, you'd know what I really wanted was my harmonica. I got along by borrowing a "C" (I play a "G" with limitation) and investing in a bottle of Listerine. I'm stealing an idea from a story from W.Va. History 1700's by McWhorter (from Buckhannon, 1915). Because I want it printed in Shenandoah mag., I'm stealing a line from "Oh, Shenandoah" for the title. Ergo the need for the harmonica.[1]

Saw Sarah[2] yesterday. Bob talked most of the time (2–6 pm), so there isn't much news. Mary Moore's car rolled down the hill and took out a nice piece of Wilson's Birthplace Wall.

Tell Grandpa not to worry about my car. It runs. I drive slowly and pray a lot, and I promise to buy a new one as soon as I get a steady job. . . .

You could do me a big favor—take my old newspaper (the Indian Fighter) out of the frame in Pop's room, put it between two pieces of cardboard and mail it to me here. Give it Library Rate because it's research material.

I've got to get a haircut pretty soon—I look like a worn out mop. And the other day my cigarette lighter was too full, and on lighting a butt in the wind, I singed one side of my chin down to a day's growth. I don't go out in public much since then. Got the brownies, but will ration them—one a day, so I won't get fat. They sure are good, and many thanks. When the weather (or if) gets better I'll start walking to school. 10 miles a day should put me in decent shape for a good long walk in May (up to Rhode Island or over to Milton). I'm eating well, but can't believe the prices. Can't wait for my tax refund! I can eat steak for a week, at least.

Give my regards to all.

Love,
[signed] Breece

1. Breece was a fairly good harmonica player and clogger. As for the story, no fragments or notes can be found.
2. Sarah Nutt, Breece's landlady in Staunton, Va.

· · · · · · · · · · · · To Helen Pancake, February 7, 1977

One Blue Ridge Lane
Charlottesville, Va.
Feb. 7, 1977

Mrs. C. R. Pancake
Milton, W. Va.

Dear Mom,
Enclosed please find some stuff Charlotte[1] sent here for reading—as if I don't have enough to read. She and Bob went on this winter trip, but as she tore a muscle, they were sent back before they could camp in the snow. When I was in the mountains in Calif. and nearly froze with my army blanket and a trench-fire, I would have been pretty comfy with all that downy crap on their backs. But the point is, I'd never have that story to tell, or the pride of having stayed alive when it was easier to go to sleep. . . .

Mostly I worked this weekend, but I did get away Sunday night for a Bogart movie. Its so funny to watch him work with Bacall—you can tell they neither one give a hoot about the acting. I saw him in Casablanca last week when he worked with Grace Kelly [sic, Ingrid Bergman], and the quality of acting was much higher.

Mary Lee Settle had me over Fri. She's working like crazy on the mine-wars,[2] and Mother Jones. Matter of fact, she's starting to talk like her . . . losing that Brit. accent from all those years in Eng. Anyway, if you can send me the correct title and ——— strike that from the record. The old guy who wrote the Pipestem book—the one you sent last year—if you could xerox the segment called "Death in the Bonepile," I'd appreciate it. I spent twenty minutes in Alderman[3] Friday and brought out scads of stuff Mary Lee couldn't find or hadn't read. Maybe I'll get a free copy, huh?

We haven't had it much better, although our weather has been sunny, and we avoided the snow. Actually, it's getting close to fishing time, and I can't get through the ice. The car is still running, and ask Grandpaw if he got that animal tail on his truck.

No news is good for the story at VQR,[4] but now that the first shock is over, I'm resigned that they probably won't take it. I'm in competition with seasoned vets like Ward Just from Atlantic, etc. Although I'm putting in to St. Joe[5] for work, I'm going to try magazines around to see if I can't get a readership or man friday job—what the heck, it's worth a try.

Hope you are feeling o.k. How do you like that dog?[6] I crack up thinking that Charlotte said in her letter: ". . . wish she could have stayed longer (without that weirdo dog, of course) . . ." Weirdo is right, and I'm convinced they are all that way. In D.C., I thought Jewell's dog was different, but by the time I left she decided to attack. Give me a bluetick.

One other thing, Mary Lee wants to meet you—she wants to meet anybody who thinks she's famous or talented. She's really funny, and doesn't drink much at all—a beer or two, but that's surprising for a writer who's in their 60's. ——— is like pouring it down a rat-hole. It takes him a fifth to feel good.

More later,

Love
[signed] Breece

Again thanks for the check.

1. Breece's sister.
2. *The Scapegoat,* by Mary Lee Settle.
3. Alderman Library at the University of Virginia.
4. *Virginia Quarterly Review.*
5. St. Joseph Central High School in Huntington, W.Va.
6. Donnetta's dog, a Schipperke.

One Blue Ridge Lane   Charlottesville, Va.
Feb. 18, 1977

Mrs. C. R. Pancake
Milton, W.Va.

Dear Mom,

I don't know what was depressing me so much—it was either being sick or the ampicillin to cure it. I was in a pretty black mood without knowing why—it was a really weird feeling. I'm a lot better now, and in much better spirits. I didn't eat much—you're right—but went to the A&P today and just finished a porkchop, gravey, bread, pickled beets, beans, milk and cookies. Back to normal. . . .

After my tax money came; my car ins. bill, phone bill, car license and sticker, etc. all came the same day, and I don't feel rich anymore. But I don't feel poor either. Actually I was thinking about coming home, but maybe I should wait until the weather is nicer. I just felt this awful pressure to get out of Charlottesville, but that passed with my cold. I swear something in those pills did that to me. I had no reason to be down—I just had a cold, but I felt like I had about as much reason to be here as a possum. Speaking of which—ALL HAIL POSSUM POWER! I told you she'd tuck her tail in a pinch! One thing I can't abide is a dog not worth its feed. I don't think even Glenn[1] could teach her to hunt.

After hearing about your gang of vandalls [sic], I'm reminded of that old guy who lived above "The Maryland"[2] [sic]—Pop said they were the only two in his "class" not to go to jail. The next will be me and Gary (Froggy) the new town cop and Troy Hatfield.[3] No hope for Scott Bias[4]— he'll shoot himself with a grease gun and call it a hunting accident.

Love,
[signed] Breece

1. Glenn Crookshank, hunting partner and friend of C. R. and Breece.
2. "The Merryland" was an ice cream parlor and coffee shop in Milton.
3. Troy Hatfield, Country and Western musician and emergency medical technician from Hurricane, W.Va. Breece wrote an article about him in the *Cabell Record* in 1975.
4. Scott Bias, friend and high school classmate.

One Blue Ridge Lane   Charlottesville, Va.
Feb. 25, 1977

Mrs. C. R. Pancake
Milton, W.Va.

Dear Mom,

Now Feb. 25, so at least I mean well. I got busy as usual and had to put more pleasant matters aside in order to get some writing done. This story[1] just started out to be homework, but I think with the proper time and effort, could be a really fine story. The only thing about writing first drafts is that it's just as much a drain as Basic Training. I've been at it since seven this morning, and at two-thirty, I feel whipped. Wrote seven pages—I know that doesn't sound like much, but I assure you I bleed with every word. . . .

Poor Richard Jones went to ask next year off so that he and his wife could go back to Wales and mourn the loss of their daughter. They told him to go ahead as they didn't have any more openings for him—ever. People here are pretty heartless.

Between being sick and all, I haven't got much of a social life together, and this will be the fourth weekend I've played the wall flower, but it sure gets the work done. Besides, I still haven't met a girl worth her salt in this place yet. I go to movies alone and when (matinee) I want, so it costs less all around. See Rocky if you can—a funny, good movie, which really should be rated "G".

Met a nice (but flighty) girl from Trinity College in one of my classes, so I asked her if she knew Matt.[2] She did, but didn't know he was dead. "What's Matt doing now?" "Pushing up daisies." "Oh."

Thanks for finding that thing for Mary Lee.[3] Haven't gotten it of this date, but that sort of thing always takes longer—the photocopy of that trial of the two cousins took three weeks. . . .

I'll write to Mary Lou first chance I get. Don't worry about my getting a job—The Navy Needs You, that's what the billboard said. Only kidding. No other news, just putting pen to paper. Give my happiest to all and tell Betty [that] Fr.[4] is making me read more than my classes do, so I'm giving up church for lent. Again, only kidding. (Why do I have to tell you when I'm kidding?)

Love,
[signed] Breece

1. Possibly "In the Dry."
2. Matthew Heard.
3. Mary Lee Settle.
4. Breece was a novitiate at St. Thomas Hall in Charlottesville studying for his confirmation classes.

One Blue Ridge Lane
Charlottesville, Va.
May 24, 1977

Mrs. C. R. Pancake
Milton, W.Va.

Dear Mom,

Many thanks for the shirts, letter, etc. I've been working so hard I dream about golf balls.[1] Got a note from Charlotte, but haven't had time to answer. As per usual, the Meades have run off to the beach, leaving me in charge. My salary must have gone up because instead of stale sponge cake, they left a 1/2 pound of hamburger in my little ice-box.

We had a little dinner for Regis at St. T.[2] last night, and a good time was had by all. Toward the middle the wine ran low, and Regis was very careful to ask me to bring some from the parish house, saying he didn't think it was time to start changing water into wine—yet. I haven't seen him in such good spirits in a long time. Then we found out Pat is leaving in August (going off to die?), so another party is in order.

Yesterday was a good day off. I swam, ate a steak for lunch, swam some more, went to mass and the party, then dinner at a friends house. Now it's back to six grinding days, but somehow I liked that steak the most, as it was the first I'd had in a while.

How is Aunt Jul and the grand parents? Tell them I often think on them, and miss being there. This is the first summer I've been out of state, and the adjustment is a hard one. I always get my best feeling for the land and the people in this season. I miss loafing with Bliss and June,[3] too.

I will argue with you about money later. And how. . . .

Miss you, and wish there was some way around all this, but I guess not. Sooner or later I've got to make my own way. Say hello to all—

Love you,
[signed] Breece

1. Breece was working an extra job at the clubhouse grill of the Penn Park Golf Course near One Blue Ridge Lane.
2. Church of St. Thomas Aquinas at Kent and Alderman Roads, Charlottesville, Va. Father Regis O'Connell signed Breece's "Certificate of Baptism" on April 11, 1977. Father Pat O'Connor would later conduct Breece's funeral service in Milton, W.Va.
3. Bliss Wallace and Junior Blake.

One Blue Ridge Lane
Charlottesville, Va.
June 6, 1977

Donnetta Pancake
Washington, D.C.

Dear Doni,   D-Day

Many thanks for your saga, and sorry this can't prove to be the same, but I'm off today, and need a haircut. My golf course is city owned, open to the public, and I don't have to charm the golfers. We get some ragged customers. Got a long talk with a guy who tried to tear his wife's jaw off—the whole time the cop who threw him in the clink is sitting there laughing along. Just grist for the mill . . . If the "girls" there want to meet me, you might warn them that I'm so horney the crack of dawn has to be careful around me. Or, as was said of old, I'd take a naked leap at a rolling doughnut. I'm dating, but these children don't do much for me—takes a thirty year-old woman to even get a good conversation going. Gloria and Libby are both getting married . . . and the other night I dreamed of Lib. She was standing on a stairway, trying to impress me with the importance of her body and mind. Oddly, I was in a Navy uniform and cowboy boots. I turned, walked away from her yakking, and one of those cold winds that takes your breath away was beating me head on. What would Freud say about that one? Pussy-whipped? Too many Tuborgs?

Have you heard of Diane Fossie and her study of the great apes in Indonesia? I'd take you up on that rt ticket if I could spend the entire time talking to that woman. I saw her on a Nat. Geo. special, and she is flipping brilliant, brave as a snake, and is dedicated as a nun. I ought to say that A. Erhart has always been a secret love of mine, and D. Fossie is alive, and therefore seems less perverse. But you should look her up—seriously—as you'd both get along. . . .

As for the news—you assisted me more than you know. Those two trips to AZ blossomed the seeds of experience, made me know myself and others more deeply, and gave me a basis to view from. Somehow, you can't look back without having been away. I think Wolfe was right—you can't go back expecting the same, but it's the re-evaluation that makes going home a truth. Not like love is a truth—that takes two of one state of mind. Going home is only something that one person can understand, making it presentable to others—trying—is the hardest part of writing. Over the past three years I've looked so far into myself and found very little I could make others understand. It wasn't until recently I found out everybody is alike on that score, too. Pontificate, pontificate. See, you even taught me that word. . . .

But a guy named Tom Waits is a new discovery of mine. His version of "Phantom 309" is a prime example that the story is in the telling. . . .

Love and miss you,
[signed] Breece

[Enclosed in the same letter]
Dear Doni,

Made it! Atlantic bought "Trilobites" for $750. Dont know when they'll print it, but Manning wrote personal congrats and said they'd have some editorial comments at a later date (?). This has really set fire to Wilson Hall and the (Cross yourself) English Department. Poor second rate citizen Pancake who can't speak the King's English, who lost the Balsch [sic] prize by one, who just never was good enough for Peter Taylor to take seriously, who (God forbid) went to work when the money ran out—that turkey made it. I went to Mass that night, work the next day, and I still put my pants on one leg at a time. I stay out of Wilson Hall, too. Since I have a letter from Little-Brown to look at a collection, I'm thinking of writing the National Endowment for the Arts. If Erica Jong can get bucks for that Fear of Flying nonsense, why not me? Hell, an Atlantic First and forty cents will buy you a cup of coffee anyplace short of New York.

I owe Jim McPherson a lot for this—he got me beyond the mail-room, and that makes all the difference in the world—otherwise it's sort of postal ping-pong. Jim's a funny sort. He's never invited me to his house or asked me to meet his wife, but I'm the only person here he'll hang around with. Everyone in the Dept. calls him "The Spook Who Sits by The Door" because he locks his office during office hours, and never sits with other teachers. He's an intense thinker—throws out heavy-duty ideas on every subject brought up, and is the only person I know who questioned the purpose of McDonalds in human existence. That is something to boggle the mind. We share a common distaste for the preppy-class and a common bond for pool halls and beer.

The funniest thing is that I'm experimenting with tenses (time in language) and images (ideal space) as making the greatest impact in telling a story, and know little about the technical aspects of either. If I've learned anything this year, it's the fact that a teller switches voices in midstream for effect, and that the words "He was walking down a darkened street" and "I am walking down this dark street" and "I walk the dark street" all mean something different in terms of time and space. I may be making TNT without knowing it. BOOM. Otherwise, all's well. Hope you get back in time to have a small party over some roast trout or bluegill (summer) and not rabbit.

Jim bought his first gun so we could hunt this fall, and I'm hoping he's quieter in the woods than in the pool halls, or we'll never see anything. He brandished the damn thing in the parking lot and said—"I want all you white-people to be in Cleveland by midnight." Told him I'd rather be in Milton. "O.K." all you white-people go to Ohio, and Pancake can stay here and be my slave." Got to go to work. Take care and come home soon.

Love,
[signed] Breece

P.S. I'm going with the name B. D'J. Pancake. J from John, my Confirmation name, and I dropped Dexter, but kept the D.

· · · · · · · · · · · · **To Helen Pancake, August 12, 1977**

One Blue Ridge Lane   Charlottesville, Va.
August 12, 1977

Mrs. C. R. Pancake
Milton, W.Va.

Dear Mom,

While I have thought of you all week, this is the first time I've had to sit down and peck out something. I know you must have thought the railroad[1] put me in jail, but I never had a bit of trouble, and the conductor was the nicest I've ever met.

All week I have been looking for loopholes to avoid paying tuition this fall, thereby collecting more of my salary. This is a "company store"—you never see what you earn, just work, starve, and don't make waves. Since that part of the system can't be beaten, I may as well make use of it and finish the degree. I found a way around two classes I don't want, and actually will learn more my way. I'm creating two courses before 1800 for myself, will be my own boss, do my own research, etc. It's much harder this way, as there is nobody to tell you how to think, but in the long run, much more interesting. So it looks as if I'm after just one more useless degree. You can be proud of me the rest of my life while I stay home looking for work.

Dr. Kellogg[2] is trying to get another course for me to teach—two pays more than one—but I'm not sure he'll come through. Meanwhile, I'll pump John for the same deal next year.

Next comes insurance. If you can put me on your Blue Cross for a year for less than 85 bucks, do so NOW and I'll pay you back. If not, tell me, and I'll buy the crap they have here. It's required, so there's no way around it. I tell you, they bleed you dry then wonder why you don't have any money. It would be O.K. if we were all rich.

I want to thank you for the good food and company while I was home—even if I got none of my favorite pie (kick that dog for me, will you?) My thumbnail is scarred from the little witch. Thank heaven that the next time I come home, I won't be bayed in my own front yard. If you get a dog, get something nice, O.K.? I've seen copperheads on the hill with better personality.

Now I'm planning classes, and should be one step ahead of them by Sept. Writing drags and drags, but that's darn good sign it will pan out to something. Nothing good was done soon . . . Otherwise I want you to rest your worry gland for me on the day of my oral exams, as Kromer[3] will probably turn in his grave. WVU has given me permission to see his papers, but I have to go there. I'm now trying to arrange a ride. All is well, and I hope you are fine and the dog has the squirts from my pie,

Love,
[signed] Breece

1. Breece occasionally travelled to Milton by rail. As a consequence, he was planning a story called *Southern Crescent*. See letter to Mary Roberts Rinehart Foundation, Mar. 21, 1978, Pancake MSS.
2. Dr. Robert Kellogg, chairman of the English department at the University of Virginia.
3. This project was continued by classmate Arthur D. Casciato and James West after Breece's death and published as *Waiting for Nothing and Other Writings* (Athens: Univ. of Georgia Press, 1986).

[Enclosed in the same letter]
Dear Mom,

If I try to kill myself, will you buy me a Volvo and a house on Jefferson Park? No kidding. Happy attempted suicide, ————. Only with my luck, I'd make it all the way to hell without a U turn. . . .

In the news: On top of my two courses in Wilson Hall, I'm thinking of taking over a ten-week course at Continuing Education. Two hours a week at night, and when it's over, I've got $420 more—also, if it works out, I could do it on a semi-regular basis. And Sub. Teaching. Not much time to hunt except weekends. But I can eat. . . .

Love,
[signed] Breece

One Blue Ridge Lane   Charlottesville, Va.
August 19, 1977

Mrs. C. R. Pancake
Milton, W.Va.

Dear Mom,

Got another class appointment—means twice as much money this term, 3 times the work, but if I eat, who cares? So, I will do quite well all considered. Writing going very well.

John and Jane[1] arrive today, but will give them time to unpack—like a week—and get over the shock of being in high prices again.

Many thanks for the History of Milton.[2] Needed that. But wanted you to read *Everything In Its Path*.[3] I have a copy I got from a reviewer (free).

Yours,
[signed] Breece

1. John and Jane Casey.
2. *History of Milton*, by Caldwell "Collie" Dudley (privately published). Breece, with the help of Collie Dudley, had planned a story on snake handlers, who are still active in southern W.Va. The sketch of that story, "Shouting Victory," is included just below.
3. *Everything in Its Path: Destruction of Community in the Buffalo Creek Flood* by Kai T. Erikson (1976) chronicles the flood disaster of 1972 in Buffalo Creek, W.Va., and reviews characteristics of Appalachia in a similar fashion to the work of Norman O. Simpkins and Jack Weller.

· Shouting Victory

"Shouting Victory," also tentatively titled "The Tongues of Men and Angels," is Pancake's most Appalachian story sketch. The idea for this story probably came to Breece during his association with Caldwell "Collie" Dudley (1903–1976) of Milton. Together, they were planning a trip to Frazier's Bottom, Helen Pancake's birthplace, to attend a glory meeting of snake handlers who were regularly active in the region. The practice of snake handling was first begun in 1909 in Tennessee. The religious practice spread throughout Appalachia and was established in West Virginia probably as early as the 1930s. Though the practice of handling poisonous snakes and drinking strychnine during religious services was outlawed in most states during the 1940s and 1950s, it continues today. Pancake had read Weston La Barre's *They Shall Take Up Serpents: Psychology of the Southern Snake-Handling Cult* (1962) and probably used this resource in conceiving the story. This handwritten early draft/sketch of the story is far from the kind of finished piece of writing Breece struggled to achieve. I have taken the liberty to change the few third-person sections of this story draft to first-person because it appears that he began to rewrite this story in the first-person, present-tense.

"SHOUTING VICTORY"
also titled
"THE TONGUES OF MEN AND ANGELS"

[Outline]
I. Speaking [in] tongues & poison (no snakes) (turned loose)
   "I felt the quickening power coming a long ways before the poison killed Mr. Todd." laying hands
II. Testimony—plea for forgiveness, shaken, jolted, man kissing man
III. Girl playing—lost in the rhythm & sway of crowd, tongues, music, etc. (droning) praying out loud, squatting.
IV. Walking girl home—stop to rest—she falls asleep, he contemplates goodness of whole world (car horn).
V. Wakes girl at dawn, takes her home—dirty look from both parents— never went shouting victory again. Ashamed for their disbelief.

[Sketch]
   We hadn't had a real Glory meeting since we turned the snakes loose back in September, so Reverend Sam mixed up a cup of strychnine and passed it around. My faith isn't holding up so good, and I never bother with drinking any, but [Darlene] is full of the ghost, and she takes some. It never hurts her neither, but [her father,] Reverend Sam, is growing a sight pale and he falls down just like he'd been stomped on.
   Everybody drops down beside him and lays hands on him and there is an awful commotion of tongues. I get me a chair and sit down and commence to pray, but I can't. I keep thinking about all the good things Reverend Sam does for folks in Cave Creek. I think about how he prays for dying folks and gives them the comfort of Jesus on their way out and how he always shows up at the mines to pray at every shift. I look up and see his eyes have gone glassy.
   Darlene, her sister, and mother are standing up, bobbing their heads sort of pigeon-like—getting socked around by the Ghost. I knew I'd done that because they said I done it the first time Glory came on me. I used to get Glory at every meeting, and be so wore out on Monday that I couldn't work and my throat would be sore from shouting in tongues. But I look at Reverend Sam, and I can't get the Ghost.
   "Shat. Hala ma shat ma te!" Darlene says.

Even in the crowd of bodies I can feel the cold soaking into the little room. Sam has stopped twitching and shouting, and lies really still while the others pray and speak in the tongues of men and angels.

I try again to pray, but my mind keeps drifting back to Sam that first day in the mine. I keep seeing the greasy blackened face, the thin line of smile.

"The snakes is God's creatures," he had said in the dinner hole. "You ain't got fear with faith in the Lord."

That night I took a serpent from Sam's hand and strung it around my neck in Glory, talking the whole time in tongues. It feels bad to remember all that and see Sam dying.

Darlene has both hands on Sam's belly, and her forehead is pressed down to them, and she is shaking from her prayers. I take her shoulders in my hands, ease her up. Her eyes are still closed, and she stands, swaying until her mother comes to hold her.

I get on my knees, put my ear against Sam's chest, hear the flutterings.

"I reckon we better get him a doctor," I say.

"He needs Jesus!" Darlene's mother says. "Don't need nothing but faith!" She looks at me [like] I've fallen from grace. Darlene's eyes are open but I'm not sure she can see me.

I walk back through the crowd to the door, step into the cold night. The air is sweet and dry. I walk up the road to Sam's house, sit on the porch swing and watch the clapboard building [with them inside.][1]

I try to think of what ugly sin Sam might be guilty of to be stricken. Sam is a godly man, a wise one to take the way of the Lord, to lead his family and their friends. Sam had smiled at me just before the blue flash knocked us to the floor and the kettles of rock fell leaving craters in the ceiling. Sam had walked me out to the main shaft, and up top Sam fell to his knees and for the first time I know why. I, too, had dropped to my knees.

I see Fred come out of the church and run down the road toward town. A few others step outside, then go back in, but I can not move from the swing. I watch the doctor's Ford pull up and the doctor get out. Two men drag Sam out and put him in the back seat. Darlene's mother gets in with the doctor and the car drives up the road toward Williamson.

In the yellow squares of the building's windows I can see the people milling around, putting on coats. The ones who pass Sam's porch on their way home see me and stop talking until they walk out of earshot.

Darlene walks by herself, and when she comes to the porch to go in, she doesn't see me.

"Who asked for the doctor?" I say.

Darlene looks up, then softly lets the screen door shut. "I did," she says. She comes to the swing, sits beside me. "I just of a sudden lost my faith and started yelling for a doctor."

"Well, nothing's wrong with having a doctor."

"But if I'd of kept my faith he'd of lived. I won't be able to stand it if he dies. It'll be my fault."

"It'll be the poison's fault. I don't trust strychnine."

"You got to have faith."

"I got faith with the snakes, but I ain't had none with the strychnine."

"But it's in the same scripture."

"I know but snakes is God's creatures. It's like he moves in them." I look at her and she is falling asleep. "C'mon, you better go to bed."

"No, I don't want to." She sits straight up. "Take me for a walk Henry, please?"

We walk along the railroad track, past the tipple and out of town. There is a new moon and we watch the ties, adjusting our steps. When we come to a low trail, we veer off up the hillside to an open world. We sit against a tree to rest and look down on the hollow-town.

She takes my hand.

"Pray with me so Daddy won't die," she says.

"All right, but we'll pray our own prayers."

She leans against me, lowering her head to her knees. I look out on the hollow and hills where the other miners have been buried—fifty-seven burned to a crisp, but Sam had walked me out and now I can't pray for the man who taught me how.

We sit there for a long time holding onto one another. Her head resting on her knees, her grip slackening in my hand. Somehow we are both warm and we fall asleep.

I awaken first at the sound of the car horn. Darlene stirs, nestled against me. I think whoever is coming down to the hollow is laying pretty heavy on the horn, just one long note getting closer. Then I think of Sam.

Sam must have lived and his wife is coming back with him, shouting victory and blowing the horn. But instead of stopping in town, the noise comes up the railroad tracks, through the brush, and blasts in my brain. I rub my face, pray it will stop. "Ke su comj klair su ke," I say. It does.

I shake Darlene. "Sam's home. I done been told."

As we walk down the path, the gray morning crosses the sky, seeps into the hollow.

I walk Darlene to her house, and as we stop to kiss, her mother and father come to the porch.

"Where you all been?"

"Just sitting out and praying for you," I say to Sam, [smiling at him.] "Angel of the Lord came upon me to tell me you was home."

Sam looks at us. I know what Sam thinks we've been doing. "If you had neither one of you lost your faith, I'd not have gone away."

"Nothing happened, Sam, " I say. "We sat up on the ridge and prayed."

"Her mother said you's first to take temptation into Darlene's heart and turn your back on God."

"Daddy!" she says.

"Go away Satan," Sam says to me. "Go to the harlots, but leave my daughter pure."

I turn to the street, already the dawn is half-over the ridges.

1. The brackets here and below are in the original.

· · · · · · · · · · · · · · To Helen Pancake, October 1977

One Blue Ridge Lane
Charlottesville, Va.
October 30? 1977

Mrs. C. R. Pancake
Milton, W.Va.

Dear Mom,

Many thanks for your long letter. The letterhead[1] was really great, only I was unclear on who gave it to you, grandpa or Uncle Tucker—and for whom you were writing. Send me and adress & I'll answer.

I don't think there is much danger in Em becoming a Catholic, so don't let it bother you—it doesn't bother me. Thanks for the sermon—I'll skip it.

Got the Alumnus[2] & read the article on H.B. Lee.[3] Actually, I figured he was dead, but he gets around as well as Aunt Julia. Maybe we ought to get them together. Also, if you could get any of his books you might have handy, I could use them. I don't need Bloodletting In Appalachia, as I've studied it, but the others might be nice.

I'm not sure the St. Andrews Society sounds too cool. It does sound racist (pro-Celt) in some sense. I'm sure there were Scots on welfare, but they just couldn't find them (or didn't look). I'd wager they are as prejudice [sic] against the Irish Catholics as Fr. Terrance is against converts. I don't like to align myself with people like that & ignore Terry along with the KKK. Basicly [sic] he's a good fellow, but he's old school—that's what your buddies at St. A's are. We've got too many good things to work with to waste time with bitterness.

Glad to hear you got to go to Bob Evans' Farm. That must have been a great break for both of you. About all I can recall is that the food is good, and they had a ground hog in a cage. Also, it is my first memory of a really big Ohio farm, the kind that made Sherwood Anderson's stories so vivid in my mind. Without Anderson, I'd never have written a word.

Letter from Doni & she is happy enough in the City. She said I was going home T-giving, which I hope, you have straight by now.

Staunton Military Academy re-opened this fall—in Newport News, Virginia. They kept the same name, added girls to the student body, and now have all twelve grades. Other than that, it is a complete mystery to me. I haven't been up there since July & that awful time I spent in Sarah's house.

I'm shanny to say anything about the Dept. Suffice it to say I'd rather be working where I have some future.

It seems something slipped from your wallet and had been folded into my last letter. Please find it enclosed. If you must, I'd like a pair of high (knee type) lace-up boots for Christmas. Put this toward them. 10 1/2 D.

Got to get to work. Don't take any wooden nickles [*sic*]—Fred Ball can't figure out how to get them into the slot machine at the VFW.

[unsigned]

1. The letterhead pictured a mule and plow.
2. Marshall University's newsletter for alumni.
3. Howard Burton Lee, Marshall University graduate, former West Virginia state attorney general, and author of *Bloodletting in Appalachia*, a recounting of the Coal Mine Wars, *Burning Springs and Other Tales of the Little Kanawha*, and other books about West Virginia history and folklore. He lived to be 105 years old.

10

1978–1979

· · · · · · · · · · · · To Helen Pancake, March 3, 1978

One Blue Ridge Lane   Charlottesville, Va.
March 3, 1978

Mrs. C. R. Pancake
Milton, W.Va.

Dear Mom,   3 AM

Guilt has the better of me, so I'd better write while I have time. It's snowing here—already 3" with more on the way. Can't say I enjoy this Vermont weather in Virginia. Interesting you should mention Plimpton's coming to Jay's party: Jay, Plimpton, and John Casey all went to Harvard at the same time. Harvard shit big that year.[1]

Will relay message re Grubb/Settle, but can't promise a return. MLS never remembers what she's doing from day to day, as she is currently preoccupied with the Paint Creek novel.[2]

Charlotte wants me to prove Indian so she can work for the white-middle-class social group trying to turn Indians into 2nd class whites. Actually, I'm looking, but not because I care whether Grandma Pancake was or wasn't part Indian: what I want to know is did they make you legally claim it at marriage? Everything else is secondary.

Sara[3] had Em and I to a really fine dinner with Mary Moore, Frank and GG,[4] Mrs. Frank, and assorted Nutts . . . all in all a fine dinner: two salads, two stews, two desserts—really good.

Doni blessed me up one side and down the other for buying a used car.[5]

I agree it is stupid, but assured her I didn't deserve the raving I was getting. At this stage in the game, used cars are the best I can do. As I recall, the Porsche is a "used car" with a VW engine, isn't it?

Did you see Awakening Land? I watched one episode with Em and when that guy grabbed Elizabeth Montgomery's tit on national T.V., I swore off the Tube for life. I guess I'm thinking of children growing up with that in their living room. Somehow learning the facts of life from Steve Spence behind a backstreet church seems right and fair now.

I'm writing to find out if I have a teaching position next fall. John is slower than steam off of shit in making position assignments and If I finish in December, I may not have work for the spring. Back to frying hamburgers and looking for schools.

Enclosed please find another will. Tear up the old one—the only thing I changed was literary executorship for your protection.

Back to work.

Love,
[signed] Breece

P.S. Regards to all.
P.P.S.: The last paragraph of the will is to insure my burial according to my beliefs. I know you'd comply with my beliefs without question, but it's hard to tell what the girls would do. Love you. B.

1. Breece is mistaken in his details, though no doubt feeling antagonistic. Jay Rockefeller, former governor of West Virginia now U.S. Senator graduated from Harvard with a B.A. in 1961, George Plimpton took his B.A. earlier, in 1950, and John Casey earned his B.A. in 1962 and L.L.D. in 1965, both from Harvard.
2. *The Scapegoat* by Mary Lee Settle. Davis Grubb (1919–1980) had also written a novel about the West Virginia mine wars titled *The Barefoot Man* (1971).
3. Sarah Nutt.
4. Frank and Gigi Pancake.
5. Breece bought a 1970 Ford Maverick.

· · · · · · · · · · · · · · **To Helen Pancake, March 1978**

One Blue Ridge Lane
Charlottesville, Va.
March 20?, 1978

Mrs. C. R. Pancake
Milton, W.Va.

Dear Mom,

Sorry I haven't written, but I'm sure you know what I've been through with this paper—yesterday I took it to my typist (don't tell Doni, O.K.?), and await the finished product. There really wasn't time to wait for D. to do it, and Jenny makes good all mistakes on the spot. Now I don't know what to do with a free Sat., and as you can tell from the type—I'm at Eisenhard's.[1] Em is working on getting an idea for her paper (she's smarter than I, so the work is finished sooner), and I've been told to come to dinner at suppertime—whatever that means, and I have no idea as to what will be served, except that it will probably be good.

Easter was wet but good. I never stop being surprised at how hard Fr. Pat works and how hard Fr. Terrance[2] works to avoid work. Together with many others, Pat and the parish put on the whole of Holy Week while Terry watched TV. I don't begrudge the old boy for being tired, but 55 is too early to retire. Terry drafted me last night to sponsor a new member Sat. Night, and got so flustered with the service that he forgot to include about one third of the Mass. It wasn't as nice as Regis's service but then Regis worked all day for one Mass. My "godson" seemed rather at odds as to how to handle himself, but I assured him later that he was in for better or worse. He's a nice kid, and I hope to do more for him than John has done for me. I didn't see or hear from John[3] the whole season, and I've grown tired of asking him to come to church. Lastly, tell Betty Holly I'm not ignoring her nice note, but will answer as soon as time allows. . . .

Again, thanks for the check, but you haven't seen the last of your money, I assure you.

Not much else is news here. Now I have to study for orals and the final in the Bible course, then find out what's going on next year (can you believe the writers have no idea what's happening until the term is over, but all others know mid-March?). Now that Peter Taylor is back from the Keys, things should move a little faster. I'm applying to a New York Foundation for a grant to write this summer, but hold little hope of getting it—grants are funny creatures, and harder to catch than a talking crow. Even if I get the grant, I should lose weight this summer.

I did get a laugh out of the clippings you sent—Milton will do its damnedest to keep from settling in one place. Are they going to move it all to 64 in hopes of getting people to stop? We could put June Blake and Bliss[4] on one of those revolving poles with red and green lights—or better yet both yellow, as one should always enter Milton with some degree of caution.

Speaking of caution: if you talk to Charlotte[5] before I do, tell her for me that the records of Tazewell County, Va. show no record of a Virginia Woodell or Waddell or Wadell marrying any William Pancake or anything close to it. It may have been any western Virginian county, in which case one might hire a geneologist at the rate of ten bucks an hour, and even then you may not get what you want. Woodell/Wadell is like Smith in London, and the chances of getting solid records in backwoods counties are slim. Just between you and me, they could have been married in a brush-arbor by a circuit preacher who probably couldn't read or write.

Well, hope this finds you in good spirits and working but not too hard. If I get, by some accident, the grant, I'll be over for a while this summer. If not, for a week in July (near the end of the month). If you want to come over, try to plan your trip for just after finals—May 1.

Love you much,
[signed] Breece

1. Breece was house-sitting in Charlottesville.
2. Father Terrance.
3. John Casey.
4. "June" Jr. Blake and Bliss Wallace.
5. Breece's sister.

To Mary Roberts Rinehart Foundation, March 21, 1978

One Blue Ridge Lane
Charlottesville, Va.
March 21, 1978

Mary Roberts Rinehart Foundation
516 Fifth Ave. Room 504
New York, N.Y. 10036

Dear Sirs:

I wish to be considered as an applicant for the Foundation's Award in order to complete five stories and thereby begin their collection and my first novel. My first story, "Trilobites", appeared in the Dec. '77 *Atlantic Monthly*, and the same magazine recently purchased a second story, "In the Dry", to appear some future time. A third story, "Time and Again", was accepted and soon will appear in *Nightwork* (Richmond's local magazine). I propose to complete the following stories:

In "Joe Holly and Buck", two hill-countrymen, one black and one white, begin their friendship on a bus migration from the hills and coal camps of West Virginia to Detroit's auto plants in search of [something] better than mining. While there, the black man readily adapts to city life, but the white man is sucked into a hill-countryman ghetto, and his only contact with the brightness of the city is in meeting his black friend in pool halls. The story is about Joe's attempt to break out of his ghetto, but the ghetto eventually breaks him, and he returns to the hills a beaten man.

"Conqueror" is a story of alcoholism and war. A fifty-nine year old disabled Vet takes his son on one last camping trip before the boy goes off to college, and for the first time in the boy's history the man goes off on a bender of vodka and Pepsi. In his stupor he relates to the boy why he once drank (due to the things he saw men do to one another in Germany), why he now drinks (because of atrocities he has never related to anyone), and why he expects the boy to do his duty in Vietnam. A tussel ensues while the boy pours out the hooch, then the old man retires to the tent, leaving the boy by the fire all night. The boy is not afraid, except perhaps for his father.

"Of Time and Virgins" is a stream of consciousness narrative as a young man tries to make a decision whether he should propose to a virgin he just met. He reviews the four great loves of his life, sees how each falls prey to sexual promiscuity in a different way, and eventually decides he is tainted, but not beyond help. Since he has been with this girl more than a year without bedding her, he decides she is more to him than the others and decides to "propose" tomorrow.

"A Room Forever" is roughly what becomes of Huck Finn when the raft is no longer a possibility. An unnamed orphan narrator temporarily works on an Ohio River tug as refuge from a recent Naval discharge. On the last night of shore leave, he encounters a young prostitute who derides everything he wants: home, family, love. After their argument in a wharf bar on New Year's Eve, she goes to an alley way where he later finds her, both her wrists slashed. The cold rain has clotted her blood, so she will live. Until now he has soaked himself in pity and whiskey, but now feels his lot is not so bad. He leaves the girl to be helped in the bar. He goes to meet his boat.

"Southern Crescent" is a tribute to the death of good passenger service and the death of a kind man. Claude, retired from the Air Force and wasted with stomach cancer, takes a last ride on a train he ran in steam days. In the club car he talks with a young college student coming up from Virginia to Washington for a job interview. En route the student is not willing to concede that Claude's life is any richer than his own. Not until the two are held at knife-point in Union Station's men's room and Claude backs the thief away with an imaginary gun does the student realize his own gutlessness.[1]

I believe I can complete these stories in as many months. My rent is $55 a month for this complete 12x12 cell (even the fox has a hole), and I spend about $125 a month to eat. I'm 25, single, and have an appointment to teach as a grad ass. next fall at the University of Virginia. I have a B.A. ('74) from Marshall University, hope to have my M.A. from Virginia next year. Before that I spent two years teaching in military secondary schools.

Many thanks for your consideration.

Sincerely,
[signed] Breece D'Jon Pancake

1. Of these five story proposals, only a fragment of "Conqueror" and the completed story "A Room Forever" are known to exist. The idea for "Joe Holly and Buck" no doubt is derived from Breece's friendship with James Alan McPherson, "Of Time and Virgins" from his relationship with Emily Miller, and "Southern Crescent" from his friendship with Wyatt "Duck" Gay.

· · · · · · · · · · · · · To Helen Pancake, March 27, 1978

[postcard]
One Blue Ridge Lane
Charlottesville, Va.
March 27, 1978

Mrs. C. R. Pancake
Milton, W.Va.

Dear Mom,

Many thanks for the Easter Gift. Consider Christmas and June 29th taken care of as well. This week finds me finishing up on the Lit. use of Bible paper after which I must spend almost all my time on Ch. 2 of novel.[1] I've applied for a Grant this summer, but hold little hope of getting it unless the foundation is crazier than I think. Emily and I had a fine Easter dinner and drew up a truce long enough to go to one another's church. Fights start again tonight! (Some of that Holy Water hit her, so she's the same as Catholic now.) Let me know your plans.

Love,
[signed] Breece

1. Breece had two plans for a novel tentatively titled *Water in a Sieve:* One plan utilized "Trilobites" and "In the Dry" as first chapters—this plan also used the working title, *Generations.* The other plan utilized a story called "Ridge Runners" and then "Hollow" as the first two chapters.

· Water in a Sieve

Pancake had actually begun writing *Water in a Sieve,* and a fragment of chapter 1, "Ridge Runner," is included here. Some additional chapters may have been written and then lost. Helen Pancake had noted: "Only Chapters I & II made it from Charlottesville–I have no idea what happened to them, if they were even started." The outline probably dates from his days in Charlottesville. The manuscript of "Ridge Runner" bears his newly adopted pen name Breece D'Jon Pancake. The novel focuses on the story of Buddy and Sally as introduced in *Hollow.*

[Plan for the novel titled *Water in a Sieve*]

[Outline]
CHAPTER I   "Ridge Runners"
CHAPTER II   "Hollow"
CHAPTER III   "Politicians" (smoke filled room)?
CHAPTER IV   "Sally Rand" (bar in Columbus)
CHAPTER V   "Just One Chance" (bargaining with Curtis)
CHAPTER VI   "Pappy's" (visiting an old friend)?
CHAPTER VII   "Good Old Boy" (mining and death of Estep)
CHAPTER VIII   "Sagittarius" (birth of Tommy)
CHAPTER IX   "The Big Top" (TV—way it's supposed to be)
CHAPTER X   "Ashes" (the way it is)
CHAPTER XI   "Deer Hunting" (finale—no deer)
[Chapters three and six had question marks indicating maybe reverse.]

WATER IN A SIEVE
A Novel by B. D'J. Pancake

Chapter I: "Ridge-Runner" [draft]

Buddy uncovered himself to get out of bed, but lay still—half-thinking, half-asleep. He tried to retrace the dream, to hook and snag the sneering way he felt; but he found only what he had seen. His family had been together again. It seemed like they had been at the old house on the ridge; just sitting, not doing anything. He had seemed a boy again, a boy who played with a toy truck at his Grandad Thacker's feet. Now that he was awake, the dream slipped and feeling fell away into times before they sold their grant-lands, moved to the hollow.

Through the trailer's slat-windows, he saw the first dark-blue sky before day, and knew the ridges would already be bright. He heard Sally's breathing. She would not make his breakfast, not even this last time. She was going, and he knew she would do nothing special about good-bye. How she was far from him in a dream, of white-powder and music, a dream busy with strange poems she wrote, a dream of things she would never tell him. He saw how slim she was; even under lumpy comforts and a wedding-ring quilt, the lines of her body lay smooth and lean. He rolled, fitted the curve of her back to his chest and belly, felt her skin and smelled of the spray on her hair. He slipped one arm around her waist, brought his hand up to the curve of her breasts, felt the slow and simple flow of her blood. She did not move to him, but drew closer into herself.

He remembered red bar-lights, the sparks they made in her hair, and he remembered the way she sat so straight on a stool in the Thunderball

Club. At first she smiled, eyes heavy with metal-flakes that caught the red lights, then her smile softened, and she mocked his hicky accent: "'Scuse me, Miss, but could I have dance?" In all the nights of dancing, she had never left the Club with him, never drank the drinks he bought. And when he was laid off his job in the railyards, she left with him, and they moved back to the hollow beneath the ridges where he was born. It rained so hard that night that leaves were knocked from the trees, and traffic on the streets crept to a drone. He had picked a sticky leaf from the sidewalk, placed it under-side the plastic umbrella, and had seen her smile, wet with the oil of lipstick.

He shook her a little. "Sal, I got a dream, to tell you."

She stirred, moaned, moved his hand away.

"It was just like when I's little. None of the folks was dead, and they's all up to the old house on the ridge . . ."

She rolled to face him. "Goddamn. Go on to work or something—the coke's still on. Just leave me alone." She turned away again, pulled the covers tight.

He got up, went down the hall to the bathroom. On a rack above the tub, his dried-out workclothes hung, stiff with shale, mud, coal grit. He dressed in two layers, spreading fine dust though the air, and pulled on his steel-toed boots, laced them to the knee.

He started at the bathroom floor, told himself Sally had to go because it wasn't her way to stay. He had been alone before he found her, knew he could take it again. He smiled. If she didn't leave tonight, he would throw her out: let her hitch-hike to Charleston for all he cared.

In the kitchen he scrambled two eggs, the last two, and ate them from the pan while yesterday's coffee reboiled. He thermosed the coffee, and built two baloney and onion sandwiches for his lunch pail. He found some cold corn-bread and raw turnip in the refrigerator, packed them. He drank off the rest of the coffee, picked grounds from his teeth with a fingernail. Curt would have to pay them next week or they would flat starve.

Putting on his miner's cap, he stepped outside. The sun struggled to sift into the hollow, and greenish fog held back the light. He crossed the foot bridge over the creek, walked past dead stalks of sunflowers Sally had planted, and slipped through the fog to the secondary. All the way to the dog-hole mine, he thought how it had started.

Over a hundred years ago Thacker's had owned the ridges around Echerton, farmed and fought on it. Only Curtis stayed, tried to dog-hole coal on his own ridge, to scrape the last life he knew into bread and beans. Buddy knew the time had come for Curtis to quit, too.

He walked through all that was left of Echerton: boarded store-fronts and rows of company houses. Weed stalks stuck between rusty spur tracks, and windows of storage areas above the store-fronts were splintered from rocks. Ahead, in half-light, he made out the rotting tipple. His father had been crushed there just ten days before the big mines shut down, and the miners were left to do scab-work and D.P.A. The tipple crackled in the cold as the sun touched it, and on a pole beside it, an unused transformer still hummed. The big coal was gone, and he did not know why he had stayed.

Sally was right to go, but somehow he wanted to stay. This place was his, had been his too long to leave, and he would stay until the last shack rotted, filled with snakes and weeds.

One light burned in the grocery store—a one room affair for the families too poor to give up, move to the cities. Buddy checked his pockets, found a quarter, and went inside. The store was warm, and he smelled fresh coffee on the hot plate.

[end of fragment]

· · · · · · · · · · · · · · · To Helen Pancake, April 3, 1978

One Blue Ridge Lane   Charlottesville, Va.
April 3, 1978

Mrs. C. R. Pancake
Milton, W.Va.

Dear Mom,

Many thanks for your letter on April Fool's. Even mail of that sort is welcome. Sounds as if you're getting along well enough, but I think you're dreading up-coming vacations where you work. I guess you won't be here for the spring—at least that's the way it sounded, but I understand. For the time involved, you could fly to Miami quicker than drive here.

I was surprised at all the ghosts you dragged out in this letter—Midget Morgan, Jim Ross, etc. Somehow it can't be real that they're married and have kids—it's like I'm frozen in time writing. I guess I'll settle down sooner or later, but it's a matter of jobs and years. Fr. Terrance told me not to worry about it so much, so I won't.

Em and I finally have enough time to run to Staunton this weekend, and I have to call Sarah[1] today. It's good to get out of Charlottesville, and see the rest of the world for a change. I think I'll take Em fishing—haven't wet a line since last summer (I'm really in bad shape), and I don't want to forget what a fish looks like.

As for the Grant: I've got enough to get through the summer, and will take a job before long as well as write.[2] As you know, I'm going west in July to make some money and take a vacation (first in three years). I want to re-visit some old Spanish missions after traveling with Doni's summer camp on wheels—that is if I survive the summer camp. My back isn't used to dirt beds. If the grant comes through, fine: I quit the job, and go west just the same. If not, fine. In any event, you needn't worry about me.

The paper's finished and turned in.[3] I told him I had some terms used in a strange fashion, but he was very receptive, and said I was safe in my argument. Em and I have a bet: if I get an A, she has to cook any dinner I want (turtle), and if not, I cook what she wants (steak). Loser pays all. I'm really hoping to place the paper at Catholic Biblical Quarterly, although that may be above my head. I can't lose by trying. Did you ever look up that passage? Luke 23: 27–31. Nobody has written much about it, so I'm that far ahead.

Also, Chuck Perdue wants me to read my Oral Narrative paper[4] at the fall meeting of the Virginia Folklore Society, and play the tapes. I'm trying to place that paper at Kentucky Folklore Quarterly, and Doni will get that to type very soon.

The Jefferson Society gave me a Jefferson Cup for second place in their fiction contest—nice of them. I didn't read my best story, but tried to keep within the page limit. As it turned out, I was the only one who did. But the first prize story was really very good, and I've got much more going with the Atlantic than an eight dollar cup.

I was glad to hear the family is doing O.K. and that Milton is still on the map. As I said in my last letter, I'll be home for my usual August visit if all works well. Give them my love. . . .

Better get this in the mail.

Love you,
[signed] Breece

1. Sarah Nutt.
2. Breece had applied to the Mary Roberts Rinehart Foundation for a grant to write a collection of short stories. He did not get the grant.
3. He had written a paper on Luke 23:27–31 for his Bible as Literature course. The passage is imaginatively explored in his story "In the Dry."
4. Breece had collected oral tales told by the men from Milton.

· · · · · · · · · · · · · · · · To Helen Pancake, April 1978

One Blue Ridge Lane
Charlottesville, Va.
April 15? 1978

Mrs. C. R. Pancake
Milton, W.Va.

Dear Mom,

Many thanks for your letter. I'm happy to hear you might be coming by next month, and will save my Mother's Day gift for then. Em and I have a couple of places we'd like to take you, and one German restaurant where they actually put more on the plate than I could eat (Fred[1] hadn't had anything all day and still couldn't eat it all.)

Please don't get the impression we're loafing in Staunton[2] every weekend... having finished my painting and spring cleaning, I'm trying to study for exams and put my dossier together for job hunting next year. Also trying to revamp old papers and stories by way of getting something else into print. On top of that, I'm teaching the last ditch of this battle for two more weeks.

By now you know that in addition to Mary Lee, James Alan McPherson won the Pulitzer Prize for *Elbow Room*. I think Mary Lee's writing is good, but I'm not ready to say Pearl Buck is a West Virginian by any fashion. Far as I'm concerned, she's Chinese. Jim lost the Nat. Book Award to Mary Lee,[3] but stole her thunder not four days later. I haven't talked to her since January, but I'm sure if there's something to be put out about with all that, she'll be down in the mouth. Somehow, Jim doesn't seem too happy—I guess because he's the type not to like reporters and the public eye. I was in the office when he got the news, and the hallway was full of NBC/CBS/ABC and every other reporter. He made statements to them about how grateful he was then disappeared. We were supposed to go fishing today, but then we've been supposed to go fishing many a weekend....

Not much else in the news, I hope all are well and send them my love. Don't brag on me so much.

Love you,
[signed] Breece

1. Fred Frazier, Breece's grandfather.
2. Breece and Emily had been escaping to Staunton and Mrs. Nutt's house on East Beverly Street.
3. Mary Lee Settle won the National Book Award for *Blood Tie* in 1978.

· · · · · · · · · · · · · · · **To Mrs. Sullivan, May 17, 1978**

One Blue Ridge Lane   Charlottesville, Va.
May 17, 1978

Mrs. Sullivan[1]
Milton, W.Va.

Dear Mrs. Sullivan,

Many thanks for your note—I hope I can keep up the pace I've set for myself. Like Wolfe, I walk a great deal (actually Richard Jones can take credit for that—Wolfe can take credit for the wasps in "In the Dry") & I just walked from my pond ten miles back. I had noticed the Canadian Goslings were disappearing and strayed until I saw a whopping snapping turtle! So much for this year's migration.

Etymologically, you're correct: "will-o-the-wisps" was the original title of "Trilobites" & Colly's mother is assimilating the syllabication—something not uncommon to daily speech (not just in Milton—something similar in Virginia is, "goddamnedyankee").

Certainly the last line is the whole point of that story, but don't you think it odd that only you and I have noticed it?

Finally, I think congratulations are in order more for you than me—after all, you put up with me in home room and Civics.

Sincerely,
[signed] Breece

1. Mrs. Sullivan was Breece's teacher in junior high school.

· · · · · · · · · · · · · · To Helen Pancake, May 27, 1978

One Blue Ridge Lane
Charlottesville, Va.
May 27, 1978

Mrs. C. R. Pancake
Milton, W.Va.

Dear Mom,

Just a note to say hello. I guess Decoration Day[1] back home is still the VFW's biggest affair—if they didn't use those old army rifles today and Nov. 11th, they wouldn't be happy. Here it's nothing much—people leave town and go to the beach.

Yesterday Emily and I took time to go out to a local lake. They rent rowboats for 50¢ an hour, so we did some exploring and had a fair time watching people. Like fools, we neither brought swim suits or a lunch, so the visit was short. She can't take too much sun at once and I don't care for going without lunch after Mass (can't eat before Mass). Spent the week studying for orals and putzing with this story—which I have to get back to very soon. Emily is still struggling with the great thinkers of 15th century England in an attempt to net some butterfly or other. She claims I'm a bad influence since my logic is so ass backwards: when she tries to argue her point, I get her so tangled up nothing makes sense.

I've arranged to read "Trilobites" at Randolph-Macon Women's College June 20th. they offered to pay me $100, so I couldn't very well turn it down.

I'll take the bus and spend the night—all at their expense—and will talk to three classes the next day. Of course I'd like to get more "readings" around the state (away from Charlottesville—one should never shit where one eats), but I'm not important enough to drag in the big money. Actually, Davis Grubb[2] has it cinched at WVU and something similar is my life's goal (as with everyone who writes I'm sure).

Glad you're reading Elbow Room—the title story is the most difficult to understand, yet in a way, they're all difficult since Jim isn't a simple man. Peter's stories are much more suited to your way of thinking than Jim's are. Peter has some degree of fame—a reputation is more like it—but the Pulitzer Prize should make people listen when McPherson talks, and in the end a writer couldn't ask for more.

The Meades are back from England and I got a verbal "thanks for taking care of the house all month." No mention of forgetting the rent or what they could do for me. Since I have to pay July rent, I "forgot" to pay May rent., and in all the rush to England, I hope they forgot too. I don't intend to mention the subject. . . .

With this wonderful postal system, it should cost me as much to write letters as it does to call home. Still, I know what it means not to get mail and I'd rather write anyway. Hope everyone is fine. Give them all my best and love to the family.

Yours,

[signed] Breece

1. Memorial Day in Milton, a memory that figures prominently in "The Honored Dead."

2. Davis Grubb (1919–1980) was writer in-residence at West Virginia University from 1978 until his death.

· · · · · · · · · · · · · · · · · **To Emily Miller, July 1, 1978**

Phoenix, Arizona[1]
July 1, 1978

Emily Miller
Charlottesville, Va.

Dear Pal,

So far the weather has been more than fair—one might say the sky is "peaches and cream." The smoking compartment on the plane gave a very-distant fine view of such skys, but upon landing, personally—I found the sun very hot and the surrounding stars not nearly so bright as imagination might paint them. I am, dear Pal, scorching with a wry smile—or a bourbon one—as you like it.

To backtrack and thereby come to the portent of this, I arrived D.C. am. 6/29 only to be rained upon while finishing—soberly—the 42nd Parallel.[2] Soaked by 9 pm., I tramped in search of a train—found nothing but a page at Union Station—"Will B. Pancake come to the desk"—trapped like the mouse in your house I hope is smarter.

But about the rain—at first I managed to seek a hole in the awning of tenement and okay, I tried to read, but kept thinking of you—said to you— "My God, Emily I miss you." In the words I heard the wisdom an unknown man uttered to Pop in his hobo days—"Boy, you got a home; you better go to it." And I said as I've always said—"I ain't got no . . . My God, Emmer, I love you." I knew I had makings for home.

Then, tonight, one of our younger tikes (alone, I tried to keep the stars from fearing the lack of sun) complained: "I'm bored with all this." All this consisted of a $16.00 dinner in a "real" western town with "real" cowboys coming in and out—a mockup to be sure—nevertheless an effort to show them a good time. The young'un is twelve with tits agreed, so I laughingly said to Ruth—"Someday my little girl will say that—and take a five mile walk looking for her head." The last part was direct, deliberate, and hells fire. I'm sure my little Burnadette would be pissed when Pop knocked her one for such a comment—I hope he wouldn't have to—and it made me mad and it made me wonder:

Would I? Am I a such a ghoul at heart? Is your papa right to ask you to re-consider?[3] He wants his boat-dream for you—what chance can a pen-pusher provide for? I want Colly in Mexico there to meet the anger of the "masses" (Marx). I want Ottie to wander the country, free from the whole great space an inch of his own, I want Colly in Vietnam's last days, a leg torn off by our own fire, to see again masses in Mexico, to say "the hell with it" and go to see his Pop. I want Ottie tired, alone, to give up the garage in Chicago, to return and finding Sheila gone—meet with the strong, good woman (a kind of you) and begin his small settling—and I believe that would be a book[4]—and a good one to read for any man of any class. The woman will be written up when I return—she must have four stories to her like the two men—and they must never be too innocent or loving or "decadent."
[The letter ends here.]

1. Breece was in Phoenix, Ariz., and in Telluride, Colo., that summer chaperoning a youth group from Washington, D.C., on a trip to the West. This letter was in one of Breece's notebooks and never mailed.
2. The *42nd Parallel* by John Dos Passos.
3. Breece had proposed marriage.
4. His plan for a novel titled *Generations*, or *Water in a Sieve*.

[Plan for the novel titled *Generations*]

[Outline]

Ch.1   Trilobites
Ch.2   In the Dry
Ch.3   Survivors
Ch.4   Colly in Nebraska
Ch.5   Ottie in Nebraska
Ch.6   Alena at bank (#2)
Ch.7   Colly in Mexico
Ch.8   Ottie out of jail
Ch.9   Alena vs. Albert
Ch.10   Colly in Viet Nam
Ch.11   Alena & Ottie (Ottie #3)

[Sketch]

Alena

1.) Survivors

 A young women left with her aged mother & no word from her prodigal preacher-brother, makes the decision to put her mother in a nursing home & sell out the timber rights and land to the incoming Chemcorp. She takes a job as a bank teller in bank handling Chemcorp account—visits her mother once—furnishes an apt. in town & waits for the old woman to die.

2.) Alena rises in status at bank and is allowed to handle Chemcorp payrole. She breaks off all former ties to her poverty—including her old boyfriend (in Survivors) who is too crude in manners to accompany her, he goes crazy—shoots at her, puts bricks through her window—follows her. She has a writ & finally he transgresses it in public & she has him arrested for assault.

3.) Alena vs. her brother Albert & his fundamental Christianity. Albert comes to visit their mother—a comatose vegetable on I.V. He tries to get Alena to admit that she has not respected her mother (violated a commandment) and that her lifestyle is of Satanic origins—he leaves cursing her to her alcoholism and whoring.

Ottie

1.) In the Dry

2.) Ottie hauling machine parts thru Nebraska's wheat harvest. Meets Collie. They talk abt. Viet Nam vs. Ottie's concern for "the real war"—survival in a country destined to make independence extinct. Action surrounds a strike on Ottie's truck—union harvesters refuse to let him through. Another character—Jeff [Berne or Beans?], a friend of Colly and rough neck—is killed accidentally by Ottie in a drunken free-for-all in a bar. Colly—seeing that Ottie's lawyer says state has no case—stops in to see Ottie before beating it out of Nebraska. He tells Ottie, finally, that the union men burned his truck. Story ends with jailer coming in repeatedly to stare at Ottie—nothing else—just stare[s].

3.) Ottie, out of jail, takes the bus to home of a friend and fellow scab trucker in Lousiville, Ky. Hill country have-nots, his friend tries to convince him to settle down (wife & kids)—pay off the unions when they threaten to picket (a man's got a right to work, says Ottie). Ottie rides shotgun with Curt on a load of whiskey bound for Richmond—in the hills of south-western Virginia they are highjacked—Ottie loses all faith in Curt (who gives up without a fight). At a nearby truckstop Curt leaves Ottie waiting for a ride—he sees a hitchhiker huddled by the pumps—Colly (Punky)—discovers he's headed to Phoenix to enlist—Ottie tells him to be a good chickenshit & go Navy. Collie says that was what he'd . . . [probably there was more here, now missing]

4.) Ottie returns top Rock Camp—everything different. Valley full of houses to shelter families working for Chemcorp—an indirect link to Dupont's napalm co. Ottie sitting at roadhouse bar debating on whether to join union so he can get a job. Meets Alena—they talk—she tries to convince him to give up & join union, talk turns to how valley has changed—he asks if she knows "Punky" Collier—comes out Colly is buried in Akron. Ottie pushes his drink away slowly. "Had enough of this swill to float a fucking battleship." Alena, "Have another." "No thanks. Have to get to work in the morning." He goes outside. She follows—"Need a place to stay?" They go to her place—talk—he decides to go union. They make love & lying after she asks him what he's thinking. He's been thinking of "Punky"—[but] he says, "Nothing."

Finis.

· · · · · · · · · · · · To Helen Pancake, August 14, 1978

One Blue Ridge Lane
Charlottesville, Va.
August 14, 1978

Mrs. C. R. Pancake
Milton, W.Va.

Dear Mom,

Many thanks for your letters and the xeroxed stuff I still haven't had time to read. The letter with the check was stuck with some other misplaced mail

on my windshield—the neighbors had picked it up—so the check is safe . . .
My summer classes are over with only one student good enough to make the
grade—the rest took advantage of my being away as an excuse to goof off,
and I encouraged them to drop rather than fail them. I later learned I should
have failed them—I get paid if I fail them, but not if they drop. It's all the
same to me, I could use the money, but not at another person's discomfort.

I assume I got the readership at Virginia Quarterly because I found a
stack of mss. with my name on them at the office today—I hope the funds
are up to date, too—should get $50 a month to defray the cost of rent. Em
and I joined our efforts in an equal battle on the cost of eating. Since I almost always eat supper at her house, I offered to go 50/50 on one meal a
day, allowing us both to eat better than we would if we cooked—or tried—
our own supper. We've found the real bargains at the Farmer's Market just
before dark, and today bought a huge round and had it cut into two small eye
roasts, fourteen swiss steaks, four pounds of stew meat, and four pounds of
ground round—all at 1.29 lb. We figure around twenty-five meals at that, and
plus a few whole chickens (how do you cut those damn things?) at .39 a lb.,
we have meat every day for a month at .60 a serving, each meal not costing
more than 1.00. I can't eat chili in a hash house for that today. Heinermann??

All things considered, God's will and low creeks, I'll be in for the gathering[1] on the 17th. I haven't priced the train, and at that point (we don't get
paid til Oct.), I might just drive in. I have emergency towing on my insurance, so don't worry. I have a credit card if anything big happens.

I was sorry to hear Lora Danford[2] died. I still think of the cold mornings, walking to school in the late fall, and speaking to her as she walked
that poor old dog of hers out by the funeral home. And I remember going
in her shop with you when I was little, and the funny tricks the sun would
play on the sheets and towels, and thinking how Uncle Abe's[3] store had been.

I've finished all but three books for my orals, and am working up the
proposal. I may postpone them, as I have a tough course to take and will
teach two while working at V.Q. I really can't bluff them off, as orals are
tricky, and I'm on shakey ground with two of the novels.

I have to give a reading in Staunton at the prison Sept. 8th[4]—I guess I
don't have to—Sara's oldest daughter asked me to, and I thought I'd like to
hear me if I was in prison. It pays a little, but I asked that the money go for
books—not enough for two these days. I know I should keep the 25, but hell,
put yourself in prison for a minute. Besides, Dad always said he and the guy
who lived above the Maryland were the only two of his class to stay out of
jail—said I was bound to make it, so he turned out right. He always had a
heart for the underdog, like he understood why a fellow would do something wrong to get by—like the war—I'm not sure if he killed anybody, but

he was the kind who felt like he'd killed a man just by looking at the body, and God knows he saw the bodies. Anyway, this is for him; he taught me to give a bum a dime because it might give the bum the last chance he needs to sober-up. So maybe a book, a hillbilly reading a story or just something to break the stay will shake one fellow into thinking it might not be so bad to get by honestly.

I ain't looking forward to seeing Aunt Julia in a such a sad shape. That's pretty selfish of me, I know. That's where your wisdom makes a big difference against my age—I get so tired of thinking that the ones I love draw up like old iris in summer. It seems like it started with Grandad and never has quit—even with Kat and Granny, and how mean they could be, I still hated to see them go. When I think of how you choke up or Grandpaw cries when you all talk about Grandma and Grandpa Frazier, I know you never stop loving them even when they've been gone a half a hundred years. I try to understand, Mom, I really try, but if I learned anything from my past, it wasn't intellectual understanding of something as deep as love and death, it was the living of love and the living of death, and now that Aunt Jul is in between, I don't know what to do, and I don't think anyone on the face of this earth can tell me.

Damn me, I'm awful depressing. I guess I'm just homesick and tired. I miss you and love you and hope you aren't working too much. Maybe for the Reunion we could have chicken and beans and potato salad for me to step in. Tell Jr. I've tied my cat to the top of the fence-post.

Love you.
[signed] Breece

1. The Pancake family reunion.
2. Lora Danford was a mortician at the Heck Funeral Home in Milton.
3. Abraham Pancake.
4. The third anniversary of his father's death (Sept. 8, 1975) Pancake gave a reading at Staunton Correctional Center, a medium security facility for men, at the request of Mrs. Nutt's daughter, Janet (Nutt) Lembke. She recalls, "[T]he guys thought he was one cool dude." Breece gave a reading of "Trilobites" to the "Creative Righters" a group of men interested in developing their own writing. Anxious to establish her trust with the men, Lembke remembers, "[B]y the time Breece made his appearance as one of our first guest writers, the Righters trusted me and the workshop. That trust was extended to Breece . . ." (letter to the author, Apr. 5, 1993).

One Blue Ridge Lane
Charlottesville, Va.
Sept. 22, 1978

Mrs. C. R. Pancake
Milton, W.Va.

Dear Mom,

This is the first chance I've had to get off my bread and butter letter. It really was nice to be home, and I hope the next time I'll have some more time to hang around and visit. The return was uneventfully fun—I picked up a stranded trucker and gave him a ride to the Sewell Mt. Gulf Station. He was my age—nothing like Ottie,[1] but a nice fellow. He told me I could get a Kenworth truck for 31 thousand and pay it off in two years. It was an interesting idea to think about, but I'm too set in my ways now to go back on the road. Also, I decided to be cute and take the back roads from Covington to Staunton (further back than my usual trail). Got to meet and talk with a lot of people along the way (one-lane roads with no signs), but didn't get here till 12:30. Still made the class the next day though.

Been enjoying the cheese and sausage and pickles—you have seemed to have given me the whole of the batch—and thanks, but wish you'd saved some for yourself. Emily, who won't eat anything but a strange selection of bland foods, gobbled down the two paw-paws and wants a paw-paw tree. I'd get her one if I could remember the leaf pattern and the texture of their bark—can you find a picture of them in the plant books??

My students are worse this year than last. They're so afraid of grades and credit, and a few of them are down-right asses. Last year things went smoothly, and there was no mention from them or me on grades. I guess the world is moving back to common materialism in favor of learning— sadly these kids have been tricked into believing there's a job waiting for them if they get four years of college. One of my seniors (a really pretty red-headed girl—I don't usually think red-heads are pretty) nearly cried when I told them not to worry about hurrying through college to join the ranks of the unemployed. Turns out she did her entire degree in two and a half years and will graduate with honors in Dec. She hasn't found a job—or a hint of one, but I ask you, what can you do with a degree in government? Or for that matter, English?

Rest assured your money will be returned to you post haste. John Casey has been really good about understanding dental bills, and I will make enough next semester and this semester to insure the return of your five hundred. I know it must seem stubbornly independent of me to refuse gifts, but your funds are so slight by today's standards, that any buffer you have between yourself and poverty should not be dwindled by your children. Besides, my profession bears the nasty condition of perpetual poverty in this life and riches for my heirs; I chose it, and I should live with it. And, I further insist, any profit you take in interest on loans, rent, or otherwise be yours and yours alone—even as cash in the box.

I don't know if you and Jack Pancake[2] have settled on any conclusion to Aunt Julia's estate, but in the event you do, remember that I said anything the two of you decide on is with my approval. I assume the distribution of personal property is in accordance with both your powers and will be done with every intention to fulfill the last will.

Better get back to business at hand. Again many thanks for the weekend, and hope to get home again soon.

Love,
[signed] Breece

> 1. Ottie is a character in Pancake's "In the Dry."
> 2. Breece's second cousin, Jack Pancake.

· · · · · · · · · · To Helen Pancake, November 11, 1978

One Blue Ridge Lane
Charlottesville, Va.
Nov. 11, 1978

Mrs. C. R. Pancake
Milton, W.Va.

Dear Mom,

Many thanks for the check—I added $120 to it and return it now—I think only owing you $100.00. Actually—although your gift is well taken, it's taken more in terms of credit to a debit. I thank you for it—and very much.

I bought two pair of pants and now try to mostly show up in class in a shirt, tie and jacket—I know it isn't much of a concession to your wishes, but I'm trying. Also—while it seems I make a good deal of money (600 compared to 200 when I first came here), it doesn't seem to go anywhere—I really do know what you're up against with your income.

As for the work—it goes on. I really can't say this instructor plays either a fair game or with a full deck. I make no promises: try as I will, he's just as apt to fail me as confer a degree on my head. What's worse is that he's my examiner on the oral exam, and his method testing isn't unpleasant if one managed to survive my Church's Spanish Inquisition (torture, burning at the stake, etc.).

I really am too busy for words, and with nothing pleasant to show for it—I can't write and teach and take what seems to be one of the hardest courses here. I guess I'm stupid—but I hope someday you might have my degrees on the wall to justify the grey hair I gave you.

That—morbidly—leads me to Glen and Katy.[1] I've so much and so often felt fond pain with them over Robert, and I had hoped some good might come of all their troubles. They are the kind of people—real people—one never finds beyond a given valley because, once out of the valley, we never have the time to know that special kind of person. Robert's death must have been a shock without mercy—their love in and pride of him was without excess. I still remember the pictures of his son's in Glen's shop, and I first learned to mouth the word "lawyer" with respect—how could Glen be any less my teacher than Katy in that respect? But Thomas Wolfe—the "great" writer—died in a cab in New York,[2] and Hemingway blew his brains out. Maybe I'd been better off a lawyer.

Well—have to get up early tomorrow—hope this finds you well.

Love you and miss you—
[signed] Breece

1. Glenn and Kathryn Perry, friends of the Pancake family. Glenn Perry was the town barber. His son, Robert Gayle Perry, was a stellar lawyer who was instrumental in bringing former West Virginia governor William Wallace ("Wally") Barron (1961–65) to justice in 1970 for bribery and corruption. Robert Perry died in an automobile accident in late October 1978.

2. Breece confuses the death of James Agee and Thomas Wolfe. James Agee died from a heart attack in a cab in a New York City, May 16, 1955. Thomas Wolfe died in Johns Hopkins Hospital in Baltimore on Sept. 15, 1938, due to complications brought on by a tubercular infection of the brain.

· · · · · · · · · · · · **To Helen Pancake, January 11, 1979**

One Blue Ridge Lane
Charlottesville, Va.
Jan. 11, 1979

Mrs. C. R. Pancake
Milton, W.Va.

Dear Mom,

We are all getting ready for the snow that I suppose hit you today. So far this winter has proven milder than the first three here, but I'm sure we're in for something yet. And I owe you a vote of thanks for the staples (canned goods) you put in the bottom of my stuff when I left—it never ceases to amaze me how kind and thoughtful you are.

I went through a pretty bad experience yesterday in Richmond. I had called to answer an ad in the paper for a Public Relations job which demanded "a flair for writing", stayed up all night writing a new resume that would make me look good for that sort of job, drive down the next morning only to be told I was "over-qualified." I don't believe that. What I think happened is that Snelling and Snelling was trying to spice-up the looks of a standard sales position, and didn't know what to say when somebody walked in qualified for the position they'd advertised. On the way down I had even decided that if they offered me the job, I'd take it on the spot and finish school at night. It's depressing enough to be turned down for a job, but it's downright lousey to be turned down for a job that probably didn't exist, and to be made a fool of.

But I'm still trying. Haven't heard a word from Alderson-Broaddus[1] or St. Joe,[2] and have about given up on them. If they were all that interested, I'd have heard by now. Actually, A-B may be so slow as to turn out something at the last minute or even two years from now—but I can't be growing moss on my feet waiting for them.

Emily is hard at work on her French, and I'm still trying to unravel and interpret a novel that seems not to want me to do either one. Apparently what was bugging me when I called was a minor case of the flu—one now over—and I just hope you didn't catch it. Also my foot is much better, and I plan to start walking two miles a day very soon, then get back to running.

I'm still disturbed by the report that Aunt Julia is being mistreated, and I hope by now the whole thing has blown over. Personally, I hope that by the time you need such care I will be in the position to give it to you. I don't think it would be fair to trust other people with your own mother.

I'm sending you a check the first of Feb., and I want you to cash it—I have enough to get me through summer, and it would really bother me to owe you money if I got down on my luck and had to bum my room and board from you to boot. So please don't argue, just cash the check. Besides, it looks as if Uncle Sam won't get my money this year either.

Better get back to work. Give my love to everybody.

Love you,
[signed] Breece

1. Alderson-Broaddus College is located in Philippi, W.Va.
2. St. Joseph Central High School in Huntington, W.Va.

One Blue Ridge Lane
Charlottesville, Va.
Jan. 20, 1979

Mrs. C. R. Pancake
Milton, W.Va.

Dear Mom,

Just a note to say I'm alive and working. Finally finished one paper for Tony Winner—one more to go, then orals and language. Believe me, it isn't worth the trouble.

I've had no contact with Mary Lee since I asked her to return *Snakehunter*[1] last year. I must say she thinks a good deal of herself, and I really didn't think the Nat'l Book Award would go to her head, but I guess it did. John Casey—who stays on her good side somehow—says she's really on cloud nine with the enclosed award . . . [enclosed clipping]

I'm now getting ready to attack the Jr. College job market. I have often thought of creating an opening for myself—I'll find a place I like, simply murder the current job-holder, then apply. All things considered, it makes more sense than robbing a bank (my second calling). But don't worry until you get a sudden postcard from Mexico.[2] I'm also into some part-time offers—will let you know if I get anything.

Was over to see Sarah[3]—she's fine, and was very nice to let us go out to the farm [Middlebrook and "Faraway" cabin] in the pick-up. Em had never been in a truck. I went out to grab a quick fish for John's[4] birthday—Other than that, nothing new.

Got to get to work—

Love you,
[signed]
Breece

1. *Snakehunter* by Chuck Kinder published by Alfred Knopf in 1973.
2. See untitled short story fragment below.
3. Sarah Nutt.
4. John Casey.

· Story Fragment

This untitled short story fragment may have been one of the last pieces Breece had written. It is a violent, dark story, reminiscent, in tone and imagery, of his last letter home March 20, 1979. The date of this story fragment remains undetermined. The idea for the story reflects Pancake's dreams of escape and his experiences in Phoenix and Mexico. "[D]on't worry until you get a sudden postcard from Mexico." See Breece's letters to Helen Pancake Jan. 20, 1979 and Feb. 29, 1976.

[Untitled fragment]

The whole thing came to him that Friday night as he lay there under five blankets with a bottle of whiskey: To do anything but make love, you needed a hell of a lot of equipment. Sweat a bug? Blankets, whiskey, T.V., hot room. Cope a mope? A cigarette without a filter so it would dangle properly from the lip. Do a dutch act? A warm bath with cold steel, a lead bead placed neatly in the brain, a tall building to jump from.

He thought of his mother. Even a good mackerel snapper had equipment—beads, a bible, all those ribbons, etc., and he thought of all the money made in the world on equipment, and he agreed with himself that there was a goodly amount of equipment involved in making love, but he hadn't gotten low enough to buy any yet.

Then he started thinking about going to confession tomorrow. He could see it now: a big hole burning in the curtain while he talked, and the holy water the priest threw on the fire gushing up like gasoline. And he thought: So this is what it's like to have some green. The lowest goddamn thing in the valley of the shadow of death, lower than whale shit in the trench, but you can afford to have the flu.

He watched Johnny Carson tell jokes, but they still weren't funny. He remembered being poor, hitch hiking all over the southwest like a good hippie. And that was where he met Martin, a wetback with a little scratch and an idea about getting more.

It was so hot in Phoenix, that at night it got down to a snappy 109. While trying to catch some cool under a bridge on the southside, he saw Martin chasing a body as it rolled into the gulch. He took out his baggy and rolled a humpish joint, watching as the Mexican leafed the wallet for green. The little man started back up the gulch, leaving the cold-cocked body, and spotted him, toking away in the shade.

"Hav-a-hit?" he said, offering the cigarette.

"You think you pretty cool, huh?" but he took a puff.

"Beats the street, man."

"The street is O.K. A few rats, not too many."

"No rats here, man."

"Where you going?" he eyed the backpack.

"Maybe Mexico."

"Very nice in Mexico. You go deep in the jungle. Is cool there," and he handed over the hot reach, disappeared to the bridge above.

In an hour the Mexican came back, but the body in the gulch still had not moved.

"I think I go with you, man," Martin said. "Big money in pottery—you know—the national art?"

They caught a ride all the way to Nogales with a bunch of freaks in a VW bus. The train was $18—sounded good, so just outside of Nogales they beat up and rolled the hippies.

Johnny Carson tried to catch a bottle of beer to hold up for an ad, missed, and Joe laughed. It was then he decided to cap the whiskey and cop a snooze until Linda came back from the hot shit political dinner for her father. He dreamed he ran up and down the sewers, looking for Linda. He carried the rusty old Mauser Martin bought for him in Mexico from an oyster salesman. A couple of kids stopped him in the sewer, asking about Martin. Blue bottle flies sucked the edges of their eyes, but they didn't wave them away, they stood there, asking about Martin. Joe wanted to wave the flies away, but they wouldn't let him, so he leveled off his Mauser. They sniggered at him, pointed, talked in Spanish, and they were still snickering when he drilled them both.

He heard Linda come in, but it was long time before he could open his eyes, and when he did, she was naked, pulling at the covers. He grabbed her.

"You'll get my bug," he warned.

"So what, I want it with you now," and she climbed in.

"How's the dinner?"

"You know daddy," she said plowing her hands through the covers to find him.

"Um," he said, and let her mount him for a change while he dreamed of the green clouds of parrots over the Mexican jungle.

· · · · · · · · · To Phoebe-Lou Adams, January 21, 1979

One Blue Ridge Lane
Charlottesville, Va.
Jan. 21, 1979

Phoebe-Lou Adams
Atlantic Monthly
8 Arlington Street
Boston, Mass.

Dear Miss Adams:

I'm working on some fiction, the likes of which you'll be the first to see when it's finished, your eye being the truest test of a story about two women.

In the meantime, I ask you to examine the enclosed. This came to me by mail through one of two sources: either DATELINE (an ad in The Atlantic which I confess to answering in a fit of lonliness [*sic*]) or GLOBTROTTER [*sic*] (an ad answered in a fit of feeling sea-worthy). In any event, I'm afraid such yellow slavery might be doing better than anyone thinks, and I'd like to do a journalistic story on it—either for "Reports or Comments" or "Life and Letters," depending upon the length desired.

I know this is a big favor to ask, so I'm willing to turn the story over to anyone you might have in mind already on the staff. I think there's some-thing here to write about, and I don't really care who writes it so long as it gets written. You'll see my cf. of two opposing points of view on the Nov. 78 issue of "Cherry Blossoms".[1] I like dogs and cats too, but I'm not sure everybody likes a sixteen-year-old looking for a pen pal in what is obviously a sickly different sort of game.

I hope this year finds both yourself and Mr. Weeks in good shape. I missed hearing from you last time, but Jim[2] assured me you were among the busy—those whose gudgons are in a constant state of grease. In the meantime, I promise to survive (by the way, I have a very nice girlfriend and promise not to answer anymore to the ads for DATELINE).

Sincerely,
[signed]Breece Pancake

1. *Cherry Blossoms,* a publication out of Stehekin, Wash., advertised "Oriental ladies" interested in finding mates stateside. For two dollars, Breece received the Nov. 1978 issue, twenty-eight pages of photographs with a brief blurb on each lady which included their age and interests. Ages in this issue ranged from sixteen to fifty-six. For twenty dollars more you could receive a list of addresses. Breece understood this to be a thin veil covering the yellow slave trade, and apparently he had plans for writing a fictional story and a "journalistic" piece. However, no fragments exist to show that he had begun work on the idea.
2. James McPherson was on the editorial board of the *Atlantic.*

· · · · · · · · · · · To Helen Pancake, February 13, 1979

One Blue Ridge Lane
Charlottesville, Va.
Feb. 13, 1979

Mrs. C. R. Pancake
Milton, W.Va.

Dear Mom,

Just a note to thank you for your letters and say all is fine. Many thanks for the underwear—getting such things in one's mail has a touch of strange-ness to it. I will wear them in good health and promise to model them for the Women's League next week. . . .

Yes, we've had quite a bit of snow—roughly 10"—and more keeps coming. I walked in and back a couple of times, but now everything but the driveway is clear, so I'm o.k. At the coldest it's only been around 8 degrees with the highs in the 20's, so a good walk can't hurt me . . . With gas promising to go $1.00 a gallon, I'm glad I got my foot fixed.

Don't worry about me and jobs: I occasionally get nibbles—the most recent from Kentucky Arts Commission (I've specifically asked for the eastern counties) where I'd lecture three days a week in high schools, North Carolina Arts Commission (same deal), and Western (North) Carolina University. West Virginia has no "Writers-in-the-Schools program" (they buy Davis Grubb a pound of Marijuana—it's cheaper).

The library dinner sounded like a joke. Do you reckon they planned for Gene McCarthy and Jay[1] to be stranded in that awful old Washington, D.C.? After all, they still get paid (I'd get paid for a reading that got snowed out.) And what can a three man band cost? $100.00 at best, with Gene and Jay sitting by the fire in the Georgetown Club talking the possibilities of Jay's 1980 nomination over Kennedy? (I wouldn't vote for either one.) Boy, I can see that one as clear as day. But your note on Carbide Parties hit home—I remember those. It's hard to keep it from eating at you sometimes, I know, and I'm not going to tell you to stop remembering—just don't stop living and being a terrific mother. . . .

I've been busy enough. My class seems bright and I think I've got good control (which probably means they hate my guts). They are writing, although only one could begin to imagine beyond the early stages (I teach writing, not imagination). I'm finishing my last paper of my life—from here, it's pure fiction. I'm also writing my orals proposal, but haven't given German much thought. Figure I can finish in a summer if I get a job. If I don't I have plenty of time. Bill Smart at Virginia Center for Creative Arts has promised me room and meals in return for my services as a painter and fix-it man (can you imagine that?) VCCA will peel, leak, and burn to the ground after I've been there a month. The point is, I won't starve and I'll have some time to write.

Saddest is this: an old, retired professor at VPI wrote me that he has written a novel and asked me if I'd read it and tell him whether or not it's publishable. He offered me $50 to read it and $450 to "fix" it. I doubt I'll get beyond the $50, but I took the job. Because of that, you'll find the enclosed. You told me you wouldn't cash a check for $100, but you can cash one for $50. Anyway, how do you tell an old man he should be writing memories for his grandchildren and great-grand children, not bad novels? Speaking of which, is it too much to ask that you send Saga of a Country Doctor?[2] I've never really read it and pretty soon I'll have a few hours to spend.

Em is fine. She's still reading a lot of French and plans to take the exam over in case she didn't score 700 (out of 800?). She's also reading for her orals and worrying about the job market next year. She's really worked hard all her life (not like me) to get to the upper levels of education, and I just hope she finds something.

Well, that's about it. Hope you survived the snow and hope all is well with everyone.

Love you,
[signed] Breece

1. Jay Rockefeller.
2. *Saga of a Country Doctor* (privately printed), by Dr. Floyd Farnsworth (1869–1946) of Milton, is a journal of his experiences in the Teays Valley.

· · · · · · · · · · · To Helen Pancake, February 28, 1979

One Blue Ridge Lane
Charlottesville, Va.
Feb. 28, 1979

Mrs. C. R. Pancake
Milton, W.Va

Dear Mom,

Even if Grandpa got fish to-go at Capt. D's, I'm sure he payed for it dearly. Emily and I innocently went to lunch at McDonald's yesterday, and for two Mac's, one order of fries and two cokes the bill was $3.25. It's getting so green baloney butts[1] are the only bargain.

We got 17" of snow, and I walked quite a bit. Now it's raining, and the snow has melted down to about four inches. While I didn't move my car for three days, I got in yesterday only to discover that I'd left the lights on during the blizzard. Hiked in, got Carl[2] to come out and jump start it, and now all is well again. Were it not for Em, I'd skip the car altogether, but she can't drive in snow and has no way to the store. When gas goes to a $1.00 a gallon, I'm walking in except to get groceries. Pretty soon we're going to be singing "Buddy, Can You Spare a Dime" again.

Alderson-Broaddus finally wrote me. The job includes an ability to teach Journalism, Composition, Literature, etc. If you could get the features (Aunt Julia, Troy Hatfield, Hinton Richmond, and any I've forgotten) I wrote for the Cabell Record and xerox them for me, I'll have that to back me up. Boy, they intend to get their money's worth out of anyone they hire. There's also a Va. Arts Commission, and I know the poet who works for them is quitting (they don't know that yet), so I'll apply to them as well. You're right: I'll get a job—it may be in a Pizza Hut, but I'll get a job—I'm too hard headed to let it get me down for long.

Funny you should mention Glazer's[3] [*sic*] salary: Staige Blackford (editor of Virginia Quarterly) does little or nothing (not that much to do when you put out four mags a year), and gets $36,000. That's the job I want some day.

Speaking of the Southern Crescent[4]—The wreck last fall that killed six, remember? Well, one of the six was a black cook. Carter had asked him to come to the White House as a cook, but he turned it down. He said he'd spent 40 years on trains, and once a train man always a train man. He was due to retire this month.

Read the first two chapters of the old guy's novel: boy, is it bad. I know he wants to fulfill his dream, but it would be cruel to tell him it's good. Now, I have to finish it, but there's no hope of it getting published. Hard way to earn $50.

Hope this finds you feeling better. We're fine. Let me know how everyone is doing, and tell Shorty and Mary Jane[5] I'm glad their granddaughter got out of Iran (I may find myself in China if this mess keeps up—gee-whiz, I thought I was too old to fight).

Got to run. Give my best to all. Love you.

B

1. The expression "green baloney butts" is from Tom Kromer's *Waiting for Nothing*.
2. Carl Beckman, one of Breece's friends in Charlottesville.
3. Fred Glazer, director of the West Virginia Library Commission.
4. Amtrak rail line, Virginia to D.C. See letter to Mary Roberts Rinehart Foundation, Mar. 21, 1978.
5. Shorty and Mary Jane Hollandsworth, family friends.

• • • • • • • • • • • • • • • To John Casey, March 25, 1979

One Blue Ridge Lane
Charlottesville, Va.
[March 25, 1979]

John D. Casey
c/0 Jane Casey
Department of English
Wilson Hall
University of Virginia

Dear John,

When you read this it really won't matter anymore, but I offer these thoughts the way a fossil comes back to haunt a geologist—but haunt isn't the right word, and I'm too stupid to think of another. But anyway . . .

Remember May, 1975? "God, why didn't you tell me . . . if I'd known you were this good, I'd have offered you a fellowship." I hadn't told you because I knew I wasn't. Then the summer of bad times when I pounded on doors, got fed-up, went fishing, and bingo they offered me a job sight unseen from Staunton, and bingo my father and my best friend croaked within a week of each other, and bingo I held on for dear life. I held on because of me, but I held on with the help of you. The night we went to see Ali murder Frazier in Manila, that night I nearly knocked your brains out with my driving into the parking-lot abutement [*sic*]. I was trying to think of some way to thank you for going with me to the fights, and I forgot to hit the breaks [*sic*].

Remember L——? "I know you want me to tell you I've had a great time, but well, I've had a good time." And there were breakfasts with wheat cakes and lemon curd and spring mornings when I'd drive the VW from Staunton. I hit a "tree-rat", as Jane called it, but nobody was up to that for breakfast with lemon curd. And I drove home thinking what a wonderful day it had been, and how my father would want me to stop for coffee at least twice on the way home. I stopped three times for coffee, but when I got home my mother called to tell me Cousin —— had dispatched his brains by a NY lake that morning. I wasn't all that sorry for Cousin ——

Remember May, 1976? Jane said: "We go to the house of my father—it has many bathrooms." I came over loaded in the VW for home, left you the things one needs for long stays away—salt, coffee, whiskey and a blanket. I spent the summer writing what would become "Trilobites," you wrote of hopes of "Liberty." Later I came to Charlottesville, worked up the story, read a good novel in galley, met one Rod Kilpatrick. L—— died and went to heaven on somebody else's cross. I died over a girl who was dry as beans in bed but full of lush [*sic*] on the phone. She moved. I stayed.

Remember May, 1977? I wrote to say a story was sold. I got no answer. I worked frying hamburgers, selling golf balls. Richard had dinner with me before late Mass. I remembered you coming all the way here to welcome me to the Catholic faith. I missed you. I went home and started a story, then I found I would teach next year, so I started my lesson-plans. I finished the story and the lessons when you returned. The story wasn't good enough, and you helped me—soon it was good enough.

Remember Emily Miller? "Then Kerrigan said there weren't any virgins left in this day and time—but—I'm afraid he—well he was wrong." So I decided she was right. I wanted to marry her, but later, when it became clear I would have no work, I wanted to become a padre. Me a padre? I loved this girl. I loved this girl. Still, I had work, and you told me I'd get none. Still, I love this girl, and time flew its course. I sold another story: I called you on a winter's night and you were happy. Still, I love the girl.

Alright—maybe not.

Remember July, 1978? I went to the Southwest, and you went to Jane's Father's house. I loved the girl. I wrote several cards to you but the Post

Office was on strike. I loved the girl. I went to a woman I knew in South Phoenix (blacks and Mexicans), but she told me I loved the girl. I went to a woman I knew in North Phoenix (lilly white), but she told me I loved the girl. I wrote you from a Big Boy counter on Central Ave., and I had no money, had no place to sleep, had no nothing. And "John, this is the last I'll ask." And it was. You were good enough to give me a clean bill of health with my dentist and then some.

So remember May, 1979? I can't. But as I see it, you'll go on as you have before I came. You're an honest man John Casey—honest at your heart—but what will you do for those who come after? Will you take a clean and simple writer like ———, and by giving him funds turn him into the slop ——— is made of? I could stay, I know, John, were I to beg—I might even have a job were I to stay one more year. Johnny, and you'll have to take a drink now, would you love me if I did? I love you. I love you because when my father and friend were dead you helped me hang on for dear life, told me I could write (and be damned if I haven't done a passing job). Alright then, the bargain is settled. I can write, now, and nothing else matters. You've fought hard for me John—fought hard for five years, and please don't think that by my gruff manner and early temper I am any less the man for you. And by your fight, I hope something comes of me worthy of calling your own name to. I'm not good enough to work or marry, but I'm good enough to write.

Can you find a tear or two in these lines they are mine, and I will hope you shed them in Ireland this summer. Maybe we'll neither of us see Heaven, but if you can bring yourself to it, say a prayer for me (not in any church) under an Irish sky.

May God Bless and Go with You and Yours Always, John Casey.

[signed] Breece

· · · · · · · · · · From Kathleen Devereux, April 3, 1979

Kathleen Devereux
Winchester, Va.
April 3, 1979

One Blue Ridge Lane
Charlottesville, Va.

Dear Breece,

If you want this job, you better make plans to come up here soon, and I mean soon, to see my editor . . . He had already, more-or-less, made up his mind about my replacement, but he agreed to see you after I talked to him . . . (I just received your letter in the mail . . .) I told him all about your work, your excellent background in writing, and how you will compare with one of our writers, Joe Bageant, who is a little off-the-wall like you . . . in fact, I can see you boys striking [it] off very well, both brought up in country settings, same type of humor . . . but he is a bit too much at times, and can have agnostic views, so maybe it won't be as great . . . loves whiskey, though.

But because Buckeye has already considered one person seriously, you should make every effort to come up here . . . of course, there is no way for me to reach you by phone, you little jerk . . . You see, Buckeye wants this person here at the Star fairly soon. . . .

Please let me know soon (as soon as you get this letter!) if you are still interested.

[signed] Kath—

• • • • • • • • • • • • From Keith Althaus, April 11, 1979

Keith Althaus
Fine Arts Work Center
Provincetown, Mass.
April 11, 1979

One Blue Ridge Lane
Charlottesville, Va.

Dear Breece D'John Pancake,

Congratulations! We are happy to offer you a Fellowship for the coming year, October 1, through April, seven months.

In terms of money these fellowships are $225 a month and an apartment at the Center or a flat $375 a month for those who do not live at the Center. . . .

The Fellowship carries no obligations but one: You must be in residence. We are not a grant dispensing organization but a community of colleagues, and if you are off somewhere we get no benefit from you, nor you from us. This is a law without a letter. It does not mean you can't go away, but the spirit is clear You must be here.

New Writing Fellows for 1979–80:

Lorna Dee Cervantes
Jaimy Gordon
John Morgan
Breece D'John Pancake
Jayne Anne Phillips
Mary Robison
R. L. Shafner
Meredith Stainbach

2nd-Year Fellows
Michael Burkard
Thomas N. R. Rogers

The judges were:
Keith Althaus, Alan Dugan, Stanley Kunitz, Vanessa Ryder, Roger Skillings, John Skoyles, Arturo Vivante and Dwight Webb.

We look forward to meeting you and hope you can come. We will be glad to answer any questions you may have. Please write or call us.

[signed] Keith Althaus, Writing Chairman

Kathleen Devereux to Helen Pancake, April 11, 1979

Kathleen Devereux   Berryville, Va.
April 11, 1979

Mrs. C. R. Pancake
Milton, W.Va.

Dear Mrs. Pancake,

It is with deepest sympathy that I write this note. It was only this morning that I learned about Breece's tragic death.

I have been a friend of Breece's since our days in fiction class. I graduated from U.Va. in 1977, but we continued to correspond with each other over the years. He provided me with suggestions and opinions about my work here at the Winchester Evening Star.

In fact, I was to meet with Breece this Monday for an interview at my paper. I had suggested to my editor that Breece would be an excellent candidate for my position, which I am leaving in May.

Breece was a very dear and considerate friend. When I experienced unhappy personal times this winter, Breece did not hesitate to share with me his own experiences to help comfort and support me.

He was incredibly perceptive and always full of humor. I looked forward to his letters.

Breece has left behind a legacy of talent, warmth and love. I will miss him.

My thoughts and prayers will be with you and your family during these times. If I can possibly be of any assistance, please do not hesitate to contact me.

Sincerely,
[signed] Kathleen C. Devereux

·· Ann-Ellen Lesser to Breece Pancake, April 20, 1979

Ann-Ellen Lesser
Millay Colony for the Arts
Steepletop
Austerlitz, New York 12017
April 20, 1979

Mr. B.D'J. Pancake
1054 Rt. 60E
Milton, West Virginia

Dear Mr. Pancake:

I am happy to tell you that you have been accepted for a residency at the Millay Colony. However, the only space presently available is November 1–28, 1979. If this time period is not possible for you, I will be happy to re-submit your application with those people applying for a 1980 residency. The enclosed sheet gives you the appropriate deadlines.

Please let me know what you decide. Unless we hear from you otherwise, we will hold your material for consideration.

Sincerely,
[signed]
Ann-Ellen Lesser
Executive Director

··· Helen Pancake to Ann-Ellen Lesser, April 23, 1979

Apr. 23, 1979

Ms. Lesser,

This would have made Breece very happy but—in deep sorrow I regret to inform you Breece died April 8, 1979. It was a terrible shock to Charlottesville, the University of Va., St. Thomas Hall and his hometown.

Breece's mother,
[signed]
Mrs. C. R. Pancake
[Handwritten]

· · · John Shaffer to Helen Pancake, February 19, 1985

John Shaffer
P.O. Box 1219
Shepherdstown, W.Va.
Feb. 19, 1985

Mrs. C. R. Pancake
Milton, W.Va.

Dear Mrs. Pancake,

I've been meaning to write this letter for a long time. Then, just about the time I was ready, there would be Breece's picture in yet another newspaper piece and I'd have to try all over again to sort out my own recollections and feelings from all that I was reading and hearing. All of that has taken on a direction and momentum of its own—a direction that has less to do with Breece than with what this society demands from its artists. So many people want to purge themselves through their deaths (or near-deaths). So many of the accounts take on an odd, almost religious, tone. I suppose there is no way to prevent this. In a way, however, it's unfair to the memory of the individual.

I met Breece while we were fellow students at West Virginia Wesleyan College. We worked together in the theater, shared some common interests, talked at length on a few occasions, and corresponded for a while after he left Buckhannon. Looking back, the point of contact was fairly brief, but my impressions of him were vivid and lasting. (When I first learned of his death, I went home and located the enclosed letter which, for no clear reason, I had saved for ten years.)

The darkness of his stories is a contrast to the warm friend I remember. Surely, he developed a craft for conveying the lives of desperate, lonely people. But it was, I think, a craft and an empathy rather than a reflection of himself. Like many, we had an interest in the "folk" music movement of the 60's which did much to romanticize the life of the travelling loner. He used to borrow my Woody Guthrie recordings, the Songs of Phil Ochs, and a book called Hard Travellin': The Hobo and His History that I later gave to the Wesleyan Library when I left town. Already, though, I had strong domestic leanings and married after my junior year. Breece, on the other hand, took some opportunities to "live out" the myth of the free spirited traveller—his reference in the letter to having been "the rounds" has that ring to it.

But underneath this presumed character was the very reasonable, highly ethical young man who could in the space of the same letter talk of family and home in the most glowing of terms—His upbringing showing at every crack in the rough exterior.

Some of Breece's Virginia friends talk about his "sizing people up" by asking people if they liked to hunt and fish. I remember the same question from an early conversation—probably because I sensed the same judgemental possibility. I don't and I didn't. I'm sure I had to admit that my fishing had ended with a certain queasiness at removing hooks from living things. But it never mattered to Breece. He took the information at face value and we went on to become good friends. While he could talk and act rough, he was capable of the most acute embarrassment and contrition if he ever thought that he had offended someone—particularly, a woman. His apologies were always more convincing than any offending act that preceded them. He was, whether he liked it or not, deeply and fundamentally a good human being.

I lost touch with Breece shortly after I graduated (in spite of our best intentions to keep in touch). I continued school at the University of Wisconsin, then worked in North Carolina and Alabama before taking my present job at the National Endowment for the Arts in Washington, D.C. I pay for the privilege of living in West Virginia with a 140 mile round-trip commute. The children Breece asked about came much later—2 girls aged 6 and 2.

It was at my desk in Washington that I first learned of Breece's death—mentioned in a newspaper clipping circulated by our literature program. Unfortunately, it was also the first that I knew of his success. Perhaps no one could have changed the course of events, but I am sorry to have missed any possible chance to help an old friend. At the time that I heard, I called others from the same circle at Wesleyan, and Professor Presar. All were shocked; all shared fond memories. None of us can begin to understand.

I thought that, now, I should just write and share these things.

Sincerely,
[signed] John Shaffer

Bibliography

Pancake's Published Writings in Chronological Order

"The Breece Pancake Report." (Huntington, W.Va.) *Herald-Dispatch*, Dec. 5, 1966.

"Country Music—More down to earth." (Milton, W.Va.) *Cabell Record*, Aug. 6, 1975.

"'I'm Thankful I Can Still Get Around' Julia Ward Is 94." (Milton, W.Va.) *Cabell Record*, Aug. 6, 1975.

"Hinton Richmond: A Man of the Woods," (Milton, W.Va.) *Cabell Record*, Aug. 13, 1975.

"Opus One: Records, Plants and a Thriving Business." (Milton, W.Va.) *Cabell Record*, Aug. 13, 1975.

"Pop Amick Is Still Going Strong." (Milton, W.Va.) *Cabell Record*, Aug. 27 1975.

"The Mark." (University of Virginia) *Rivanna*, Feb. 25, 1976.

"Hollow." (University of Virginia) *The Declaration*, Sept. 30, 1976.

"The Way It Has to Be." [Under the title "Cowboys and Girls."] (University of Virginia) *The Declaration*, Oct. 21, 1976.

"Trilobites." *Atlantic Monthly*, Dec. 1977.

"In the Dry." *Atlantic Monthly*, Aug. 1978.

"Time and Again." *Nightwork*, Sept. 1978.

"The Honored Dead." *Atlantic Monthly*, Jan. 1981.

"A Room Forever." *Antaeus*, Dec. 1981.

"Hollow." *Atlantic Monthly*, Oct. 1982.

"The Way It Has to Be." *Rolling Stone*, Apr. 14, 1983.

The Stories of Breece D'J Pancake, first ed. Boston: Atlantic Monthly Press/Little, Brown, 1983.

The Stories of Breece D'J Pancake, first paper ed. New York: Holt, Rinehart and Winston, 1984.

"Trilobites." Anthologized in *Stories of the Modern South*, edited by Ben Forkner and Patrick Samway. Exanded ed., New York: Penguin, 1986.

"The Honored Dead." Anthologized in *Soldiers and Civilians: Americans at War and Home*, edited by Tom Jenks. New York: Bantam Books, 1986.

The Stories of Breece D'J Pancake, German ed. Neuer Malik Verlag, Kiel, East Germany, 1990.

"Trilobites." Excerpted in *Out on the Porch*. Chapel Hill: Algonquin, 1992.

Trilobites and Other Stories, British ed., new title. London: Secker and Warburg, 1993.

"First Day of Winter." Anthologized in *Appalachia Inside Out: A Sequel to* Voices from the Hills, edited by Ambrose Manning, Jack Higgs, Jim Wayne Miller. Knoxville: University of Tennessee Press, 1994.

Contos Cortantes (Stories of the Heart), Portuguese ed., new title. Translated by Jose J. Veiga. Rio de Janeiro: Bertrand Brasil, 1994.

"The Honored Dead." Anthologized in *The Other Side of Heaven: Post-War Fiction by Vietnamese and American Writers*. Edited by Wayne Karlin, Le Minh Khue, and Truong Vu. Curbstone Press, 1996.

• • • • • • • • • • • • • • • • • Letters and Unpublished Works

Foster, Ruel. Letter to Helen Pancake, May 5, 1995, Pancake MSS.

Glazer, Fred. "West Virginia Literary Award." Paper presented at the annual awards meeting of the West Virginia Library Commission, Science and Cultural Center, Charleston, Feb. 7, 1984.

Higgs, Robert J. Letter to author, July 20, 1994. Pancake MSS.

Lembke, Janet (Nutt). Letter to author, Feb. 22, 1993.

Nutt, Sarah. Letter to author, Oct. 10 1992. Pancake MSS.

Pancake, Breece D'J. Papers. (#10975), Special Collections Dept., Univ. of Virginia.

Pancake, Helen. Letters to author, 1986–96. Pancake MSS.

Pancake Manuscripts. Letters, diary, notebooks, and manuscripts. West Virginia Univ. Library, Morgantown.

Perdue, Charles. Letter to author, Sept. 21, 1994. Pancake MSS.

Welch, Jack. "Davis Grubb: a Vision of Appalachia." Ph.D. diss., Carnegie Mellon Univ., Pittsburgh, Pa., 1980.

• • • • • • • • • • • • • • • • • Interviews and Recordings

Benedict, Pinckney. Interview by Marty Buchsbaum. Videotape recording. Lewisburg, W.Va. July 26, 1988.

———. Interview by Thomas Douglass. *Appalachian Journal* (Fall 1992): 68–74.

Blenko, Rick. Interview by Marty Buchsbaum. Videotape recording. Milton, W.Va., July 28, 1988.

Breece Pancake. Video broadcast by Russ Barbour. WPBY, Huntington, W.Va., Jan. 7, 1987.

Casey, John. Interview by Russ Barbour. Videotape recording. Huntington, W.Va., Nov. 5–6, 1986.

Currey, Richard. Interview by Thomas Douglass. *Appalachian Journal* (Summer 1993): 374–82.

Foote, Shelby. Interview by Noah Adams. National Public Radio broadcast, Nov. 3. 1994.

Giardina, Denise. Interview by Thomas Douglass. *Appalachian Journal* (Summer 1993): 384–93.

Harshbarger, Sam. Interview by Marty Buchsbaum. Videotape recording. Nov. 5, 1986, Milton, W.Va.

Hendricks, G. C. Interview by author. Tape recording. Wake Forest, N.C., June 30, 1995.

Jackson, Robert. Interview by Russ Barbour. Videotape recording. Nov. 4, 1986, Milton, W.Va.

———. Interview by Marty Buchsbaum. Videotape recording. July 28, 1988, Milton, W.Va.

Jones, Richard. Interview by Russ Barbour. Videotape recording. Nov. 6, 1986, Huntington, W.Va.

Kinder, Chuck. Interview by Thomas Douglass. Tape recording. Sept. 29, 1992, Pittsburgh, Pa.

Koger, Lisa. Interview by Thomas Douglass. Tape recording. July 28, 1992, Glenville, W.Va.

Maynard, Lee. Interview by Thomas Douglass. Tape recording. Jan. 20, 1993, Wake Forest, N.C.

Morgan, Julia. Interview by Russ Barbour. Videotape recording. Aug. 1988(?), Milton, W.Va.

Pancake, Breece. "The Big Break." Interview by Chuck Hyman. *The* (U.Va.) *Declaration*, Dec. 1, 1977, 12.

Pancake, Helen. Interview by Russ Barbour. Videotape recording. Nov. 4, 1986, Milton, W.Va.

———. Telephone conversation with author, Nov. 9, 1992.

Phillips, Jayne Anne. Interview by Thomas Douglass. *Appalachian Journal* (Winter 1994): 182–87.

Taylor, Eleanor Ross. Letter to author, Dec. 21, 1995, Pancake MSS.

Teel, John. Interview by Russ Barbour. Videotape recording. Huntington, W.Va. August(?) 1988.

Willis, Meredith Sue. Interview by Thomas Douglass. *Appalachian Journal* (Spring 1993): 284–93.

· Secondary Sources

Alvarez, A. *The Savage God.* New York: Random House, 1972.

Anderson, Sherwood. *Tar: a Midwest Childhood,* edited by Ray Lewis White. Cleveland: The Press of Case Western University, 1969.

Barrett, Sharon. "A Posthumous Voice from Somewhere Deep in the Hills." Review of *The Stories of Breece D'J Pancake. Chicago Sun-Times,* Feb. 6, 1983.

Battersby, Eileen. "South Forks." Review of *Trilobites and Other Stories* by Breece D'J Pancake. *Irish Times,* Feb. 6, 1993.

Bell, Carolyn Wilkerson. "The Stories of Breece D'J Pancake." *Magill's Literary Annual* (1984): 824–27.

———. "Pancake Wouldn't Have Minded at All." *Herald-Dispatch,* Dec. 13, 1993.

Bosworth, David. "A Writer's Death Haunts His Stories of Pain and Beauty." Review of *The Stories of Breece D'J Pancake. Boston Globe,* Mar. 13, 1983.

Butterworth, Tom. "Review of Trilobites and Other Stories," (London) *City Limits,* Oct. 29, 1992.

Casey, John. Afterword to *The Stories of Breece D'J Pancake.* Boston: Little Brown, 1983.

Cheuse, Alan. "A Greatly Gifted Storyteller and Tales Not Quite Ripe." Review of *The Stories of Breece D'J Pancake. Los Angeles Herald Examiner,* Feb. 27, 1983.

Cole, Thom. "Young Writer Was Haunted by the Troubles of the Less Fortunate." Review of *The Stories of Breece D'J Pancake. The Stuart Florida News* (UPI), Jan. 2, 1983.

Curtis, Michael. Foreword to *Contemporary New England Stories.* Old Saybrook, Conn.: Globe Pequot Press, 1992.

Davis, Bolton. "The Stories of Breece D'J Pancake." *San Francisco Review of Books*, May–June 1983.

DeFrancis, Robert. "West Virginia Writer Celebrated." *The* (Parkersburg, W.Va.) *Parkersburg News*, Feb. 20, 1983.

Dent, Jim. "Presence of Death Lurks in Pancake's Stories." Review of *The Stories of Breece D'J Pancake. Charleston Gazette*, Feb. 20, 1983.

Dieckman, M. K. "The Stories of Breece D'J Pancake." (Ithaca, N.Y.) *Grapevine*, Aug. 25–31, 1983, 34, 36.

Domini, John. "Crying the Beloved Country." Review of *The Stories of Breece D'J Pancake. Boston Phoenix*, Mar. 15, 1983.

Dudley, Caldwell "Collie." *History of Milton*. Privately printed, 1976.

Edwards, Grace Toney. "Memories of Breece." *Appalachian Heritage* 13 (1985): 112–14.

———. "Place and Space in Breece Pancake's *A Room Forever*." In *The Poetics of Appalachian Space*, edited by Parks Lanier Jr. Knoxville: Univ. of Tennessee Press, 1991.

Eige, Eason, and Rick Wilson. *Blenko Glass 1930–1953*. Marietta, Ohio: Antique Pubs., 1987.

Eliade, Mircea. *Myth and Reality*. New York: Harper and Row, 1963.

Fiedler, Leslie A. *Love and Death in the American Novel*. New York: Criterion Books, 1960.

Foote, Bud. "The Pain of Creation, Pancake's Legacy: Simple, Direct, Honest Prose." Review of *The Stories of Breece D'J Pancake. Detroit News*, Mar. 13, 1983.

Foster, Ruel. Interview by Marty Buchsbaum. Videotape recording, Aug. 1988, Morgantown, W.Va.(?).

Fox, Edward. "Pancake's Imagination Rooted in West Virginia Soil." *Charleston Gazette*, Apr. 23, 1984.

Frakes, James. "Your Choice: Stories Hard or Soft." Review of *The Stories of Breece D'J Pancake, The Plain Dealer* (Cleveland), 20 March 1983, C19.

Harpham, Geoffrey Galt. "Short Stack: the Stories of Breece D'J Pancake." *Studies in Short Fiction* 23 (1986): 265–73.

Harrington, Michael. *The Other America: Poverty in the United States*. New York: Macmillan, 1962.

Hazo, Samuel. "A Dozen Good Stories." Review of *The Stories of Breece D'J Pancake, Pittsburgh Press*, Mar. 13, 1983.

Hendrickson, Paul. "The Legend of Breece D'J Pancake." *Washington Post*, Dec. 10, 1984.

Hogan, Randy. "Review of *The Stories of Breece D'J Pancake*." *Village Voice*, May 3, 1983.

Kadohata, Cynthia. "Breece D'J Pancake." *Mississippi Review* 18 (1) (1990): 35–61.

Kakutani, Michiko. "Books of the Times." Review of *The Stories of Breece D'J Pancake. New York Times*, May 15, 1984.

Kirby, Martin. "Stories of Life's Grim Side by a Gifted, Tragic Artist." Review of *The Stories of Breece D'J Pancake. Philadelphia Inquirer*, Feb. 13, 1983.

Kromer, Tom. *Waiting for Nothing and Other Stories*. Edited by Arthur D. Casciato and James L. West III. Athens: Univ. of Georgia Press, 1986.

Lutwack, Leonard. *The Role of Place in Literature*. Syracuse: Syracuse Univ. Press, 1984.

Maurice, Johanna. "Station Once Hub of Commerce." *Charleston* (West Virginia)*Daily Mail*, Apr. 18, 1981.

McPherson, James Alan. Foreword to *The Stories of Breece D'J Pancake*. Boston: Little Brown, 1983.

Merkin, Daphne. "The Aura of Suicide." Review of *The Stories of Breece D'J Pancake. New Republic*, May 9, 1983, 36–37.

Merritt, Robert. "Writer Leaves an Earthy Legacy." Review of *The Stories of Breece D'J Pancake. Richmond Times-Dispatch*, Feb. 20, 1983.

Miller, Jim Wayne. "A People Waking Up, Appalachian Literature Since 1960." *Appalachian Symposium: Essays in Honor of Cratis Williams*. Boone, N.C.: Appalachian Consortium Press, 1989, 47–76.

Monroe, Robert. "A Single Flame." Review of *The Stories of Breece D'J Pancake*. (Cambridge, Mass.) *Harvard Crimson*, Feb. 28, 1983.

Montrose, David. "In a Melancholy State." Review of *Trilobites and Other Stories* by Breece D'J Pancake. *Times Literary Supplement*, Oct. 23, 1992.

Morris, Gregory. "Bare Gaping Wounds." Review of *The Stories of Breece D'J Pancake. Prairie Schooner* (Fall 1983): 89.

Nelson, Raymond. "The Hills of Home." Review of *The Stories of Breece D'J Pancake. Virginia Quarterly Review* (Winter 1984): 169–75.

Oates, Joyce Carol. "The Stories of Breece D'J Pancake." *New York Times Bock Review*, Feb. 13, 1983.

Pennebaker, Ruth Burney. "Remembrances of a Young Writer." (Charlottesville, Va.) *Daily Progress*, Feb. 20, 1983.

Peyton, Dave. "Troy State Can't Have Pancake—He's Ours." *Herald-Dispatch*, Dec. 8, 1993.

Reuschel, Cynthia. "Milton Friends Remember Talented Author." (Milton, W.Va.) *Cabell Record*, Aug. 24, 1983.

Review of *Trilobites and Other Stories* by Breece D'J Pancake. *Glasgow Herald*, Dec. 5, 1992.

Rice, Otis K. *West Virginia: a History*. Lexington: Univ. Press of Kentucky, 1985.

Ritchey, Mike. "Stories That Give Clues to Their Young Author's Despair." Review of *The Stories of Breece D'J Pancake. Ft. Worth Telegram-Star*, Feb. 20, 1983.

Santos, Carlos. "'We Teach Them to Rewrite' at U.Va." *Richmond Times-Dispatch*, Jan. 7, 1979.

Settle, Mary Lee. *The Clamshell*. New York: Lawrence/Delacorte, 1971.

Short, Randall. "Pancake's Vivid Stories a Fit Legacy." Review of *The Stories of Breece D'J Pancake. Virginia Pilot-Ledger Star*, Feb. 27, 1983.

Shutt, T. B. "Bright Hosannas and Eyes in the Night: Breece D'J Pancake, Writer." *Virginia Country* (June 1983): 38–45.

Simpson, Lewis. *The Dispossessed Garden: Pastoral and History in Southern Society of the Old South*. Athens: Univ. of Georgia Press, 1975.

Stephens, Tim. "Director's Attempt at Humor Falls Short." (Huntington, W.Va.) *Herald-Dispatch*, Dec. 7, 1993.

Still, James. *Hounds on the Mountain*. New York: Viking, 1939.

Tanner, Tony. Review of *Trilobites and Other Stories* by Breece D'J Pancake. *The Guardian*, Nov. 3, 1992.

Taylor, Peter. *A Summons to Memphis*. New York: Knopf, 1986.

———. *A Woman of Means*. New York: Frederic C. Bell, 1950.

Taylor, Thomas. "Breece D'J Pancake and His Literature of Last Words." (Marshall University) *Parthenon*, Mar. 22, 1990, 6–8.

"Three West Virginia Writers: He's Gone, He's There, and She'll get There—Breece D'J Pancake, the Writer Who Was." (Summerville) *West Virginia Hillbilly*, May 21, 1983, 1.

Tompkins, Jane. *Sensational Designs: the Cultural Work of American Fiction, 1790–1860*. New York: Oxford Univ. Press, 1985.

Towers, Robert. "Violent Places." Review of *The Stories of Breece D'J Pancake, New York Review of Books*, Mar. 31 1983.

Vigderman, Patricia. "K-Marts and Failing Farms." Review of *The Stories of Breece D'J Pancake. Nation*, Mar. 19, 1983, 345.

Wagner, Erica. "A Dead Poet's Fossils." Review of *Trilobites and Other Stories* by Breece D'J Pancake. *London Times*, Oct. 20, 1992.

Welty, Eudora. *The Eye of the Story: Selected Essays and Reviews.* New York: Vintage, 1979.

Wilhelm, Albert. "Breece D'J Pancake." *Dictionary of Literary Biography: American Short Story Writers Since World War II.* Oneonta, N.Y.: SUNY, 1993.

Wilson, Edmund. *The Wound and the Bow.* Cambridge, Mass.: Houghton Mifflin, 1941.

Wilson, Robert. "Tales from West Virginia Hills and Hollows." Review of *The Stories of Breece D'J Pancake. Washington Post Book World*, Mar. 6, 1983.

Index

Adams, Phoebe-Lou, 90–91, 97; letters from Breece Pancake, 238–39; letter to Helen Pancake, 91
Agee, James, 27, 147n
Agrarians, 110
Algren, Nelson, 27, 42
Amick, "Pop," 33, 140n, 171
Anderson, Sherwood, 18, 27, 103, 213; *A Storyteller's Story*, 142–43n; *Tar: a Midwest Childhood*, 138–39n; *Winesburg, Ohio*, 95,133
Antaeus, 90
Appalachia Inside Out, 13, 105
Applegate, Anne, 13
Arnow, Harriette, 121; *The Dollmaker*, 109
Atlantic Monthly, 14, 71, 73, 90, 91, 159, 205
Atwood, Margaret, 92

Ball, Fred, 26, 33, 36, 66, 213
Bannon, Barbara, 93
Barnes, Jane, on Pancake's personality, 8
Barrett, Sharon, 101
Battersby, Eileen, 95, 103
Beasley, Mike, 159, 170
Beckett, Samuel, comparisons to Pancake, 96
Beckman, Carl, 4, 60, 241
Bell, Carolyn Wilkerson, 101, 102
Benedict, Pinckney, 6, 104, 121, 127; on Pancake's fiction, 7–8, 13; *Town Smokes*, 127
Blake, Junior, 26, 33, 66, 171, 176, 197
Blenko, Rick, on Pancake's death, 4; on Pancake's fiction, 34, 35, 122
Blenko, William, 19, 139n
Blenko Glass, 19

Bloss, Suzanne, 38–39
Bosworth, David, 96, 99, 123
Buckhannon, W.Va., 127, 157–58
Butterworth, Tom, 103–4

Cabell Record, 241
Carver, Raymond, 93, 112
Casciato, Arthur, 70
Casey, John, 29, 56–57, 58, 72, 73, 78, 88, 107, 109, 178, 179, 192, 193, 208, 214, 215, 216, 232; letters from Pancake, 177, 242–44; on Pancake's conversion, 82; on Pancake's death, 5; on Pancake's drinking, 87; on Pancake's fiction, 45, 52, 97, 104, 117; at Pancake's funeral, 4; on Pancake's personality, 8, 11,134; *Spartina*, 104; works toward posthumous publication, 90, 92
Caudill, Harry, 29, 69; *Night Comes to the Cumberlands*, 126
Chappell, Fred, 121
Cheuse, Alan, 101
Coffindaffer, Bernard, 17
Conroy, Jack, 42
Cornstalk, Chief, 22–23
Crane, Stephen, 13, 95
Crews, Harry, 93
Currey, Richard, 6, 121, 124, 126
Curtis, C. Michael, 120

Dailey, Fred, 34
Davis, Bolton, 99
Davison, Peter, 90, 93
Debs, Eugene V., 19, 139n

The Declaration, 67, 73, 89, 91
The Deer Hunter, 83
DeFrancis, Robert, 125
Dent, Jim, 100
Depta, Vic, 121
Devereux, Kathleen, 60; letters to Breece Pancake, 83, 244–45; letters to Helen Pancake, 246
Dieckman, M. K., 98–99
Dos Passos, John, 27
Dubus, Andre, 13, 93
Dudley, Caldwell "Colly," 69–70, 208

Edwards, Grace Toney, 8–9
Eliade, Mircea, 114
Ensey, Tom, 121–22
Erikson, Kai, *Everything In Its Path*, 208

Faulkner, William, 6, 94, 103, 109, 110
Fiedler, Leslie, *Love and Death in the American Novel*, 95–96
Field, David, 60
Foote, Bud, 98
Foote, Shelby, 107, 151n
Forche, Carolyn, 13
Foster, Ruel, 13, 114
Fox, Edward, 109
Frakes, James, 123

Gay, Wyatt "Duck," 74, 219
Giardina, Denise, 6, 13, 121, 130
Ginsberg, Allen, "Howl," 163
Glasgow Herald, 103
Glazer, Frederic, 6
Gold, Mike, 27, 42
Grubb, Davis, 14, 36, 121, 214, 226, 240; *The Barefoot Man*, 215n; *The Night of the Hunter*, 133
Guthrie, Woody, 36, 248

Harrington, Michael, *The Other America*, 123
Harshbarger, Sam, 179n; on C. R. Pancake, 26; on Pancake's death, 5
Hazo, Samuel, 96
Heard, Matthew, 48, 51, 53, 165, 168, 171, 172, 173–74, 175, 180–81, 182, 202; death of, 54, 60
Hemingway, Ernest, 27, 90; comparisons to Pancake, 6, 13, 80, 94, 103, 115, 148n; *The Old Man and the Sea*, 140n
Hendricks, G. C., 13
Hendrickson, Paul, 104
Higgs, Robert J., 13
Hogan, Randy, 93
Holbrook, Chris, 6, 13
Hollandsworth, "Shorty," 12, 33, 66, 164

Jackson, Robert, on Pancake's boyhood, 33, 35; on Pancake's personality, 9–10
Jacobson, Wendy, 73
Jennings, Mike, 4, 60
Jones, Richard, 8, 14, 58, 62, 64, 82, 83, 202, 224; on Pancake's fiction, 107
Joyce, James, *The Dubliners*, 92, 96, 133
Just, Ward, 72, 146n, 200

Kadohata, Cynthia, 13, 104
Kakutani, Michiko, 109
Keene, Laura, 85
Kilpatrick, Rod, 60, 243
Kinder, Chuck, 13, 121, 132–33; *Snakehunter*, 236
Kirby, Martin, 99, 100
Koger, Lisa, 6, 121, 133, 134
Kromer, Tom, 27, 42–43, 70, 71, 94, 121, 142n, 207; *Waiting for Nothing*, 42–43, 94, 207n, 242n

La Barre, Weston, *They Shall Take Up Serpents*, 70, 208
Lawrence, D. H., 36
Lee, Howard Burton, 42, 141n, 212–13n
Lembke, Janet (Nutt), 28, 31, 230–31n
Lightfoot, Gordon, 36–37, 172
Little-Brown, 5, 71, 91, 92
London, Jack, 95
Lumpkin, Grace, 27, 42
Lutwack, Leonard, *The Role of Place in Literature*, 107

Macauley, Robie, 145n, 194
Manning, Robert, 70, 72, 90
Marshall University, 121–23
Mason, Bobbie Ann, 6; comparison to Pancake, 101
Maynard, Lee, 6, 64, 121, 124–25, 136; *Crum*, 124
McCarthy, Cormac, 6
McCullers, Carson, 103
McPherson, James Alan, 7, 8, 29, 58, 69, 78, 82, 144n, 205, 206; *Elbow Room*, 224, 226; on Pancake's personality, 60, 65, 102; reaction to Pancake's death, 85
Meade, Everett, 84–85
Meade, Virginia, 62–63, 83, 84, 88, 196, 226
Meadows, Bill, 33–34
Mencken, H. L., "Hatrack Scandal," 142n
Merkin, Daphne, 97–98, 123
Merritt, Robert, 89
Millay Colony for the Arts, 14, 87, 247
Miller, Emily, 77–80, 212, 214–15, 216, 219, 222, 223, 224, 225, 232, 235, 236, 240–41,

243; letters from Pancake, 226–27; on
Pancake's death, 4
Milton, W.Va., 17–19, 138n
Monroe, Robert, 96
Montrose, David, 103
Morgan, Julia, 38–39; on Pancake's death, 5;
on Pancake's personality, 9–10
Morris, Gregory, 102
"The Mothman," 22–23

Nelson, Raymond, 60, 63, 149n; on Pancake's
death, 85, 99
Norman, Gurney, 13
Norman, Marsha, 6
North Carolina Arts Council, 87
Nutt, Sarah, 55, 140n, 186, 187, 188, 189, 193,
195, 196, 198, 214, 222, 236

Oates, Joyce Carol, 94, 97, 117, 125
Ochs, Phil, 36, 37, 53, 100, 164, 248
O'Connell, Regis, 203, 216
O'Connor, Flannery, 6; comparisons to
Pancake, 94, 103, 116
O'Connor, Pat, 3, 4, 203, 216
Orr, Greg, 13

Paint Creek Miner Songbook, 69
Pancake, Breece D'J
—Life: ancestry, 20; birth, 16, boyhood, 21–23,
33–36; Catholic conversion, 73, 77, 82, 147n,
202, 216, 243; choice of vocation, 33–35, 68–
70; C. R. Pancake's illness and death, 53–
54, 80, 158, 177–78, 244; dreams, 4–5, 204;
East Beverly Street (Staunton, Va.), 31, 53–
57, 186–94; Fork Union Military Academy,
30, 36, 46–52, 161–74; grave, 3, 82–83;
influences, 29, 30–32, 35–45; letters, 161–94;
Marshall University (Huntington, W.Va.),
28, 34, 38–39, 41, 70, 87; Mexico, 26, 39, 74,
149n, 189; Milton, 9–10; name, 16–17, 206;
One Blue Ridge Lane (Charlottesville, Va.),
61–62, 195–244; political attitudes, 65–66,
168; Randolph Macon College, 80; religious
attitudes, 163, 165–66, 180–81; romantic
imagination, 7–8; sense of place, 107;
sexual attitudes, 75–79; Staunton Military
Academy, 52–57, 177–94, 196, 213; suicide,
83–88; temper, 77, 143n, 162, 165; travels in
the West, 30, 39–41, 159; University of
Virginia (Charlottesville), 30, 58–73; West
Virginia Wesleyan College (Buckhannon,
W.Va.), 36, 32, 158, 248
—Works: Books
Contos Cortantes, 103; *The Stories of Breece
D'J Pancake*, biblical allusions, 128–
29,141n, 142n; characters, 7, 14, 94, 110–11;

127–28; criticism, 95–105; myth in fiction,
113–14; Pulitzer nomination, 103; *Trilobites
and Other Stories*, 103
—Works: Poems
"The Carver," 44; "[Ghosts]," 10; "He
scratched and stirred . . .," 160; "It is fear,"
11; "Let It Flow," 12; "Song of the Road,"
12; "Starlings," 11–12
—Works: Stories
"Cowboys and Girls," *see* "The Way It Has
to Be"; "First Day of Winter," 13, 67, 90,
97, 113, 128, 133; "Fox Hunters," 9, 41, 52,
56, 67, 89, 97, 112, 113, 114, 116–17, 133,
134, 182; "Hollow," 29, 62, 67, 68, 90, 93,
97, 112, 113, 114, 117–18, 129, 134, 194;
"The Honored Dead," 68, 82, 89, 90, 108,
109, 113, 114, 139n, 141n, 145n, 172n, 226;
setting, 19, 22, 25, 28; "In the Dry," 67, 68,
72, 80, 81, 97, 113, 114, 128–29, 139n, 202,
222, 224, 232; "Keeper of the Flame," 34;
"A Loss of Tone," 70, 90; "The Mark," 7,
23, 29, 56, 58–59, 97, 112, 113, 114, 129–30,
131, 134, 145n, 189–90, 192, 193; "Rat Boy,"
34, 141n, 159–61; "A Room Forever," 7, 67,
86–87, 90, 97, 112, 134, 218; "The Salvation
of Me," 9, 56, 67, 90, 113, 119, 132, 133,
140n, 141n; "The Scrapper," 52, 56, 90, 113,
115–16, 131, 175n, 179, 181, 188; "Time and
Again," 25, 56, 80, 97, 127, 129; "Trilobites," 7, 17, 19, 22, 25, 28, 41, 56, 67, 68,
70, 71, 73, 75, 81, 97, 131, 132, 133, 145n,
146n, 205–6, 225, 243; discussed, 110–14;
sources, 74; "The Way It Has To Be," 56,
67, 97, 112, 134, 193; "Will O' the Wisp,"
see "Trilobites"
—Works: Story Drafts and Fragments
"The Conqueror," 183–86, 217–18;
"Generations," 14, 227, 228–29, *see also*
"Water in a Sieve"; "Joe Holly and Buck,"
217; "Of Time and Virgins," 79, 218;
"Shouting Victory," 70, 208–11; "Southern
Crescent," 218, 242; "Stuart," 41; "Toy
Soldier," 45, 143n; Untitled Fragment, 236–
37; "Water in a Sieve," 219–22
Pancake, Charlotte, 10, 24, 31, 36, 75, 199,
203, 214, 216
Pancake, Clarence Robert ("C. R."), 3, 16, 66;
advice to his son, 19, 38, 42; death, 53–54;
family, 19, 24–28; letters, 25, 27, 157
Pancake, Donnetta, 12, 24, 30–31, 36, 38, 41,
76, 83, 88, 159, 195, 214, 215, 222; at
funeral, 4; letters from Breece, 41, 204–6
Pancake, Gally, 17
Pancake, Helen Frazier, 16, 66; comparisons to
Olive Steinbeck and Julia Wolfe, 29, 197;
family, 20, 28–30; letter to Breece, 71; letter

Pancake, Helen Frazier, *cont.*
to Millay Colony, 247; letter to Phoebe–Lou
Adams, 90–91; letters from Breece, 178–241;
on her son's writing, 6, 15; reaction to her
son's death, 4, 83, 85; working toward
posthumous publication, 89, 90
Pancake, Robert, 3, 17, 31
"Pancake," Ward, Aunt Julia, 31–32, 80, 171,
179, 190, 232, 233, 235
Percy, Walker, 93, 109, 110
Perdue, Charles, 60, 63, 70, 82, 195, 222
Peyton, Dave, 122
Phillips, Jayne Anne, 6, 13, 14, 92, 121, 126–
27, 128, 130, 133, 134
Plath, Sylvia, xii, 90, 100, 104
Poe, Edgar Allan, 36
Presar, Charles I., 36, 249
Provincetown Fine Arts Fellowship, 14, 87,
245–46
Pulitzer Prize nomination, 5

Ramsey, Nancy, 60, 63, 196–97
Remarque, Erich Maria, *All Quiet on the
Western Front*, 34
Rinehart Foundation, Mary Roberts, 217–18
Ritchey, Mike, 100–101
"Rock Camp," 17, 18, 35, 71, 95
Rockefeller, Jay, 240
Rush, Tom, 37

Santos, Carlos, 44, 67
Settle, Mary Lee, 59, 69, 121 191, 199–200,
202, 236; *Blood Tie*, 224; *The Clamshell*, 64;
on Pancake's drinking, 87; on Pancake's
personality, 10, 64; *The Scapegoat*, 146n, 214
Shaffer, John, 158; letter to Helen Pancake,
248–49; on Pancake's personality, 248–49
Sharp, Ronald, 93
Shepard, Sam, 13
Shutt, T. B., 60, 63
Simpkins, Norman O., 42
Simpson, Lewis, 7
Smith, Lee, 121; *Oral History*, 109
Snyder, Bob, 105
Soldiers and Civilians, 105
St. Thomas Aquinas Catholic Church
(Charlottesville), 73, 77, 203
Steinbeck, John, 27, 36, 95, 103, 128; *Of Mice
and Men*, 115
Still, James, 121, 126

Stories of the Modern South, 105
Stuart, Jesse, 121, 160–61

Taylor, Eleanor Ross, 61
Taylor, Peter, 8, 58, 59, 61, 62, 67, 68, 71, 75,
78, 83, 194, 195, 197, 216, 226; comparisons
to Pancake, 107–10, 119; *The Old Forest*,
151n; *A Summons to Memphis*, 110; *A
Woman of Means*, 108
Teays River Valley, 138n
Teel, John, on Pancake's personality, 9
Thompson, Earl, *Tattoo* and *Garden of Sand*,
66, 67, 145n
Toole, John Kennedy, *A Confederacy of
Dunces*, 92–93
Towers, Robert, 94, 102

University of Iowa, 53, 57, 58, 69
University of North Carolina at Greensboro,
52
University of Virginia, 53, 57, 58, 63

Virginia Pilot Ledger-Star, 98
Virginia Quarterly Review, 72, 73, 200, 230, 242

Wagner, Erica, 104
Waits, Tom, 37, 76, 147n, 205
Warren, Robert Penn, 7
Weatherford Award, 5
Weeks, Edward, 14, 71
Welty, Eudora, "Place in Literature," 151n
West, James L., 70
West Virginia Hillbilly, 98
West Virginia Literary Award, 6
West Virginia University, 52, 166, 171
West Virginia Wesleyan College, 248
Wilhelm, Albert, 94
Williams, Tennessee, 74, 98
Willis, Meredith Sue, 6, 125–26, 135–36
Wilson, Edmund, 114
Wilson, Libby, on Pancake's personality, 8, 60
Wilson, Robert, 107
"Wobblie," 41, 141n
Wolfe, Thomas, 36, 80, 121, 147n, 204, 224;
comparisons to Pancake, 6–7, 91; *Look
Homeward, Angel*, 6; *You Can't Go Home
Again*, 6

Yount, John, 121

A Room Forever was designed and typeset on a Macintosh computer system using PageMaker software. The text is set in Palatino and titles are set in Stone Sans. This book was designed and composed by Sheila Hart and manufactured by Thomson-Shore, Inc.

www.ingramcontent.com/pod-product-compliance
Lightning Source LLC
Chambersburg PA
CBHW020353120726
47904CB00002B/544